Most of These Stories are Somewhat True

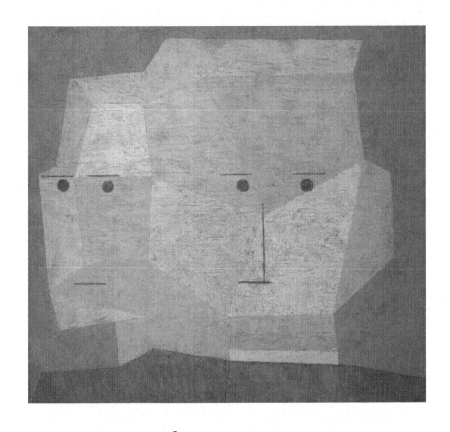

(Naughty and Nice)

Jeff Mackwood

Library and Archives Canada Cataloguing in Publication

Mackwood, Jeff, 1959-, author
    Most of these stories are somewhat true / Jeff Mackwood.

Issued in print and electronic formats.
ISBN 978-0-9949310-0-9 (paperback)
ISBN 978-0-9949310-1-6 (pdf)

1. Mackwood, Jeff, 1959- --Anecdotes. 2. Mackwood, Jeff, 1959-
--Travel--Anecdotes. 3. Pembroke (Ont.)--Anecdotes. I. Title.

FC3099.P44M32 2015   971.3'81   C2015-907856-3
                                            C2015-907857-1

Front cover:
'Two Heads' by Paul Klee, 1932, (Norton Simon Museum)

Ron

I like the company
you keep!
All the best.

[signature]

To Steve and Amelia Mackwood.

Wish you were still around to read this.

A Note About the Book's Title

Two of my favourite books have incredibly neat titles, at least by my standards.

Dead Lawyers and Other Pleasant Thoughts (1993) is a great collection of *Non Sequitur* cartoons by Wiley.

Some of the Stories I Told You Were True (1981) is a superb collection of oral histories of the Ottawa Valley, as told to author Joan Finnigan (1925-2007) by many old-timers.

I wanted to somehow pay tribute to these books with mine.

I couldn't fit *Dead Lawyers* into this book's title in a way that would truly fit its content. However I would refer you to *Bank it Off His Left Nut* within these pages for a lawyer-related story.

So in the end, the title of this book was chosen as an unabashed homage to Joan Finnegan's, which I fully acknowledge.

I must also acknowledge that, without the wonderful Ottawa Valley traditions of storytelling and tall-tale telling that have so affected me and infused my character, this book would never be.

Cast of Characters

Gen:

> Someone who really did not want to be mentioned in this book, but given that she's been married to me since 1982, how could she not be? An avid and accomplished open water swimmer. (You get to be called accomplished if you swim completely around Manhattan Island!) A very caring mother and grandmother. She's also the only person I know who has committed the entire British royal family genealogy to memory.

Natasja:

> Our oldest daughter; a teacher who has travelled the world widely.

Nicholas:

> Our son, who now lives on Canada's West Coast; a commercial diver, welder, fisherman, and volunteer member of the Prince Rupert Marine Rescue Society.

Alexandra:

> My most favourite youngest daughter; the reason we're grandparents.

Kirk:

> My lifelong friend. He was my best man and a month later I returned the favour. The fourth of a five-boy family, all of whom are great storytellers and humourists. (On his 25th anniversary: "I coulda been out by now!") An early blooming mesomorph, his job was to buy beer for the rest of us at a very early age (and carry the two-four under one arm as we rode our bikes to where we were going to drink it.) Since almost as long as I've been married, he's been in business with Gen's brother Mark.

Wayne:

My younger brother by nine years. I'm pretty sure he was too young at the time to remember all the cruel things his jealous older brother (me) did to him. I've long described him as the taller, smarter, and "good" one; to my own handsome, evil persona.

Steve Mackwood:

My father who passed away way too soon after a long battle with cancer. The greatest father that ever lived. A very smart person, with little formal education. For reasons that I'll never fully understand, he only ever bought Chryslers.

Amelia Mackwood:

See the story *A Son's Duty*.

Bruce:

A former work colleague and travel buddy. The straightest straight-shooter I've ever met; he has no trouble speaking his mind, and when he does, folks should listen. Tough as nails. An avid hunter and sportsman. A fine storyteller who loves a good laugh as much as I do.

Tony:

Another former work colleague and travel buddy. An engineer who has worked on dozens of aircraft programs. A lover of good beer, wine, spirits, and food. A great friend who also does not suffer fools gladly.

Table of Contents

Opportunity from Tragedy...1
Snap of Rubber Gloves 4
The Ruby Ring...6
Hockey Heaven on Howe Street...........................9
Pie ! 10
Paintings – The Lessons...12
Hooligans' Game 13
A Never-Solved Mystery...14
Super Mike..17
A Crasher's Tale – Part 1 19
Wine Opener and Oven Mitt...................................23
Border Crossing...25
Walking To Chicago Stadium 27
London Pub Crawl..30
Honda Meet Datsun...32
I'm Not Dreaming Terror 38
Under The Rainbow...39
The Christmas Turkey 40
Cycling in Italy 41
Rumble in Toronto..43
The Poo-Pee Flush..46
Chiropractic 48
Go Grayson Go!..50
Hilton Hookers...52
Flipping a Quebec Bird 54
There's Quartz in Them Thar Hills!....................55
Lights, Camera, Cut! 56
Cream Pie 59
Bank It Off His Left Nut...60
Nightmares of 256 Supple Street 62

Mind The Gap 65

D'Oh! 67

Quick Clay 70

Jack and Bill 71

Interspecies Love 72

Frog Astaire 74

Yes Minister(s) ! 75

Americans Spying on Americans 78

Crop Patterns 80

8-Tracks, Shotguns and Rifles 82

Maxi-Me 83

Singapore Satisfaction – Part 1 88

'72 Ski-Doo 91

A Son's Duty 93

Risky Business 99

Double-Barrel or Doberman? 100

Swimming – The Hot and the Cold of It 103

Corporal Punishment 106

Broken Noses 108

Stroke One – Having a Sharon Stone 110

The 21-Year-Old Springbank 112

Low-Hanging Exit Sign 115

Incoming! 117

The Kilts 119

The Thinkers 122

The 155-Pound Subwoofer 123

The Best Darn Margaritas in the World 125

The Perv 127

Pembroke Pub Crawls 129

Proud Father 132

Great Pyramid of Giza 134

Coliseum 137

Cold, Darn Cold! 140

The Scotch Night 143

Paintings – The Self-Portrait 144

Boeing, Boeing, Gone! 145

Paris Shower Stall 149

The Last High - Thai Sticks 150

Good Relations 151

How Much For That Guy in the Window? 153

The Amber Necklace 156

The Boyfriend Killer 157

A Crasher's Tale – Part 2 159

The Robert Grahams 162

The Sea of Tits 163

You're Still An A-Hole Watson! 165

Obituary 166

Lucky's Lake Swim 167

Bavarian Beer Tour 169

The Idiot Vote 172

Stroke Two – I Smell Curry 173

Fight or Flight 175

The Pearls 178

Recollections of the Hofbrauhaus 181

Singapore Satisfaction – Part 2 182

Pain Relief 183

Paintings – The Avenue 184

Chevy Chevette Chills 186

Turkey Thief 188

The Tradition 189

Muddy Footprints 190

No Officer 191

Lock-in at The Royal Exchange 194

Slow Motion Rollover 196

Just Swish It Around 198

Flying Drunk 200

Four Floors of Whores...202
Swiss Alps 205
The Richard-Out Award 208
The Vasectomy 209
Cuban Cigar Hangovers..212
The Pool That Wasn't 214
Paintings – Vermeer...216
Arab Conflict..217
The Dive Knife 220
My Standard Fee 223
Zap Three Times..225

Acknowledgements and Credits

About Me, the Author

Opportunity from Tragedy

In January of 1986 I was just over a year into a new, and exciting, job at the Government of Canada's Atomic Energy of Canada, Chalk River Nuclear Laboratories.

As told in another tale in this book, I spent my first few years after graduating from university working in nuclear reactor operations at CRNL. However that was shift work, and with my also shift-working wife pregnant with our first child in 1984, one of us needed to secure a steady "day job" to make things work. So I somehow managed to convince a manager to hire me into a relatively new group at CRNL tasked with the business development, marketing, contracts, and sales related to its nuclear technology, services, testing etc. I would spend the rest of my working life in similar positions.

While I fit right in with the group and quickly became quite good at it, I really did not do much to distinguish myself.

Also in January of 1986, NASA's Challenger space shuttle was destroyed 73 seconds into its last mission. I remember a senior executive walking down the hall of our building, ashen-faced, saying "They lost a shuttle." We gathered in a conference room and watched the coverage on TV, shocked at what we were seeing.

Later that year the Rogers Commission Report on the disaster was delivered.

A physicist (whose name I unfortunately can't remember) at CRNL got a copy, read it, and attached a note suggesting that maybe there was something we could do to help. It made its way down the line until it ended up on my desk.

One of the groups at CRNL that I supported in their business activities was the Fluid Sealing Technology Unit. In the nuclear business, leaks (and leaking fluids) are not a good thing. FSTU did the research and design work that stopped leaks from happening in Canada's Candu reactors, and was teaching others how to do the same with theirs.

The Rogers Commission Report focussed its findings on all aspects related to the O-ring seals in the solid rocket motors. Escaping hot gas is just another fluid. Hence the question as to whether FSTU might be able to help.

Some of the Post-It notes on the copy of the report that hit my desk seemed to cast doubt on whether we could, but after reading it I was left with a feeling that we could. I took it down to the head of FSTU. While somewhat cautious, he agreed that it was worth pursuing but the real key would be what we could bring in terms of quality control. We talked about that for some time and then I headed back to my office.

The question then was how the heck to approach NASA? I knew that you could always submit an unsolicited proposal, but I also knew that it would either get rejected outright or buried for years. I went to the CRNL library and searched for NASA solicitations on the subject (remember, there was no web back then!) but couldn't find any. So I decided on a direct course of action: call NASA. But who?

I figured I'd start at the top. So I put a call in to the head of NASA. The assistant who I ended up talking to told me that it was not possible for me to speak directly to him. I told her that I was calling from the Government of Canada and that I had information that was vital to the successful and safe re-start of the shuttle program. After quite a long time on hold she transferred me to a very senior NASA executive.

His immediate approach was to thank me very much for calling, and welcome me to submit a proposal to NASA for their consideration. It was at that point that I made a very bold decision –I can trace all of the success that I've had in the rest of my career to that decision. I told him no. Absolutely not. We would not submit a proposal because that proposal would never get acted upon by NASA. And because it would never get acted upon there was a very big chance that future shuttle launches would not be as safe. That we had knowledge and technology that nobody else in the world had, especially as it related to quality control of fluid sealing, and that I could not in good conscience allow him to make the mistake of not making use of it. I was sweating by the end of my rant.

He took down my name and number, thanked me, and hung up.

I thought I'd blown it. I started walking up and down the hallway, muttering to myself. I stopped at my assistant's office and told her I'd come on too strong. I walked back to my office and sat there, staring out the window at nothing.

A few minutes later she came running down the hall. "NASA's on the line for you!" It was a senior person in charge of the re-design. We spoke. He asked if he could come and visit us, along with his team and a team from Morton Thiokol and Parker Seal. A week later they came, and FSTU was more than prepared for them. Two weeks later we had an initial contract in place, which I negotiated with the help of our legal counsel, for $1.8 million US (which was a BIG contract for us in those days) and by the end of the multi-year project, that amount would grow, via additions and extensions, to $3.3 million US.

It was that deal that established my reputation, and which led to subsequent positions that set the course for the rest of my working life.

But the tale's not done. There's something I left out.

You see there was a glitch in the contract negotiations. At that time the United States Government was only offering indemnification (call it protection) for liabilities in excess of $1 billion US. In other words, if the next shuttle exploded and the lawsuits started flying, AECL (and by extension, the Government of Canada) would be potentially liable for up to that $1 billion limit. The other quirk is that, unlike private-sector companies, the Government of Canada does not protect itself via third-party insurance policies. It self-insures – which is just another way of saying it will have to find the money from its own budget in the case of problems.

And we were told that the only way to waive that limit, and secure what is known as "first dollar indemnification" (meaning we were fully covered) was to get a waiver signed by the President of the United States.

So my legal counsel and I reached agreement with Morton Thiokol (who was the prime contractor to NASA and subcontracted work to us) that they would pursue and obtain said waiver, and that we would proceed "in good faith" with the work. Which we did.

Flash forward to the next launch. We've done a ton of work, the results of which form part of the launch check-off. In other words we had to certify certain results and things that were critical to the launch proceeding. We've assembled a news team at our site with our technical people available for questions and live shots of their reaction when the launch happens. The clock is ticking. The launch time is fast approaching.

Huddled in another office in another building in front of a fax machine are me and my lawyer. You see for months and then weeks and then days before the launch we kept asking for the waiver. We still did not have it. That morning we told Morton Thiokol's contracts specialists that unless we got it, at T minus 10 minutes we would release a fax message stating that we do not support the results of the work and that we disavow ourselves from it utterly and completely. That would have the effect of scrubbing the launch and potentially setting back the program for a long time. Not what we wanted but, given the risk, it was something we'd decided had to be done.

So we waited and waited. At T minus 20 minutes our fax machine starts to print (ever so slowly!) a message from Morton Thiokol. We read it as it emerged. It contained all of the legal documentation to confirm that the waiver had been signed and that we were now fully indemnified. We tore up our draft message. Walked over to the main auditorium. And at 11:37am on September 29, 1988 we gleefully watched the successful launch of the space shuttle Discovery. Nobody knew how close we'd come to halting it.

Snap of Rubber Gloves

I was returning to Canada via Ottawa International Airport. I collected my luggage from the carousel and was about to exit the Customs area. The next thing I know I'm in a room hearing the snap of rubber gloves behind me.

Rewind.

There's more to the story than that, so let's back up and fill in a few blanks.

First off, it was the middle of winter and as the plane touched down in Ottawa I could see swirling snow and feel the cold already.

Rewind some more.

I'd been visiting some hot destination on business. Before leaving for the airport that morning I had packed all of my winter clothes in my big checked bag: ski jacket, toque, mitts, and boots. I was travelling in a t-shirt and jeans with sandals on.

When you arrive from abroad you need to clear Canada Customs.

You fill out a Customs Card on-board the plane and after deplaning the first thing you do is get interviewed by a Customs agent who asks a few questions then writes some cryptic letters and numbers on the card. (Just once I wish it was the winning numbers for the next day's lotto.) You then proceed to collect your baggage.

So I waited for my bag to descend, likely missing another wheel or some such piece of itself. Mine was easy to spot: I always duct tape a large silver "X" to each side. My bag dropped and I yanked it off the carousel. I then retrieved my winter gear from the bag, put it on, and headed to the exit where I presented my Customs Card to the agent. The next thing I know I'm in a room hearing the snap of rubber gloves behind me.

Rewind again. To the point where I'm putting on my winter clothes.

You see even though I'm a fully developed example of *Homo sapiens*, I still maintain some mannerisms of my primate cousins. I don't have a prehensile tail for grasping objects when two hands are not enough, but I do have a perfectly functional mouth - too perfectly functional it will turn out. As I was going through my bag and getting dressed, I put my Customs Card between my lips for safekeeping.

As I'm leaving the Customs area, I present my card to the female Customs agent. With a look of shock and horror on her face, she makes a big "Ewww" sound and says "You expect me to take that! After where it's been!" The next thing I know I'm in a room, with a big guy behind me, hearing the snap of rubber gloves.

Ok, last rewind. I left out a thing or two.

When the female agent reacted in disgust and said, "You expect me to take that! After where it's been!" my too-fully functional *Homo sapiens* mind flashed back to the card in my mouth and concluded that's what had upset her: the possibility of contact with my bodily fluid.

Fair enough, but I was more than a little pissed off at her theatrics. Of course I should have said "I'm sorry Ma'am. I have the utmost respect for people such as yourself and the valuable job you do protecting us and Canada. I'll see that it never happens again. Please accept my most sincere apologies."

Well, I could have said that.

Instead I said, "Then I guess the chances of you and I having unprotected sex tonight are pretty slim."

And that's why the next thing I know I'm in a room, bent over a table, jeans at my ankles, while a big guy by the name of Bruce snaps on rubber gloves up to his hairy forearms, telling me to "spread 'em."

But you know, as I left that room, I couldn't help but tell myself that I'd won. That I'd stood up to the tyranny of power over us little guys. I keep telling myself that. I figure if I say it enough times, it will be true.

The Ruby Ring

It's pretty easy, to misquote Monty Python, to always look at the dark side of life. Just look at the "comments" section of any web site to get your fill of hating trolls. It's easy to forget the many instances where one is reminded of the inherent goodness of people. This is one of them.

In the earlier years of my career, when I was frequently away from home and Gen was left to tend to the flock (of kids), there was a toll to be paid to cross back over the front door's threshold upon my return. It could be flowers. It might be chocolates. A bottle of wine, or some crystal to drink it from. Jewelry was a possibility; gold bangles were de rigueur at one point. And then there was the ruby ring.

I guess things must have been tough at home during the first few days of a February Ottawa - Detroit - Washington D.C. trip that I was on, because when I called to see how things were going back at the ranch, the only words I heard were, "Bring home a ring. A ruby ring. A really nice one." Click. Gauntlet firmly thrown down.

Luckily for me I was staying in downtown Windsor and commuting daily to an event in Detroit. Luckily, because there's a great store in downtown Windsor called Shanfields-Meyers Jewelry & China Shop, which I knew quite well, having gone there many times on previous trips.

It's a riot of a store. It rambles along several storefronts, and has a huge storage / warehouse area upstairs. It's got everything from new and old jewelry, to dinnerware, to china, crystal, you name it. And it's got, or at least it had back then, Lima.

Lima ran things. No deal was done or sale made without her blessing. She was a tiny lady, old back then, but with a vice-like grip. You wouldn't shake hands with her; she'd reach out and grab your pinky finger – and not let go until she had led you around the store and you'd agreed to buy something. Anything to get her to let go! On previous visits it was stainless steel flatware, china, and crystal. (How many husbands actually know "their" patterns? I do!) I once took my brother with me, and gladly offered up his pinky to Lima, rather than mine.

While I'd never bought jewelry there before, I knew that they had a large selection of estate pieces. So it was over to the display cases to look for ruby rings. I looked at dozens and dozens of them but none of them were just right. Then Lima retrieved a small collection from under the counter and I saw it immediately: a big beautiful ruby flanked by two diamond baguettes. It was all over but the haggling.

The ring was put into a small black case, and then into a small plastic bag and then into the inner pocket of my long winter coat. When I got back to my hotel I called Gen with the news. I'm sure she was pleased with my description of the ruby ring but all I remembered were the words "don't lose it!"

The next day it was off to D.C. for a quick meeting and an overnight stay at the Mayflower Hotel. Upon checking in I asked the desk staff to store the ring in the hotel safe, which they did. The next day I checked out, had them bring me the ring which I put in my overcoat's pocket, and then stood outside chatting to the doorman as he called up a cab from the line to take me to Washington National Airport. The cab pulled up, the doorman opened the door, I handed him a one-dollar tip, he loaded my bag into the cab's trunk, and off I went. It's a very short trip to Washington National from downtown D.C.

We pulled up to the terminal's curb. I paid the driver, hopped out of the cab, and met him at the trunk to get my bag. As I'm walking through the doors to the terminal I'm suddenly overtaken by a disquieting sense of dread. I've just remembered Gen's last words to me and can't remember if I retrieved the ring from the hotel's safe. I do a quick pat-down of my coat pockets and can't feel it. I rush outside to see if I left it in the back seat of the cab, but the cab is long gone. Now I'm in a mini state of panic.

Ahead of me there's a traveller's aid station. I explain that I think I've just lost something valuable and ask to use their phone. I call back to the hotel and the operator puts me through to the front desk. I tell them what's just happened and tell them that I can't remember for sure getting it from them on check-out. They look and confirm that I did; I signed a chit to that effect. I give them a description of the ring and my full contact information. They tell me they'll keep looking, just in case, although I'm sure they're just trying to calm me down. I tell them my flight leaves in an hour or so and I'll call back before boarding.

So I check in for my flight and 20 minutes later phone the hotel again. This time the operator is expecting my call and connects me directly to the hotel manager. He comes on the line, introduces himself and asks me to describe the ring. I don't ask why, I just do. He then tells me that he's holding the ring in his hands as we speak. Apparently, right after my first panicked call, they alerted all staff to look out for a small plastic bag containing a small black jewelry case.

The doorman had gotten the message, then taken the initiative to search the back seat of every cab in line at his hotel, and every cab that pulled up. Apparently cabbies have a habit of returning to the same hotel after an airport run. And in one that had just pulled up, he found the bag on the back seat. The driver would never have noticed it. It must have somehow fallen out of my coat pocket. He then took the bag directly to the hotel manager, who alerted the hotel operator to put me through directly to him when I called back.

He told me that it was no problem for them to ship the ring to me, but that he'd very much like to try to get it to me before I left. He said to wait out at the curb until the last possible moment before I had to go back, clear security (very different back then) and then board my flight. So I waited.

In what seemed to be an eternity, but was actually record time, a long limo pulled up directly beside me, the hotel's name and crest on the passenger's front door. The tinted window slid down and the manager handed me the small bag. Still stunned from the journey to panicville and back, I was at least able to reach for my wallet and pull out the only bill I had left, a hundred, and hand it to him, with a request that he give it to the doorman. He said the doorman would appreciate it very much, and the limo pulled away.

I boarded my flight and was met at the airport by Gen. As soon as we got home, I presented her with the ring, which she loved. I told her the tale about its near-loss and how badly I had felt at the time. While she still loved the ring, the tale had the effect of greatly reducing the number of special requests on future trips. Besides that small side benefit, the whole experience, and especially the doorman's actions, honesty and integrity, continue to remind me of the inherent goodness of people.

Hockey Heaven on Howe Street

I grew up in the East end of Pembroke, Ontario, on Howe Street. As hockey-crazed kids we convinced ourselves that it was named after the legendary Gordie Howe - which it wasn't.

Mind you, besides the dozens of kids who at one time or another played road hockey on Howe Street, it really did host a few genuine hockey stars.

After his first season with the Boston Bruins, defenceman extraordinaire Bobby Orr came to Pembroke for a week, along with a couple of his teammates (right winger Wayne Connelly, and a goaltender whose name I'm not sure of) for a summer hockey school program.

Howe Street is a short street, with more major streets at each of its ends. It's quiet and perfect for road hockey, in winter or summer. It was also the home of the (Dennie) Labine family.

Now Gilbert Labine of Parry Sound (Bobby's hometown) happened to be good friends with Bobby's father Doug Orr, and Doug asked Gilbert if he could get his brother Dennie to billet Bobby for the week at his house - which was basically right across the street from mine.

At the end of the street, a few houses down, lived Wayne Connelly's brother. So he stayed there - along with the goaltender (whose name I forget.)

Anyhow, from the second he arrived, all of the neighbourhood kids showed up at the Labine's to meet Bobby and to get his autograph. After the first day he upped the pleasure and joined us, morning and night, for the rest of the week, for ball hockey games on Howe Street. As an eight-year-old Canadian kid it was like dying and going to hockey heaven!

I still have, somewhere, one of the autographs he signed for me back in 1967.

Flash forward to a few years ago, to an aerospace trade show that I was attending.

I get word that Bobby's at someone's booth signing autographs. I race over and just miss him. He's done for the day – and the show. Seeing the look of disappointment on my face, one of the booth staff comes over. I tell her that I was hoping to get Bobby's autograph for my grandson Grayson. I tell her how I played hockey with Bobby – and relate a brief version of the Howe Street story to her.

She tells me to wait a second and goes back into their storage room, emerging with a copy of a signed photo of "The Goal" for me. She explains that Bobby signed a few for booth staff and they have one left over.

It now forms part of the very small, but special, collection of sports memorabilia that I have assembled for Grayson, my grandson.

Pie !

My first trip to Barcelona was for business and I was accompanied by Bruce, my regular business partner-in-crime. For this one we decided to take our wives along with us.

We were staying at the almost-new Hilton Diagonal. It's a gorgeous property with rooms, food and service that greatly exceeded expectations of a Hilton. I managed to get both of our rooms upgraded for free to the very swanky executive floor, which came with the benefit of access to an incredible executive lounge. For the first three or four days that's where we did all of our eating and drinking.

One day later in the week, as a change of pace, we decided to hit the city. We walked from tourist spot to tourist spot. Starting at one end of La Rambla, a tourist street / pedestrian mall, we visited store after store. By that evening, as the now-usual 9pm dinner time approached, everyone was hungry. I was famished. Actually in-pain hungry. It took a while to find a restaurant that could seat us.

We struggled a bit with the menus that were either in Spanish only, or whose English translation was not much better. I ordered what I thought was described as a ham dinner; the others something else. We sipped on wine while the food was being prepared, my hunger growing ever more acute.

The others' platters of food (definitely not tapas size) arrived first, to my stomach's rumbles of approval. And next came my "ham dinner."

I should explain that in Spain there's something called Iberian Ham. It comes from a special breed of pig whose meat is cured. It is very expensive. Perhaps because of this expense you typically don't get very much of it at a time; it's served as very thin slices. That's what my "ham dinner" consisted of.

Not a mound of ham with all the trimmings and veggies etc. A white plate onto which were spread, radially, the thinnest, sheerest slices of meat known to man. If you were to roll them all up into a tight ball it would easily fit on a soup spoon. While the others dug into their meals with gusto, my heart (and stomach) wept in sad frustration. I tried to make it last, but it was all over in a flash. It only made me hungrier. Some weird sense of pride kept me from begging for the others' scraps, no matter how delicious the aromas that were wafting my way. I did sense that they knew I was casting a tortured glance at them, given how they adopted protective postures over their plates, much like a wild animal protects his kill from others.

Come time for dessert, the others were too full but I NEEDED something! Again consulting the menu I saw what was described as "apple pie," which I ordered. After what seemed like way too long a time to wait for someone to slice me a slab of pie, it finally arrived. The same master of the transparent pig slices had been at it again: he'd somehow managed to slice what was at most half an apple into slices so thin that he covered a whole plate with them. Those slices had then been sprinkled with cinnamon and "baked" on-plate before arriving at our table.

The look on my face must have been funny, because my table mates could no longer hold it back and broke out into fits of laughter. Sure it hurt to do so, but I couldn't help but laugh along with them.

Paintings - The Lessons

I love old paintings. I've spent hours and hours walking through museums around the world. I've spent hours sitting in front of just one painting. The more "realistic" a painting looks, the more I like it. I think I know why.

During our first visit to New Orleans in the mid-'80s, Gen and I were wandering the French Quarter and happened upon the galleries of Kurt E. Schon, Ltd., which we at first mistook for a museum, rather than the private business that it is. Before we could get back out the door a rather distinguished gentleman, with a heavy accent, asked if he could help us. I apologized and said that the obviously fine works of art hanging on the store's walls were far beyond our means and that we were sorry to have simply walked in and started looking around as we had done.

Nonsense he said. Fine art needs to be seen and appreciated. And there began one of the best couple of hours of education that I think we'd ever had. He took us from room to room and explained each piece to us. He talked of the artists, and where the works were painted, and for whom. He taught us a little trick to better appreciate a painting: start some distance away and take it in. Then take a step closer, stop, and see what new details emerge. Keep doing this until you are at arms' length. It's amazing how your perspective changes.

He did not try to sell us anything. (I'm sure it was obvious to him that this young couple could not afford any.) But he did offer another piece of advice: when you are just starting out as a collector of art, find a painting that is not only affordable, but one that you absolutely love to look at. We thanked him and said it would probably be years, if ever, before we could buy. He said not to worry, that <u>his</u> store would still be there when we were ready.

We had just been toured and schooled by Kurt E. Schon himself. And his store is still there! We've made good use of this education over the years, buying several pieces of original art by a number of local artists.

Hooligans' Game

It is said that soccer is a gentlemen's game played by hooligans, and that rugby is a hooligans' game played by gentlemen. While I have very limited personal experience playing either game, given what little I have, I'd tend to agree.

In the early '80s, after graduation, I was living in Pembroke, Ontario and working for Atomic Energy of Canada at Chalk River. A sizeable number of the professional employees there live in a nearby town called Deep River. It's so named after the depths of that part of the Ottawa River, beside which the town is situated. You might also assume it's because of the very deep roots that its inhabitants have to the UK. Canada's nuclear industry was initially populated by a large number of scientists and engineers from the UK. They stayed and several waves of additional employees from there followed over the next few decades.

Given the accents and local traditions found in Deep River when I was growing up, it's no wonder that we, from Pembroke, considered it to be "not of the Ottawa Valley."

Most of my managers came directly from the UK, and one day one of them approached me to ask if I'd played high school football. I told him I had played a few positions, and my favourite had been middle linebacker. So he said something about me probably being able to run and tackle. He then asked if I'd ever played rugby. Nope, I answered, although I think we might have tossed a ball around once in gym class. No matter, he said. Would I like to join him, some co-workers, and residents of Deep River, in a "friendly" match against a visiting team? It seemed he was desperate for players and could use me as another body. What the heck! I agreed.

A few days later, after a few minutes of prep time, I found myself on a pitch getting pummeled and beaten like never before.

He had failed to mention that the "friendly" game was against what I seem to recall was the Welsh "National" Team. Apparently a few of them had relatives in Deep River, were touring Canada anyhow, and decided to stop by for a visit, bringing the whole team with them. Naturally (to them) they would do everyone a favour and play a match while in town.

Yes, I could run, and yes, I could tackle. I could do the former as fast as most on the pitch that day, and while I quickly learned how to "properly" effect a rugby tackle, I had never done anything like it without a full set of pads and helmet. My body, arms and face were hammered. I was stepped on and punched, and I think someone bit my ear (or maybe that was a set of cleats passing by). I was cut and contused. And the play never really stopped. No sooner had you tackled someone, or been tackled (and had your face pushed into the hard turf), than you were running after or away from someone else. I never quite caught on to any of the finer points of the game, but I don't think I embarrassed myself too badly.

Except for possibly my nose, I ended the game without anything broken. A small miracle of sorts.

What was most amazing, however, was how, while we were lined up and shaking hands at the end of the game, there was such a sense of warm and genuine camaraderie amongst the players from both teams. We had pounded the crap out of each other, but as soon as the game ended that was all put aside. I, and my fellow gentlemen, retired to a local bar and the game was replayed, to great amusement, many times over. Much less painfully!

A Never-Solved Mystery

I don't believe in ghosts.

Nor spirits. Nor a thousand and one other such things.

But one event has come close to making me a believer.

When I was in grades seven and eight, there was a large group of neighbourhood kids who hung out together all the time. We'd sit at the end of Howe Street and dream up pranks and ways to cause mischief.

Now I'm not talking gang-style crime here. It was more like "Whose apple tree are we going to hock from tonight?"

One such night there were at least a dozen of us, maybe more – both girls and boys. I don't recall who suggested it, but someone said we should prank Mr. Fields.

Mr. Fields was a high school science teacher, and beside the fact that he had a very strong British accent, I can't think why we singled him out. (As I learned a few years later in high school, he was a great teacher, and was blessed with a tremendous sense of humour.)

So we set off to the other end of the street.

It was very late at night, probably midnight or later. We were a large group, but we were good at being very quiet. We saw that Mr. Fields' Datsun was parked in its usual place: at the far end of his driveway, with the front against a thick cedar hedge, and with that hedge also running down the driver's side. On the right, alongside the front half of the car, was the side of a poured concrete set of steps leading to the side door of the house. (Garages and carports were rarer than Yetis on Howe Street!) There was plenty of room for driver and passenger to open their doors.

Again, I don't recall what inspired us, but like a flock of swallows diving in unison to roost as the sun goes down, the group surrounded the Datsun, picked it up and silently carried it backward out of the confines of the end of the driveway. Then we turned it ninety degrees and walked it back into its cove, this time with the front bumper almost touching the concrete steps and the rear tight against the cedar hedge. It was locked in place. It would take either a huge forklift to extract it – or a group as committed as us. The whole operation took just a few minutes, and not a grunt nor a squeak of metal could have been heard.

We retired back to the other end of the street to replay the successful operation to each other.

I was the first to call it a night.

My place was a couple of houses away. Mom and Dad had left the back door unlocked for me and after I went in, I locked it, and checked the front door to make sure it was locked as well.

I tucked myself into bed and was soon asleep.

That morning I was the first in the house to wake up. As I opened my eyes, something was not quite right.

My bed was a simple thing: non-attached headboard, box spring and mattress, six screwed-on wooden feet on the bottom of the box spring, with a separate rubber "cup" under each foot, to protect the carpeted floor.

Problem was, the headboard was not where it should have been. Actually it was. It was my head that wasn't. It, and the entire bed, were turned ninety degrees in place – just as we had done to Mr. Fields' car! All six rubber cups were in place under the feet – and they would normally pop out of place if I so much as bumped the bed hard.

I got out of bed and checked the house. Both doors locked. No signs of entry anywhere.

I put the bed back in place – which took some effort – especially to get the cups back under the legs.

I never told my parents, nor my friends.

I could not imagine how anyone could have entered our small house and not woken me, or the rest of the family. (We all slept with our doors open. We could hear each other get up to go to the bathroom in the middle of the night.)

It would have taken at least four people to lift the bed and rotate it with me on it. But even then I would have woken up. In the pitch dark of the room there's no way that anyone could have ensured that the rubber cups were put back in place, let alone even know they were there in the first place.

Over the years, none of the group ever came forward to fess up. I didn't ask, but the nature of that group was that someone would have broken up laughing the next day, when we first got together again, had they done it.

To this day it remains a puzzling never-solved mystery. Karma?

Super Mike

The Dutch seem to have a very different attitude toward sex than we Canadians. At least that's what I concluded on a trip to Amsterdam, and a tour of their Red Light District.

My travel buddy Bruce and I decided to visit it one day and were very surprised to see all manner of "normal" citizens, tourists and locals alike, walking along the canals and over the footbridges in what is actually a very scenic locale. Older teenagers (mostly women), older couples, and everything in between.

Of course an awful lot of the scenery is taken up by numerous storefront windows in which sit the ladies of the night in the hopes of luring customers in. And judging from the action, business was brisk. There seemed to be a size, shape, colour, what have you, for every taste.

After a circuit or two, we passed what looked like the entrance to an old movie theatre. It might have been at one time, but now the marquee was advertising continuous live sex shows. There was a statue of an elephant out front, nose raised. (This would turn out to be very prophetic.) And every so often, the doorman would activate a spray of water from it to the delight of passersby.

Bruce and I turned to each other and said, what the heck, you only live once. So we bought our tickets, got our "free" drink that was included in the (rather steep) price of admission, and waited in the foyer as the crowd built. We would eventually learn that the theatre is divided into four sections – two on each side of a main aisle, one front and one back. Every fifteen minutes an entire section is asked to leave and are replaced with the waiting crowd. The acts "loop" every hour, so no matter when you come in, you eventually get to see them all.

We ended up in the front row of the front left quadrant, with barely room for our legs – or drinks, which we placed on a rail in front of us. Every time there's a crowd change, the curtain is closed and there's an admonition not to try to peek under it while the next act is being prepared. We ended up in a little spot of trouble over that rule, when we had to move the curtain to sit our drinks on the railing. A spotlight illuminated us, a loud voice yelled in Dutch, and a bouncer appeared. We managed to convince him of our innocence.

And the shows began. Use your imagination but yes, this did involve live people, some in costume, having real sex, but it came across more as a bawdy skit-based vaudeville theatre production than anything else. Part-way through I remarked to Bruce that, to date, I was unimpressed with the male "talent." He agreed. Then the last act (for us) came on. He was introduced as Super Mike.

He was dressed in work boots, and a Tarzan-like loincloth, and not much else. He was of medium height and ripped. Mustache and long hair capped it all off. He started to dance around the stage to the music. At one point he wrapped a large silk cloth around his waist, dropped his loincloth, and (sort of) danced in place doing pelvic thrusts towards the audience. To the delight of all of the women in the audience (more than half), something started to bounce off that silk cloth, which he held further and further away from himself, until it was at arms' length. Then he dropped the cloth.

Bruce and I (and everyone else's) reactions were of utter

amazement. Super Mike indeed was. I can only describe him as being hung like a baby elephant! Now at 6'3", I'm a big guy, but even my ... forearm and fist combined were shorter and smaller.

After a little more dancing on stage, Super Mike pulled out a bottle of baby oil and completely soaked his "trunk." He leapt off the stage and headed up the aisle to the back right quadrant. There, to squeals of delight, he danced on the seat backs over a large group of women. We then realized why the oil: every one of them was trying to get a handhold on him, perhaps wanting to be Tarzan's Jane and swing on his vine. The oil foiled their attempts.

He soon raced back up to the stage, took a bow: show's over, and our quadrant got escorted out.

Bruce and I knew we had seen something special, but given its surreal nature, I think my mind soon let the memory slide in order to protect my sanity.

Then one year, at a big family Christmas get-together at my mother-in-law's place, we were all, adults and children alike, lounging around after dinner, presents having been distributed and opened, with a TV playing in the background. It was showing a Lonely Planet travel episode featuring Amsterdam, and right there on screen, being interviewed standing beside that elephant statue, was none other than the long-forgotten legend. "Hey, it's Super Mike," I blurted out, mouth engaging before brain! I chose to not answer the questioning gazes that ensued.

A Crasher's Tale – Part 1

Over the years I've become pretty adept, almost legendary in some circles, for my ability to crash "private" business social events and parties. I'm prepared to share two of them with you.

In October of 2004, I was in Las Vegas for the annual National Business Aviation Association event. That year we had an expanded presence at the event: some media briefings and a larger trade show booth. A handful of colleagues from our labs were there in support.

As is the custom, after a day at the show we all headed to a variety of events, parties and receptions, some open and some for which we had received invitations. Back then I'd try to cover a few of them every night, quickly "working" the room in search of clients and business contacts. (In later years I tended to pick one big event and hunker down there for the evening.) This one night I ended up talking to a friend who sold advertising space for a major aerospace publication. He told me he was heading over to Bombardier's Learjet Owners' Appreciation event at the Bellagio. I was intrigued. I'd not heard of this obviously exclusive event.

He had an invitation, I didn't. I asked if I could tag along, and told him I'd figure out a way to get in once we were there. No problem, he said and we set out on foot. We hadn't gone very far when we happened upon four of my colleagues who wondered what was up. I told them about the event and said they could come along and, while I was making no promises, if they followed my lead (whatever that was going to be) they'd stand a chance of getting in as well.

We showed up at the Bellagio and I immediately spotted the lovely hostess holding a sign for the event. Now at this point I should add that the first rule of crashing an exclusive event like this one is to look like you belong. My business-suited advertising friend and I did; my just-out-of-the-lab colleagues in tweed sports coats and khaki slacks? Not so much. This was going to be tough and I was already estimating the odds of at least partial failure as high.

I asked the hostess for an escort to the event check-in, which was quite some distance back into the massive Bellagio. She called over a colleague who took my arm and led us on. A key rule of crashing is having someone working at the event on or at your side. A hostess will do in a pinch.

The check-in consisted of six "will-call" windows. My advertising friend took the wicket on the far left. I was immediately to his right and the rest of my crew the last four slots to my right. They were all fearfully trying to watch what I was up to. I avoided even acknowledging them. (Rule number three: help where you can, but don't sacrifice your own attendance at a great event!). I hoped that with my own official entry, theirs could follow.

My advertising friend presented his invitation and was quickly given a name tag and lanyard and was ready to proceed. I, of course had no such invitation, so instead I presented my business card, and said to the nice lady at the window: "Hi. My name is Jeff Mackwood. This morning at the show, I was invited by a Bombardier rep to this event. He told me you'd have my name on file by the time I showed up." She did a search of her up-to-date list and naturally did not find my name. She then asked me who the rep was.

Next rule: use that request not as a reason to panic, but rather as an indirect route to legitimacy. I told her I could not remember; that I had left his business card in my other suit coat. And as they will almost always do, trying to be helpful, she then asked if it was "Bob?" At this stage, crashers-in-training, the rule is: always say no, you don't think so. "Fred?" She asked next. Again, you decline. But three's the charm, so when she said "Was it Leo?" I said yes, to which she said "Oh, that Leo. He's always inviting people and not telling us. Here you are, Mr. Mackwood" (handing me a printed pass and lanyard). "Enjoy the evening."

At this point I turn to my left, with my back to my colleagues, and another hostess takes me by the arm and leads me towards the ballroom. As we're walking away I hear a plaintive cry from behind from one of my colleagues: "But we're with HIM!" I keep walking.

Many minutes later, they too were escorted into the event. For whatever reason, my new-found legitimacy was enough to get them in as well.

But that's just the beginning of the tale, because the night was young and the best still to come.

The organizers had split the massive Bellagio ballroom in two. We were taken to the half without the stage. There was found any manner of drink, and mounds and mounds of food. And scattered between the food and drink stations were dozens of gaming tables. They had set up a casino within the casino and we got to play with funny money – the idea being that you could take your fake winnings and use them to bid on great real prizes befitting a Learjet owner, or his wife.

Speaking of which, I'm really not a casino gamer, and almost never with my own real cash. I just don't understand the games well enough. But I can get by at blackjack, so I took a seat between two couples at a table. As I quickly learned, they were Texas billionaires with their wives. Quite nice people and we chatted and laughed much more than we played. As I knew would happen, they got around to telling me what kinds of Learjets they owned. And, again as I knew they would, they asked me which one I owned. (Assuming I owned one, at such an event, was normally a safe bet on their part.) For this I was prepared.

Next rule: stretch the truth as much as possible; it's much harder to keep track of big lies.

So I told them sheepishly (in hushed tones, like a confession) that I did not own a Learjet. And after a slight pause I then said that I had a Dassault Falcon 20 instead. (The partial truth is that my employer did in fact own a Falcon 20 and that I was pretty familiar with it.) They then clapped me on the back and said "Heck, that's nothing to be ashamed of; that's one damn fine aircraft."

After a while it was announced that the first part of the evening's festivities were coming to an end and that we should now proceed through the big doors that were opening to the other side of the ballroom, which was kitted-out in magnificent theatre style, with large semi-circular booths facing a huge stage, each booth already well-stocked with champagne on ice. I sat with a couple of my colleagues and three legitimate invitees. I think the "pressure" had gotten to the other two of my colleagues and they'd already left the event. Too bad because the show was about to begin.

To the sounds of a big band supporting his entrance onto the stage strode none other than David Foster, our host for the evening. In this capacity he was not just a hired performer for the evening but, as he was quick to tell us all, he was also part-owner of a Learjet. He played a great, but too short, opening set and then introduced the President of Learjet who gave an appropriately short welcoming "thank you" to all of us.

Then David took over. He made reference to his discovery of Celine Dion, and said that he had just recently stumbled upon the next greatest thing. That thing turned out to be Renée Olstead, an amazing singer whom I had not yet heard of – nor had very many others. David said that we were in for a treat because Renée was going to be on Oprah later that week and would be performing one song on the show. Tonight she was going to do two songs and we, by our applause, would get to choose which of the two Oprah got to hear. She led off with an incredible Ella-like performance of "Mack the Knife." To tell the truth, I was so blown away that I can't remember what the second song was. Mack it was on Oprah.

David then introduced the next performer. If Renée was the future, then this man was the present. And on came Michael Bublé. He performed a full set, including a finale of singing impersonations that he used to do more often earlier in his career. He was amazing.

As David was starting to introduce the final performer, white-tuxed musicians came on stage to replace those who were already there. Whoever it was, he was bringing his own orchestra! David tells us that we've now heard the future and the present and that we should now get ready for ... not the past ... but Mr. Las Vegas, Wayne Newton!

On strides Wayne, and the band launches into the opening notes of "Danke Schoen." But almost as soon as it begins Wayne starts saying "no, no, no, that's not right" and they stop. "Let's try it again." Now I'm pretty quick on the draw, so as soon as they do, I jump up and yell "Yeah!" at the top of my lungs, to which Wayne points to me and says "that's what I'm talking about," which then gets the crowd to break out into thunderous applause.

Next rule (which I had just violated completely): don't draw unnecessary attention to yourself!

Anyhow, Wayne finishes a great set (although, to be honest, his voice sounded almost like Buddy Hackett's to me). David thanks everyone for coming, the house lights go up and he reminds everyone to make sure to pick up a lovely parting gift bag on the way out.

As we move to the exit and approach the loot bag table there's a matronly-looking staffer who makes direct eye contact with me and transmits the "don't you dare" look. I gave a slight nod of understanding and exited the ballroom. I guess my encouraging yell was noticed by more than just Wayne. Oh well, it was still one of my best crashes ever.

Wine Opener and Oven Mitt

Ever have one of those moments where you suddenly understand something that, for most of your life, you've failed to grasp? Maybe it was quantum physics. Darwin's theory of evolution? Why your tee shot always slices?

Over the years I've shared more than a few bottles of wine with good friends Kirk and Annette. In the early days there were no screw-top bottles; at least none with contents worth drinking. Nope, it was cork, and only cork.

To open those bottles we had a sommelier's wine opener that somehow came into our possession – sans instructions. It had the corkscrew and handles that we extended to form a "T" with which we would then grasp and yank out the cork. In our hands there was always great danger of lacerating your fingers as you did so, because of a number of sharp edges. We assumed it was missing some protective plastic or wood parts. Many drops of blood were spilled before we came up with the solution: wear an oven mitt when performing the operation.

And so it went. For years, bottle after bottle was opened using that wine opener and an oven mitt that, over time, began to look like it was in successively worse knife fights.

Then the day came when we were out to dinner together at a restaurant. We perused the wine list and, with the help of the waiter, picked something that was sure to satisfy. He arrived back at our table with the bottle and proceeded to open it.

He produced a wine opener that was identical to ours. We exchanged knowing glances and sniggers: there was no oven mitt in sight! Ready the first aid kit! He extended the opener's appendages, including a knife with which to cut and remove the capsule. Call 9-1-1! He inserted the corkscrew into the cork and twisted it a few turns. Then, at the moment when we would have been applying Mister Over Mitt, he folded one of the appendages down to rest on the lip of the bottle and pulled upwards on the other, lever-fashion, and out popped the cork with no loss of digits.

After all of those years, we now understood how the common wine opener worked. Not exactly the meaning of life, the universe and everything. But close enough for us.

Border Crossing

Life on September 10, 2001 was good. I was in Seattle for a conference that was to start the next day. By chance, two of my colleagues, Bill and Kris, flew into Seattle the day before on the same flight, even though they were going to a different event. We'd agreed to meet up and now we were cruising through some back-country roads looking for yet another winery on our wine tour list.

I'd never toured that region before and was impressed with the quality of the wines. So much so that I'd ended up buying a dozen or so bottles over the course of the day. We took pictures as we travelled and laughed, while Kris and I took turns reading articles from a copy of The National Enquirer that someone had left under the seat of the rental. That night, back in Seattle, we enjoyed a superb seafood dinner, a few bottles of wine, and each other's company.

I woke up in my hotel room bed the next day to some fading rumbling sound and a ringing room phone. It was another colleague, Tony, who'd driven down from B.C. the day before for the same event as me. "Turn on your TV. They've attacked New York." I muttered something and hung up the phone. Minutes later that rumbling sound was back. I opened my 22nd floor window curtains to see a fighter flying combat patrol around the Space Needle. I turned on my TV.

And like almost everybody on the planet who could do so, I sat transfixed for hours, not believing what I was watching.

That afternoon, the organizers of the conference met and, from the speakers and session chairs who were already in the city, cut and pasted a programme together that would start the next day. It was an amazing undertaking. I would see several staff members break down in tears over the next two days, the combined stress of the attacks and the effort to re-do the conference pushing them to that point.

Downtown Seattle, as I'm sure with most cities, was a surreal place at that time. Armed soldiers stood at every corner and almost nobody was out. Unable to sleep, I took a stroll through the downtown area at 3am; the first time I'd ever felt completely safe at any time in downtown Seattle.

The conference wrapped up and it was time to get home. The

problem was that nothing was flying in the US, although Canada had just started to allow some domestic flights. I found out that if I could get to Vancouver on time, I could catch my previously scheduled return flight to Ottawa. So very early that morning we loaded up Tony's big truck and headed for the border.

There were massive lineups and it took us hours to crawl to the front of the line. We could see what was taking so long: Canadian border agents were being extremely thorough in their questioning. More so in the line we ended up in. Here the agent was emptying vehicles completely. Luggage was strewn and its contents spilled everywhere. Items opened. Toothpaste squeezed from its tube. The full monty of inspections.

As we are watching this happen to the vehicle immediately ahead of us, I say to Tony: "Would this be a good time to tell you about all the wine I'm smuggling in the back of your truck right now?" Wish I'd had a camera to record the look of abject terror on his face.

He doesn't have time to start yelling at me (I think he's still in inhale mode) when the car ahead of us moves on and we are waved ahead by the agent. We pull up, Tony now on the verge of panic, and an agent tells us to wait. That agent then goes into the building and out comes another. Shift change! She approaches Tony's window and asks to see our passports. "Anything to declare?"

Tony squeaks out a "no" and I respond in kind. "Have a nice day," she says, and waves us through.

I'm pretty sure Tony was suffering from PTSD for the rest of the ride to Vancouver airport. But he held it together and made great time, almost great enough for me to make my flight. I was just as happy to end up on another: an overnight red-eye into Ottawa, some eight hours later.

It had been a surreal week. Unfortunately I had just enough time to get home and hot-swap my luggage for another set. Flights were now flying in the US and I had to head to Houston later that day for another event.

Walking To Chicago Stadium

Of all of the professional sports events that I've ever attended, the most memorable has to be a Bulls – Celtics game at the old Chicago Stadium. But not because of the game.

It was my first trip to Chicago. Most likely in the '86-'88 time frame. I had not travelled much up until then. I might as well have had the words "Travel Newbie" stencilled to my forehead. Or a big target painted on my chest.

One morning I read that the Celtics were in town to play the Bulls in a playoff game that would feature Michael Jordan and Larry Bird. I was staying at the Chicago Hilton and Towers in the Loop District across from Grant Park. Knowing that I had nothing booked from late afternoon on, I checked with the concierge to see if he knew how I might get tickets to the game.

Like any good concierge, he knew a "ticket broker" and later that day there was a message on my phone that he had a ticket at his desk for me. I paid him cash and grabbed a map of Chicago. I had plenty of time to kill and, after looking at the map, figured the best way to do it would be to walk to the game. (Chicago natives are now rolling their eyes.) I headed north on South Michigan Avenue and hung a left onto West Madison St. - from there it was to be a five mile or so rifle shot to the stadium.

At this point I should explain that part of a being a travel newbie, at least for me, was that I took all the money I would need for the trip, not including airfare, with me in cash. The other part is that I felt it was a much better idea to keep all of the cash on me, as a bundle of large bills in my front pocket. Safe and sound that way. Yup.

As I left the loop area, things started to thin out. There were fewer and fewer people on the sidewalks. The ones that were, were lying down on the sidewalk. There were fewer and fewer of what I would call habitable buildings as I continued west. Cars sped by but even then traffic was pretty light for such a wide street. I also appeared to be the only white person. Still, the weather was great and I was enjoying the walk.

About halfway there, things were looking more and more sketchy.

The locals were starting to notice me; or maybe my bulging front pocket. I was on the south side of Madison and a few blocks ahead I could see a gang of teenagers milling about on the sidewalk. As I got closer, a little more than a block away, they noticed me. In unison the pack turned and started walking in my direction. At that point I started to wonder about the wisdom of walking to Chicago Stadium, and whether using a hotel safe might not have been a bad idea.

I stop. They start running towards me. Now one thing I have going for me is that, at least back then, I could run fast. Very fast. And with a little help from Mr. Adrenaline Rush, even faster. I doubted that any of them could take me in a sprint, but I wondered how good they were at middle distances.

I start back the way I came, briefly, until I notice that the pack's shouting and screaming has alerted some of the other locals to my presence. For reasons unknown, my body decides to leave the sidewalk, accelerate to near warp speed, and cross the six lanes or so of traffic. I get to the other side and almost run into a sign for a bus stop, and as I turn to see the gang leaving the sidewalk in hot pursuit, the view gets blocked suddenly by a bus that pulls up and stops with its front door inches in front of my face. Door opens. I get on. Door closes. Bus pulls away.

I notice the fare box, reach into my pocket and pull out the wad of bills to pay. (Of course the hundreds are on the outside!) As I'm about to fan the stack and find some ones the driver glances over at me, shakes his head, and waves me on. I put the cash back into my pocket and start walking down the aisle. It's only then that I notice that the bus is full except for one aisle seat way at the back. I also notice that nobody's talking; they're all looking at me – the only white person amongst them.

(Now I need to say that I'm mentioning "white" and, by implication "black," only as statements of fact. It is germane to the story only insofar as it highlights the fact that I stuck out like a sore thumb and was obviously not from around there.)

I walk to the back of the bus and take a seat beside a very big guy who, having no doubt noticed I'm now in a post-adrenaline state of panting and sweating, asks if I'm ok. I tell him I'm just out of breath – having just run to catch the bus (which was a bit of a stretch.) He asks where I'm going (probably wondering what the heck I'm doing out there in no-man's land) and I show him my ticket to the game. That gets us into a great, but all too short, conversation about basketball, Jordan, and Bird. He eventually lets me know when the next stop is Chicago Stadium.

If I recall correctly, the scene that greeted me upon exiting the bus was of a stadium surrounded by parking spaces, around which was a cordon of police officers. I was early for the game, but there were still lots of people heading to the entrances. Inside I was directed to an upper section and my seat. The place filled up and got very noisy. It turns out that my seat, and the one next to mine, were both sold by the same broker, only the other one was sold to a local: a giant white guy who easily had 60 pounds on me and, as we shook hands, a grip that could crack walnuts. He and I struck up a conversation. I also talked to the father / son combo who were sitting directly behind us, mostly because, as far as I could tell, they were the only ones in sight wearing Celtics swag. The Bulls crowd was giving them a bit of a hard time over it. (Truth be told I was a Celtics fan as well, but felt a need to lay low at that point.)

As the game goes on, my seat mate and I have been chatting to each other quite a bit, when he asks how I got to the game. I told him how I had walked, at least part way, to the game. That drew a look. I then mentioned the short chase. Another look. I then mentioned the wad of bills in my front pocket.

Sometime later he asks me how I'm planning to get back to my hotel. Now up until then I had pretty much recovered from my trip to the game, and not even considered the inevitable trip from the game. So I told him I'd probably take a cab. He said that was a bad idea: that there were lots of instances where cabbies took people for a ride, robbed and killed them, and disposed of the body. I thought he was pulling my leg, but the seeds of doubt were sown – and quickly taking root.

A little later he says he'd give me a ride back to my hotel. I jumped at the offer. The game went on but that beanstalk of doubt was getting taller. What if his cabbie statement was just a way to lure me into his car? What if he planned to take me somewhere, rob and kill me, and dispose of the body? Questions like this kept popping into my head so fast that I considered telling him that I'd take a cab instead. But what if the cabbie took me somewhere...? I was locked in an endless loop of doubt. So I did the only reasonable thing. When he got up after the third quarter to get a beer I flipped a coin. It told me I was leaving with him.

Now firmly committed, I pulled out one of my business cards and handed it to the Celtics fan behind me. I told him that if he read in the papers that my body had been found in a ditch somewhere, that he (pointing to the empty seat beside me) did it. That drew a strange, but perhaps appreciative, look.

The game ended. (I couldn't tell you who won, who scored, nothing. I was too rattled by that time.) We headed to a parking lot and got into his car – a great big 500 series Mercedes. As we leave the lot and past the cordon of cops, he tells me to not be surprised if he doesn't stop for any red lights on the way back east on Madison: too much of a risk to come to a stop. So we went the whole way back to the Loop District without once stopping for a red. Where the intersection and traffic permitted, we didn't even slow down. Somehow we (and I) arrived back at my hotel – safe and sound. I thanked him and headed to my room.

I picked up my phone to place a wake-up call. The operator made the mistake of asking me how my day went. I then proceeded to tell her the whole story, from leaving the hotel to returning several hours later. "Sir," she said after listened patiently, "you sure are one lucky person." Or maybe it was "dumb SOB." She was right either way.

London Pub Crawl

If, after an evening of pub crawling in London, you're perusing the morning tabloids and happen to see your picture in a few of them, you might expect to be doing so from the local lock-up. Not so the day after my friend Arnim and I did one for the scrapbooks.

We'd been at a business reception in a swankier part of town. I was dressed in my usual business suit, and Arnim in his military uniform. The reception was winding up early and, with no more official duties ahead of us for the night, we decided to start our own two-man pub crawl.

We hit quite a number of typical locals, and it became my custom to walk up to the bar and ask the bartender for a pint of whatever he wanted to recommend. That worked out just great, with quite a number of mostly British ales being consumed. We would only do one pint each per pub and then it was off to find the next source of libations.

We were walking along a typically narrow London street (where, I could never remember) when to our left was an even narrower street that looked like it ended in a dead end. Well, not completely dead because it looked like there was a pub at the very end.

About halfway down the street, there was a small restaurant off to the side and a throng of paparazzi milling about in front of the establishment. I stopped and asked them what was up. Was there someone important in the restaurant? Perhaps it was the Canadian accent (or the slight slurring of that accent) but we got the not-so-royal brush off from them. Oh well, I guess they just weren't friendly sorts.

So we continued to the pub.

Once again I approached the bar and asked the bartender what he would recommend. "Well," he says, "tonight I would recommend the Guinness." Interesting. We'd not had a Guinness all night long. So I asked him why the Guinness? "Sir, because Guinness are running a promotion tonight and it's free." As last call was fast approaching, and because the price was right, we each ordered two.

When mine had properly settled, I grabbed a pint and turned to the rest of the establishment. Emboldened by the liquid courage already in the tank, I announce to all that I'm a Canadian and I believe I have just arrived in Heaven, as surely to heck, if one finds oneself in a London pub where the Guinness is free, one must be at least at the pearly gates. This brought a huge cheer and a few friendly slaps on the back.

Once we finished our pints, we bade the bartender goodnight and went back onto the street. As soon as we cleared the pub's front door, however, we could not help but notice the flashing of cameras up the street at the restaurant we'd passed earlier. The paparazzi were in full operation. Without thought (my natural state by then) I broke into a sprint towards them; Arnim just behind me. As I got closer, I saw there was a big Bentley parked to our right, and standing at the curb, back door open, was the unmistakable Rod Stewart. Next day we would learn from those same tabloids that his then-wife, Rachel Hunter, had just left hospital, having given birth to their child. But all I could think of as I closed the distance fast was "it's Rod Stewart."

Now I don't know what part of my brain decided that the best thing to do would be to jump onto Rod's Bentley and slide across its roof with my hand extended yelling "Rod! Rod! I'm a Canadian and a big fan!" but it did. Amazingly, he did not duck, flinch, or anything like it. He simply met my extended hand in mid-slide, grasped it, and we shook hands. The paparazzi went nuts! Cameras flashing like crazy.

Now I suspect that Rod might have had a glass or three at dinner, or maybe he was always so calm. But we actually chatted for what seemed like quite a while. I couldn't let go of his hand. I told him he'd have to drop in the next time he was in Canada. He said he would. (Oops. Forgot to exchange contact info!) I disengaged, got off his car by sliding back down the street side (only to realize that Rachel, had she been looking out her window, would have been staring at my crotch.) I waved bye-bye as they sped off.

The vacuum left by the Bentley's departure was fast-filled by the paparazzi who demanded to know who I was, how I knew Rod, etc. It was our turn to practice the royal brush off. I suppose if we'd been a little more forthcoming, more of them would have run the photo of me sprawled across the Bentley with Rod's hand firmly locked onto mine. The few who did would only refer to me as a crazed fan in a good suit – or something like that. Not surprisingly, Rod never has dropped by.

Honda Meet Datsun

My motorcycling days came to a sudden end in 1988. Sudden as in tear-the–ass-end-off-a-Datsun-B210 sudden. But up until then it had been pretty uneventful.

Other than a few minutes on a dirt bike in the middle of a big Saskatchewan field in 1980, I had no experience riding motorcycles. However I had the itch to own one. Gen and I had been married for less than a year when we decided to get rid of my 1973 Mercury

Montego MX Brougham land yacht for the much more practical 1982 Honda Accord hatchback. I'm sure it was during the visits to the Honda dealer that my eyes strayed to the room next door, and the bikes therein.

It wasn't too long after that I was back and signing the paperwork for a brand new 1982 Honda CB900C. It was a gorgeous bike; powerful, shaft drive, dual range transmission, and comfortable as all get out. I was to pick it up the next day. The only problem was that I had no motorcycle driver's licence and, as stated earlier, had never really ridden one. So I went to the local library and took out every book I could find on motorcycles. In my dreams that night I was visualizing myself riding a bike.

The next morning I wrote my test for my learner's permit and passed. I then made an appointment to take my driver's test that afternoon, after I'd picked up the bike.

At the dealership the salesman wheeled my candy-blue beast out to me, handed me the keys, and shook my hand. I then told him there was just one more thing I needed from him: a quick walk through as to what was what (like which handle was the clutch, gear shifter, throttle, brakes - just the basics). He looked dumbfounded. I told him I'd never ridden before but assured him that with a few extra minutes of his time I'd be good to go. And I was. After a slow-go around the lot I waved goodbye and headed to the motor vehicle office for my driver's test.

I passed it with flying colours. Mind you it was a lot easier back then. My brand new bike was parked in front of the building. The examiner came outside with me and told me that I was to mount and start the bike, drive down the road and turn right, then the next right, then the next right, then the next right, and then park it on its centre stand, and then turn it off. Other than the fact that the salesman had not shown me the centre stand, I figured I could handle it. The examiner would stay standing at the front of the building the whole time, with me mostly out of sight circling the block.

So I took off, carefully signaling all of my turns, and successfully got it up on its centre stand upon my return. I now had my licence.

I put well over 13,000 km on that bike that season, including a trip to Toronto with Gen on the back. For the return trip we bought a backrest with luggage rack and installed it. I would later add a fairing shell. Gen showed enough interest in biking that soon after the Toronto trip we bought her a new 1982 Honda CM250C. But she took a full motorcycle riding course before ever riding it. She rode that bike around town and took one trip to Ottawa with me and me on my 900, although I think we swapped for a while. This convinced her that she needed something bigger, so the 250 became a Honda CB450. She did not get much riding out of it since she was soon pregnant with our first child (must have been the biker leathers!) and decided to sell it. She's never ridden since.

I, on the other hand, was in the mood for something sportier. So after a season of riding, the 900 was sold and a 1983 Honda CB1100F took its place.

This was a beast. One of the most powerful and fastest bikes available at the time. A true supersport in its day. I had a blast riding it all over the back-country roads. By then we'd moved to our first house, and with it and our first child needing a lot of attention, my riding time dropped off. After a few years of very little riding, including one whole summer when it sat in the garage, and with two kids in the house, I decided to sell it. My last ride was going to be down to Ottawa where there was a bigger potential market. The bike was now five years old but still in mint condition, having only 4,400 km on it and never having been ridden in the rain.

The plan was to go down and stay at Gen's Mom's place, leave the bike there, and Gen's brother Mark would help sell it for me. I decided to wear full leathers for that last ride: boots, pants, jacket, and gloves, topped off with the full-face helmet. Gen kidded me that my leathers fit a lot tighter that day than when I'd first bought them years before. It's a good thing I don't embarrass easily, because I kept them on.

I set out. It was a great summer day. Warm. No wind. Sunny. I opened it up and sped down Highway 17, Gen following in the Accord with the two kids in the back. She was soon ten minutes or so behind me. As I was going down a long straight stretch, I approached a busy intersection of the highway. There was oncoming traffic and cars stopped on each side of the intersection waiting to either turn, pull out and merge, or cross. There were no traffic lights, just stop signs for the road that intersected the two-lane highway.

From a distance the intersection was clear as I approached. The cars to the right remained stopped. But the first one in line to the left misjudged my speed and decided to pull out and cross the road, directly into my path. I went hard on both brakes, flicked on my high beam and laid on the horn, all while dropping gears like crazy. That amazing Honda tracked beautifully throughout, not a hint of wanting to lie down. I moved close to the centre line, hoping that the car, a blue Datsun B210, would get far enough to my right to allow me to pass just behind it, and still avoid oncoming traffic on the left. But the driver, a 16-year-old girl with a learner's permit, missed the shift from first to second gear, and was now coasting through the intersection. There was no place to go and no way to stop.

At the very last moment, while lined up for impact with the Datsun's rear wheel, I pushed up from the foot pegs and handlebars in the hope of going over the car rather than head first into it. I almost made it. Unfortunately the roof of the B210 is pretty high and while I cleared it from the waist up, my thighs hit the roofline. Luckily the impact was somewhat lessened by the bike first making impact with the B210's rear wheel and pushing the car sideways and into a spin. But the thigh impact was still enough to put me into a fast mid-air cartwheel.

I don't know whether it was this high-G head-over-heels spin that caused me to black out, or the impact of my helmet on the pavement, but I did. Not for very long because I remember sliding, feet first, down the highway, on my back, the sound of the back of my helmet scraping on the pavement loudly in my ears. I came to rest on the centerline with oncoming traffic trying to swerve to avoid me. I forced myself to roll back into my lane and passed out again.

I came to with a woman screaming above me that "he's dead, he's dead." So this is what the afterlife was going to be like: more women screaming at me! Well I wasn't having it so, lying absolutely still, I went through a quick systems' check, sat up and exclaimed "Not quite yet!" Don't know if they got the Monty Python reference or not.

I then said "I feel horrible." I was helped to my feet and noticed that my leathers were shredded in places and worn almost through in others. But other than a little road rash on one elbow, one hip and a knuckle, I'd kept all of my skin. As far as I could tell, I had no obvious broken bones, but the shock was preventing me from feeling much pain from the multiple bruises and sprains. That would come later.

I was walked back to the impact site, 150 yards in the direction I had slid from. As I got closer I could see that the bike lay in the middle of the highway, bent so that the front and rear wheels were almost side-by-side. The Datsun had fared much worse: the bike had sheared off its rear end. The rear wheels and axle were in one place and the rest of the car, judging by the marks on the highway, had done a few 360s before coming to rest. I asked if the driver was hurt. My escort pointed to a young girl standing by the side of the road, hugging herself and shivering. She was obviously in some state of mild shock herself and I wanted to help.

So I walked up to her and told her it was ok, everything would be fine, and that I was not that badly off. Then I passed out and rolled into the ditch. Apparently this did not help her shock situation much.

When I came to, I was helped back up onto the highway and walked towards my bike. By then bystanders had been directing traffic around the crash, and I saw Gen approach in the Accord. She didn't see me but she saw my bike, all scrunched-up and leaking fluids. She swerved and pulled over to the side where I greeted her with "Nice day for a ride, isn't it!" I think she was happy to see me alive.

Just then the ambulance pulled up and the attendants were extremely surprised to see me standing. I guess whoever had called it in had given them a description of the crash that led them to believe that a body bag cleanup in aisle 17 was all that would be needed. I assured them I was alive, if not completely well. I was placed on a stretcher and taken to a nearby hospital, the attendants sharing stories with me of some messy spills they'd previously cleaned up.

As the stretcher was being unloaded from the ambulance, a cop appeared. He had a few questions for me since he'd missed me at the crash site. What had happened? How fast was I going? ("No more than the posted speed limit, officer. I checked my speedometer regularly".) Those sorts of things. It would be my only contact with the police, but at that moment it set off some legal alarms. Or maybe it was a head injury. In any case, as I was being wheeled into the emergency room I noticed a payphone on the wall and told the attendants to stop. "I have the right to make a phone call and I want to call my lawyer!" Yup, head injury. But they did. And I did.

I got him on the line. He wasn't my personal lawyer. Rather a lawyer who was a work colleague and friend. (The same one in *Opportunity From Tragedy*.) I gave him a rundown of the situation and asked for his advice, which turned out to be "don't leave the hospital without a neck brace!" I asked why, and he said I'd get more from the insurance claim that way. I'd not thought along those lines before. "How much can I expect in total, all in?" I asked. "About $2,000" he said. I filed that bit of info away and we continued to the ER.

For one heck of a crash, the medical exam was pretty slapdash. A cursory physical exam. No X-rays. And a discharge with no neck brace. Gen was told to watch me for signs of concussion. We continued on to Ottawa for the weekend but I felt pretty horrible. By Monday, I was in my own doctor's office and he produced pages and pages of notes detailing all of my sprains, bruises, and scrapes. By then there was probably not a spot on my body that wasn't showing some bruising. He ordered a full series of X-rays and luckily they showed no breaks. But I felt like crap.

Later that week I started to deal with the girl's insurance company. I told the adjustor that all I wanted was a fair price for my bike. Prices of new bikes had soared over the five years that I'd owned mine, and given its mint condition (pre-crunch) and low mileage, I said I'd settle just for the amount that I originally paid for it, which was something like $3,300. The adjustor's offer was $1,800. Big mistake. Now I was pissed. All deals off the table, I went to work.

I costed everything. The bike. Pain and suffering. Future medical costs. Full set of bike leathers and helmet. Time off work. Possible future time off work. You name it. I escalated it up to the regional manager of the insurance company. In the end she was happy to pay me $10,000, which she had to do via two cheques, because she could only sign for $5,000 at a time. Back then $10,000 was a hefty sum. To this day, whenever I meet my lawyer friend, I remind him of his lowball estimate, and he, in his defence, says he had forgotten who he was dealing with.

While Gen was able to use it for new drapes for the house, and I bought an expensive Sony video camera (which is why I have videos of our kids), I think the insurance company got off easy with what they paid. You see, for the next ten years I suffered from daily migraines. I was on and off all sorts of medications, some of them mood altering. Those migraines did not really end until I suffered a brain hemorrhage in 1999. (see *Stroke One – Having a Sharon Stone*.)

Other than sitting on one or two in a showroom over the years,

I've not been on a bike since. But a year ago the Honda CBR250R got my attention. Naw. Maybe. Who knows?

I'm Not Dreaming Terror

A paraphrasing of the Wiki definition of "night terror" yields "A night terror (or sleep terror) is a sleep disorder causing feelings of terror or dread during sleep."

Also from Wiki we get "Sleepwalkers arise from the slow wave sleep stage in a state of low consciousness and perform activities that are usually performed during a state of full consciousness. These activities can be as benign as sitting up in bed, walking to the bathroom, and cleaning, or as hazardous as cooking, driving, violent gestures, grabbing at hallucinated objects, or **even homicide**." (My emphasis)

A number of years ago, I had an experience that combined both of these.

Imagine yourself in bed, lying flat on your back, deep in sleep, dreaming very pleasant thoughts. Then imagine that, while still asleep, your dream grows somewhat darker. It's not one of those "I'm running away but getting nowhere" dreams; more like an "I can't breathe" dream. You feel you are choking and that there's a huge weight on your chest. As you arise to consciousness you wonder if you are suffering a heart attack. You open your eyes and in the gloom of faint moonlight that's barely penetrating the room, you realize that your spouse is atop you, straddling your chest, with both hands clasped firmly around your throat.

If you're like me you wonder if it's because you forgot to take out the garbage, or that perhaps she'd finally figured out that you are worth way more dead than alive because of all the insurance coverage you've got, but I digress...

With the remnants of what little air is left in my lungs I manage to croak "Gen...what...are...you...doing?" To which she responds, "Must...stop...the...bleeding." A likely story! Maybe a jury would buy it but I'm doubtful.

Regardless, my now oxygen-starved brain manages to quickly put two and two together. You see Gen's a dialysis nurse. She must be sleepwalking and performing a task that she would as a nurse. She isn't really trying to kill me. So lethal force is not called for. I instead roll her off me, which brings her closer to being truly awake. After I draw in a few life-saving breaths of air, she explains (if you're buying it, members of the jury) that she thought my central line had blown and I was bleeding out fast. Only direct pressure to the jugular would save me.

She drifted back to sleep and it was only later the next day that I broached the subject. She seemed to vaguely remember it. But I wasn't sure if she really did, if she was faking that she did, or if she was already devising "Plan B" to off me!

Under The Rainbow

I don't know anyone who is not fascinated by rainbows. Who doesn't stop and look at one when it appears? Who doesn't think back to tales of finding pots of gold at their end? I've experienced one that was so beautiful that I might perhaps trade a pot of gold to see another one like it in my lifetime.

On most summer Thursday evenings you'll find Gen and I swimming at Blanchet Beach at Meech Lake. There's normally a good crowd of fellow swimmers present, all doing laps around an island. Meech Lake's not that big: about four kilometres in length and much less so in width. Blanchet Beach is at the west end of the lake and the tiny island that we swim around lies about two-thirds of the way across, or about 350 metres from the beach.

On one such evening, severe thunderstorms rumbled through the area and most people stayed home. But Gen and I showed up and when the storm passed overhead and down-lake, we, and a handful of others, headed for the water and started our swim.

On the way back from circling the island, the skies to the west cleared and the evening sunshine poured through. Immediately to the east, the air was still misty and the storm could be seen pounding the other end of the lake. As we arrived mid-lake, we could not help but be distracted by an extremely bright colourful glow to the east.

A rainbow had formed. Easily a hundred times brighter than any I had ever seen. It was close: 200-300 metres away at most. Its ends could be seen touching the water on each side of the lake, right at shore, forming an amazing arched portal to the rest of the lake beyond. Each individual band of colour was incredibly thick – and richer and deeper than anything I'd ever seen. The half dozen or so of us stopped swimming and treaded water, transfixed by what was surely a once-in-a-lifetime sight.

It still comes up in conversation when any of us lucky ones are together at Meech. And while I sometimes wish I'd had a waterproof camera with me that evening, that rainbow's memory has been so powerfully engraved in my mind that no photo is needed.

The Christmas Turkey

For over a decade, we've been cooking our Christmas turkey on the BBQ. Those in warmer climes are no doubt wondering what the big deal is about that. But if you're from Ottawa you can appreciate that things can be quite cold, and snowy, at that time of year. And so it was in 1999.

Earlier that year we'd bought some new appliances for the kitchen, including a $1,200 self-cleaning Whirlpool stove. We'd also bought a $1,400 natural gas Weber BBQ and put it on the back deck. Long before Christmas, the BBQ was covered over with snow and ice, and the deck had at least three feet of the stuff on it.

It was our turn to host the big family dinner and Gen had a huge bird ready for the oven. She'd stuffed both ends with her incredible sausage stuffing. A half-hour into the cooking, the oven died. Not a breaker trip. A full-fledged circuit board failure. Leaving us with a warm, raw 25-pound bird.

There's no way to get hold of a repairman on Christmas day. The neighbours were all no doubt using their ovens to cook their own Christmas dinners. And the guests would be arriving in a few hours.

Panic was starting to set in. I was wondering if KFC was open.

As I sat in the family room staring at the snow on the deck, the shape of the snow-laden BBQ caught my eye. Wait a sec! Why can't a $1,400 Weber BBQ cook a bird as well as a $1,200 Whirlpool oven? It's worth a shot.

So I get dressed and grab a shovel and a half-hour later the deck and BBQ are cleared of snow and ice. I wheel it close to the sliding glass doors so that it can be tended with feet still inside. I fire it up, and with upper grille and warming rack removed I'm very pleased to find out that the turkey roaster fits perfectly inside the BBQ. I'm easily able to get the temperature up to 350 degrees and then back it off to 300 degrees during the latter stages of cooking. With some trial and error with the three burners I can get it to any temperature and have it stay there.

With the roaster cover off, the bird gets basted and skin crisped-up for the last 30 minutes. With the guests all arrived, the bird is done, carved, and unstuffed. The Weber has done an outstanding job and the bird is pronounced the best ever. And from that day forward, I've always kept the deck and BBQ clear of snow all winter long, and besides using it regularly throughout the winter, every turkey that we've cooked has been done on that same BBQ, easily putting the Whirlpool stove to shame.

[Note: the author has not received any compensation from Weber for writing this story. That's a hint, Weber!]

Cycling in Italy

Gen and I love to cycle together. From spring through early fall we set aside Sunday mornings, and part of the afternoon, to hit the road together. And on occasion we'll bring our cycling gear with us on vacation. Such was the case when we spent a week in the Lake Garda region in Northern Italy.

We travelled by train from Munich, after a week of business there, past Verona, to Peschiera del Garda, where we caught a taxi to Bardolino, and the wonderful "Color Hotel" where we stayed. This is

a busy tourist area and because of it there are plenty of stores and restaurants in Bardolino and all of the towns around Lake Garda.

On one of our first days in town we took advantage of the hotel's stock of good road bikes for rent, got into our gear and set out on a northward loop around the very large lake. Even though we'd not gone more than several kilometers, I found the main road to be a bit too narrow, the shoulders (if any) too small, and the traffic too close. We'd been told that all Italian drivers watched out for and respected cyclists, but I was having my doubts. So we crossed the road and headed back through Bardolino and southward towards Peschiera del Garda.

As luck would not have it, the weather turned on a dime. Warmth and sunshine turned to cold rain. By the time we got to the town, we were soaked and chilled to the bone. But as luck would have it, we decided to stop at a small café that made the world's greatest hot chocolate. I'm talking pure liquid hot chocolate. Add some biscotti and we were warm in no time.

Even though the sun came out again, we figured things could change again, so we headed back to Bardolino. The shoulders on that side of the road were again non-existent so we were always moving in the single lane of traffic, where most vehicles were doing at least 80 kph. At one point on the trip back, a big tour bus passed so close to me that its rear view mirror passed over my shoulder and "ticked" the side of my helmet. I'd come within inches of literally losing my mind. Time for an underwear change!

When we got back to the hotel, luckily without any other really close calls, we decided that that would be our one and only cycling outing during that trip. To some extent that was a very positive thing since it meant that we rented a car on a couple of occasions, something we'd not planned on doing, and one of those rentals was for what turned out to be a very memorable day trip to Venice.

Perhaps the cycling is much better in other less-touristy areas, but while I'd love to go back to Italy sometime, I'd never risk cycling there again.

Rumble in Toronto

Natasja, our oldest daughter, married a fine lad named Dave, whom she met in Korea while they were both teaching English at the same international school. He's a great guy and we like him a lot. But as many marriages nowadays do, theirs has ended. And while we don't get to see Dave anymore, we certainly have fond memories of him and his family.

We still talk about their Toronto engagement party.

The evening started off normally enough. Dave's mother had arranged the party, which was held in a rented basement hall. As well as Gen and I, my brother and sister-in-law were there to represent our side of the family, and Dave's parents, uncle and cousin, friends and old neighbours, as well as others, were there as well. There was a nice meal, music, dancing, some speeches, and an open bar.

Apparently the open bar is a must at any such event, and the attendees made good use of it. My daughter had told me that at previous parties with Dave and his friends, there had been heavy drinking and a few heated arguments. I filed that piece of information away for future use.

By later in the evening, most of the older relatives and neighbours had left, as did my brother and his wife. I'd not been drinking due to my self-appointed designated driver status. Back at the bar, there was a good-sized gathering when some pushing and shoving broke out. I was on the dance floor with Gen at the time. The shoving escalated and soon there was yelling and wrestling. Dave was in the thick of it. Combatants were separated and more drinking ensued, until it was time to call it a night.

As we were gathering on the sidewalk outside the hall entrance, things heated up again. One of Dave's friends grabbed a case of still-full liquor bottles as they were being loaded into a car and started smashing bottles all over the busy street. This led to punches being thrown (although given the state of those doing the throwing, it was no surprise that none landed). Traffic came to a stop as pitched battles erupted outside the hall. Within minutes, several squad cars of Toronto's finest pulled up. Police were restraining people as wrestling matches continued. (My thought at the time: I wonder if the suits these combatants are wearing can be repaired and cleaned in time for the wedding?)

Gen, who might have had a drink or four as well, and who had no previous experience with drunken brawls and the police, was lecturing two cops that, as a nurse, she could tell them their restraining techniques were not safe to the recipient. I went and grabbed her and made her nice and comfy in the back of our car, which was idling in front of the hall.

With her safely in place, it was off to retrieve my daughter, the bride-to-be, who was inches away from a much-shorter male Asian cop, wagging a finger in his face, and telling him how she has a degree in criminology and that's how she knew how badly he was handling the situation. I got her into the back seat of the car before the cop applied pepper spray or a Taser.

Then it was off to get Dave who was in the middle of a scrum. Instead of grabbing hold of him, I stood back several feet from the mêlée and yelled: "Dave! Into the car! Now!" He bowed his head like a chastised puppy and complied. With my crew all strapped in, I bade goodnight to the nice police officers and drove off.

By the time we got back to my brother's place, Nat and Gen were in good enough shape to help get Dave up to bed. My brother set my niece and nephew up to sleep on the floor in his room, so that Dave and Nat could each have one of their rooms; not for propriety reasons, but because the kids only had twin beds. Unfortunately Dave saw fit to be sick all over his assigned bed, and Nat spent some time getting him, and it, cleaned up, and set with fresh sheets, which my brother provided.

Sometime during the night, Dave found his way to the bathroom, but, being as it was a strange house, and he was still far from sober, he had trouble finding his way back to his room. He kept walking into my brother's room to hear a chorus of "wrong room, Dave!" from the occupants. After several attempts he somehow found his way onto a couch in the upstairs family room. My brother, concerned about his wanderings, got up to see if he was ok and found him in the loving embrace of a giant life-sized stuffed monkey by the name of Mr. Bananas. When my brother tried to pry the two apart Dave refused to move. So my brother left him there.

A few days later, Dave would find the following email in his in-basket: "I hope this email finds its way to my new friend Dave. I realize it was probably the alcohol, but what we shared last night, while brief, was nothing short of wonderful. The way you held me close, the heat we shared, nobody has ever treated me that way before.

I know that you won't remember it but I will cherish our time together forever. Mr. Bananas."

A couple of months later, the wedding in Ottawa went off without a hitch. Both the bride and groom agreed to a cash bar to minimize the risk of trouble breaking out. The DJ I hired was a massive friend who would help me control things if they got out of hand. But they didn't. No mention was made of the rumble in Toronto and I was left with the impression it had been nothing particularly unusual amongst that group, and therefore not worth rehashing.

The Poo-Pee Flush

One of my many job responsibilities at Canada's National Research Council (a part of the Government of Canada) over the years was managing a portfolio of intellectual property cases. Everything from identification of inventions, through to patenting, maintenance, licensing etc. An important element of this responsibility was to train staff in how the process works and to get them to fill out the necessary disclosure-of-invention forms.

At one point in my standard training presentation I talked about how all inventions, whether made on personal or company time, must be disclosed. (It's a requirement under the Public Servants Inventions Act.) In the case of inventions made on personal time, it was the usual practice for all rights in the invention to be assigned to the employee, if the invention had nothing to do with their work, and was of no direct use to NRC. I recall one skeptic challenging this, claiming that it would be a huge amount of paperwork with a never-positive (for the employee) outcome. So I decided to prove him wrong, and have some fun doing it. I decided I would go home that evening, invent something, and write it up the next day. I would then see how long it would take to receive the assignment paperwork telling me it was all mine to do with as I pleased.

As I was sitting at home on my throne of inspiration (toilet) that proverbial light bulb went off above my head. As I flushed the toilet the lever broke and there was only a small partial flush. My first thought was, boy, that was useless. Then I realized that for "liquids" it was just the right amount to clear the bowl, while a full flush was required for solids. So I sat down (at my desk) and sketched out a mechanism that would allow a person to choose full or partial flush, described it in full, and filled out the two-part disclosure of invention forms. Which I signed and handed in the next day.

Now I know you're all thinking that I could not have possibly invented the dual-flush toilet. Well I did; at least a way of doing it. The thing is that others, unbeknownst to me, had done so well before I did. The internet was just emerging as a source of information, and I'd never seen a dual flush toilet, so I was none the wiser. And because my disclosure of invention asked for immediate assignment of all rights to me, there was no need to have anyone incur the cost of searching the patent databases. It was only quite some time later that I saw my first dual-flush toilet in action; surprisingly similar in design to what I had come up with.

But all was not lost. As well as proving to that skeptical staff member that the process could work fast and in the employee's favour (the assignment documents arrived on my desk two weeks later, which is lightning fast in the inventions world), I became probably the only employee to ever have the President of the National Research Council of Canada sign off on a document containing the words "poo" and "pee" in both its title and body of text. You see, in one section of the disclosure form, the inventor is asked to give his invention a name. I just couldn't resist the very apropos "Poo-Pee Flush" for mine, and the President executed an assignment that clearly stated that all rights in the Poo-Pee Flush hereby belonged to me.

Chiropractic

My Mom was a long-time believer in chiropractic services. For years and years I remember her visiting the office of one on the next block over from our home. As a kid I figured it was just like going to any other "doctor" and thought nothing more of it. Until my own first experience with the profession. Recent events have got me thinking back.

It was the last shopping day before Christmas. I was out at my local mall, just starting my shopping as is my usual practice. My back was killing me. Specifically my lower back. It had been sore for a few days but now it was much worse. Could have been any reason for it (sports, bad posture, who knows) but I didn't care. I was in agony and considering a visit to the closest ER.

As I was driving out of the mall's parking lot, I passed a small strip mall where a branch of my bank was located. Up until then I had not noticed that the "store" right next to the bank was a chiropractor's office. I recalled Mom visiting one and figured if it (whatever "it" was) worked for her, it could work for me. So I pulled in.

It was quiet. The chiropractor was just about to close up for the day, and heading out for Christmas holiday. I got the feeling that he still had shopping to do as well. Anyhow, he sees that I'm hurting and agrees to see me. I spend 10 minutes filling out a questionnaire, which he then reviews with me. He then does a very thorough physical exam of my body, and then x-rays my spine from tip to tail. He tells me that if I come back after the holidays he will have a treatment plan ready and we will begin treatments.

I ask if there is anything he can do right away. He says it's a bit unusual but that some lower back "adjustments" shouldn't hurt. Prophetic.

Now recall that I've never had chiro done and hadn't even seen my Mom being treated. I honestly had no idea what was about to be done to me. Which was to be placed on one of the back-cracking tables, face-down, and have him place both hands firmly on my lower back and then... push down hard and fast, slamming the table down. It happened so fast that I didn't have time to scream! Not sure if it was the sudden bending like a twig or the slamming of the table against its stops that scared me the most.

After a moment he said that's it and had me slowly stand up. I had to admit: my back felt much better. The pain had diminished quite a bit and, while it felt strange, in the way that a brand new experience feels strange, I was very relieved to no longer be in distress. I paid him and we scheduled an appointment for a week or so later.

I finished my shopping, went home, wrapped presents, set out Santa's treats, and hit the hay. I was the first up the next morning and, feeling pretty chipper, went down to the kitchen to brew a pot of coffee for Gen and to set the table for breakfast. I poured the hot java into a cup, placed the cup on its matching saucer, and then headed to the table where sat the cream and sugar. And then it hit!

It was like a bolt of lightning had passed through my lower spine. Massive pain (and I swear the smell of seared flesh) followed by total paralysis from my waist on down. At least that's what passed through my mind as I slammed into the table, smashing the cup and saucer, ending up in a heap on the floor, unable to move.

I debated yelling for help, but was probably in too much shock to do so. So I lay there, contemplating life, and wondering what Santa might have brought me this year. After about 15 minutes I started to feel some tingling in my toes, which gradually turned to a raging burning sensation in both legs, which eventually subsided. I very carefully got up, cleaned up the mess, poured fresh coffee into another cup with saucer, and delivered it to Gen in bed.

It was only later that day that I told her what had happened. For the next week, the same thing happened again every morning, only not as severe, and diminishing every day until after a week, it never happened again. During this time I made sure to not be carrying anything at the time, and to always be holding onto something like a chair or the counter. The episodes, as I called them, finally went away, just in time for my follow-up appointment!

So I showed up and we exchanged the usual pleasantries of that time of year. And then he asked how the back feels and how did it feel over the holidays. I said that, other than the complete paralysis of the lower body that sent me crashing to the floor, everything was pretty good. His jaw dropped. We then agreed, by mutual consent, that he would not be treating me anymore, and I left.

Why am I thinking back to this time, many many years ago? Well, about four years ago my back pain returned, and was seriously affecting my quality of life. I kept hurting it while playing basketball and hockey, which (I know, I know) I refused to stop playing. I'd been to see regular doctors and they just kept saying to rest it. So, only because she had been to see him, I went to see the chiropractor that Gen had been seeing. She assured me that he was not the "typical" bone-cracking chiropractor; rather he did deep tissue massage, A.R.T., and developed very effective exercise and home treatment plans.

And it worked amazingly well for me. He works in concert with a sports med doc, who was able to order an MRI, which showed some serious issues, which led to a change in treatment plan and exercises, which has my lower back pretty much completely cured. But here's the thing. Now that all of the treating of the immediate problem has worked, we are just now starting a new phase: traditional chiropractic "adjustments" targeting the long-term health of my entire back. It was with some trepidation that I signed the consent form today, placed myself on one of those tables, and had him do several adjustments.

I feel great right now. However I won't be making coffee for Gen tomorrow morning. You can call me superstitious if you want; I figure I'm just erring on the safe side.

Go Grayson Go!

As of the writing of this story, my children have produced one grandchild for us to praise and adore, with none that we know of currently on the way.

Grayson was born to my daughter Allie, and his father, Chris. He turned four the year I began writing this book, and is an amazingly bright, fun, and big young boy. In fact, today was his first day of school.

First day of school!? It seems like only yesterday that he almost did not get past his first breath of air.

He was born in the Montfort Hospital in Ottawa, which had recently undergone a massive renovation and expansion, including the addition of a great maternity wing.

The pregnancy had gone mostly okay, but in the last few weeks there were signs of trouble: big variations in fetal heart rate etc. Once contractions started, things got progressively worse; something was not right. It turned out that the cord was wrapped around his neck.

During delivery, you are allowed two attendees in the birthing room, besides the father. My oldest daughter, Natasja, camera in hand, was one of them. My wife Gen, a nurse, was the other. I, and Allie's very good friend, Verena, stood in the doorway, technically not in the room.

The one doctor, perched between Allie's legs, was tasked with getting the baby out and handing it off to two pediatric nurses. He would then be concerned exclusively with Allie.

Now we knew it was going to be a boy, and that boy had already been named Grayson. (Chris, the father, is a big comic book and Batman fan. You figure it out!)

Calmly and very professionally, the doctor delivered Grayson, even though all the monitors were signalling trouble. He emerged, purple as a grape, uttered one pitiful cry, and then hung limp and dead in the doctor's hands. Grayson was very briefly placed in Allie's arms, but seconds later was whisked away by the nurses, over to their station right in front of Verena and me.

My heart was pierced as I heard Allie cry out, "Where's my baby. Why can't I hear him?"

I looked at Chris and Natasja, who were both focussed on Allie, and perhaps not yet in tune with the gravity of the situation. But Gen's face was one of abject horror. She knew!

When Allie first told us she was pregnant, Gen did not take it well at all. "This is not happening" and "I am not going to be a grandmother" went on throughout the first trimester. But after that she came around and was nothing but incredibly supportive, and expectant.

She came over to me in the doorway and burst into tears. "No. No! This can't happen!" The pediatric nurses were doing all that they could – slapping him, rubbing him, and starting compressions. A code was called over the PA and I realized it was for Grayson. Another doctor appeared immediately and went to work.

I've never seen anything so professional in my life. She was quickly given the short history to date, asked why they were doing compressions, and took control. She whacked and slapped that little purple body. Intubated him again. Grabbed his balls. Rubbed his chest. Everything to get him to react – to breathe! Just prior to that I had, without knowing it, started a quiet chant of "Go Grayson Go!" which built in volume with each iteration. Pretty soon I was yelling it at top volume.

Then there was a cry, and another, and another. That purple dead boy turned a living bright pink. I let out a loud "Yeah!" The room broke out into cheers and ecstatically welcomed Grayson into the world of the living.

He gave us quite the scare right off the start. We are reminded of how lucky we are every time we see him.

When I am long gone from this world, I want him to know that I have written this book in very large part so that he can read this story of his birth, and read it to his children and grandchildren as well.

Hilton Hookers

To be fair to Hilton (the hotel chain, not the heiress) I could have chosen the name of probably any of their competitors for the title of this story, but the fact is that I was a Hilton Diamond member and stayed pretty much exclusively with them for years. During some of those stays, and especially at the Hilton London Metropole Hotel, it was fairly easy to spot working girls, well, working.

The lobby area is a favoured hang out. They don't dress like Julia Roberts in Pretty Woman. They don't have any specific distinguishing features. But if they're not already occupied with a business prospect, they're checking out the comings and goings intently, if discreetly. And if you happen to be a big unsuspecting goof like me, when you make eye contact with them and they do not disengage that eye contact, it's not because you're a dead ringer for Richard Gere, it's because you've now been targeted.

How do I know? I've seen it happen, from a safe vantage point in the lobby bar, on many occasions, and on two separate occasions my good friend Tony and I have had first-hand experience.

We'd just gotten checked in to our rooms and headed down to

the bar. As we strode across the lobby, eye contact was made with a very pretty brunette. She latched on and eventually followed us to our table. "Mind if I join you fellows?" she said. I said there was no problem with that, that we'd even buy her a drink if she wanted. But I also added that's all we were planning to buy. She took it all in stride, the door being at least partly open, the pro that she was.

After a half-hour of idle chit chat and a couple of drinks (into us, not her) she suggested that we should "get together." I played dumb and said we already were. She then said we should call her. Why call when we're already here talking? After several more such exchanges she passed me her mobile number. I asked Tony if I could borrow his phone. I called her. She was sitting right there. She then proceeded with the true sales pitch: rates and what those rates got. I respectfully declined. She excused herself and left the hotel.

It seems that solicitation in person was a crime back then (it might still be), however by phone it was okay.

A short while later, Tony's phone rings. (Now you know why I borrowed his.) She's got a new proposal. Half the price and a cheaper hotel with a girlfriend of hers included as well. Still a "no, thank you" and the call ends. Tony and I chuckle about the whole thing, and while sitting there the rest of the evening we watch others plying their trade.

Flash forward six years. That's the next time Tony and I find ourselves sitting in that same lobby bar when another brunette sits down with us. We go through much the same routine with her – minus the phone call. Then she makes a call. It's to her "friend" who she asks to join us. Minutes later, another brunette appears and Tony and I can barely suppress the urge to laugh out loud: it's the same girl as six years before! We tell her how nice it is to see her again and ask how things have been... and she can't place us. "Was it last week?" she asks. Nope. Longer. "Last month?" Nope. We then remind her of our meeting six years before. We say that offer to join us for drinks still stands.

The two girls exchanged professional glances and within minutes disengaged and joined two other guys at a nearby table. Tony and I enjoyed another chuckle.

Flipping a Quebec Bird

Ottawa sits on the Ottawa River, across which you will find the Province of Quebec. If you live in Ottawa long enough, you will be able to spot a driver from Quebec before you see their licence plate: they're the one doing something stupid. (Sorry friends from Quebec; I speak nothing but the truth.)

I had a bunch of friends staying at my place one summer and I decided to take them across the river and up to Meech Lake for a picnic dinner. Before we set out in our cars I gave them some words of warning: if you see a Quebec plate on the Ottawa side, be extra cautious since the likelihood is high he'll do something totally unexpected like turn left across three lanes of traffic from the right lane, or slam on his brakes for no good reason, or refuse to yield, or... [insert transgression here].

By the time we drove there and back, any skepticism they had about my warnings were put fully to rest.

And so it was but a week before I typed this tale for the first time that my observational theory was once again proven right.

My street is a very "deep" u-shaped crescent with a T-junction at a more major road. As I approached the end of the road there was a landscaping truck and trailer at the stop. I pulled up behind him and after waiting for a good thirty seconds or so as the lone occupant of the truck was clearly busy texting (and it not being safe to try to pass at the corner) I gave a light tap of my horn to get his attention. He looked up from his device and at me through his rear view mirror and then hammered the gas and cut hard left onto the next road, while at the same time flipping me the bird with his left hand out the window. It was then that I noticed his Quebec plates.

His trailer was one of those flatbed types with really low steel mesh sides and a ramp at the back. Sitting on the trailer was a large industrial ride-on lawn mower. The problem was that it was just sitting there – not tied down. So as he flashed his sign of defiance and accelerated hard while turning left, good old physics came into play. While the trailer swung left with the truck, the ride-on mower continued pretty straight, smashing through the side screen of the trailer and rolling off across a lawn, coming to rest upside-down on a driveway.

I pulled out around the corner very slowly in time to see the Quebec driver hop out of the truck holding his head and yelling every Quebec curse word that I'd ever learned, and then some, as he hopped onto the trailer and jumped up and down.

I always stop to help someone in need, but in this case I must confess that I instead slowly cruised by, opened my sunroof, and raised my own one finger salute, as I continued on my way.

There's Quartz in Them Thar Hills!

I've had the good fortune of visiting plenty of museums in my travels. One thing that I never get tired of is visiting gem and mineral collections. And whenever I do, and see displays of quartz geodes, I am taken back to a time when I was kid growing up in Pembroke, and we were allowed to pretty much roam wild and explore and enjoy its great outdoors.

My neighbourhood was at the edge of development in the east end of the city. When I was eight or nine years old, two big construction projects were taking place in the nearby fields and forest we would play in: a six-story retirement home and a high school. Roads were extended and built and large earth moving trucks deposited huge amounts of excavated material, which was largely rock and clay, in long high mounds that were, to us kids, like mountain chains separated by valleys. This was both a good thing and a bad thing.

Bad because in so doing, the only three trees in the field, which stood along the highest ridge, were taken down. We had named them the papa, momma, and baby trees. By the time it was removed, however, papa tree had already met its match in a lightning strike, and all that stood was a hollow trunk some twelve feet tall, and the rest lay on its side. Of course that made for great climbing and fort building, which we did.

Good because the mountains of excavated material gave us a new play area. And one day dozens of us neighborhood kids were doing just that when one of us discovered something really neat: a partially broken-open hand-sized rose quartz geode. While I say rose quartz because it's a known mineral found in the Pembroke area, the actual mineral material was closer to a dark purple, almost like amethyst. In any case, I'll just call it quartz.

Well, that find set off a few days of prospecting that, at least to us kids, was bigger than the great gold rush of 1849. We found more of the stuff. Rocks were smashed together, at first, to reveal inner deposits. But we soon figured out that we could more easily do so with our fathers' tools. I don't think Dad's wood chisels were ever able to cut wood again. Hammers, screwdrivers, shovels, sledges, axes and mauls, were all pressed into rock-breaking service. Mothers' clothes hampers, milk crates, and even suitcases were filled with the stuff.

Some specimens were football- and even basketball-sized. While all of the "mountains" were explored, it was actually just one section of one that had almost all of the finds. Some excavator must have dug up a deposit and it was mostly moved all at once. After a few days, we'd dug into quite a bit of that section of mountain and new finds petered out. But it was quite the impressive haul.

My collection sat on Mom and Dad's basement storage shelves for years. They came in handy for school show-and-tells. I tried a few times to make things with it, like gluing crystals to an old hockey helmet. (For what purpose I do not know.) But after a while, the collection just gathered dust, and probably like most fathers in the neighborhood did, eventually Dad loaded what was left of it into the car, and dumped it somewhere out in the country.

A shame. It would have been nice to have kept at least one good sample from that great find. If only to remember the excitement that we kids all felt over its discovery.

Lights, Camera, Cut!

By pure luck, if you could call it that, I have stumbled onto Hollywood movie sets while movies with big stars are being filmed. It's kind of neat to be able to pull out a copy on DVD and say "I was standing right here when that was being shot."

I was in Los Angeles for a conference in the late '80s and staying at the Westin Hotel downtown. One of many things I liked about that place was its rooftop pool, which was great for lap swimming. I'd been going every evening during my stay. I'd been out to dinner one night with my buddy Roy, and as we were headed to the lobby elevators I suggested that he meet me up top for a swim.

The elevator door opens and we step in. Standing there is Henry Winkler, AKA The Fonz. I tend to be very respectful of celebrities' privacy and space (for a notable exception see *London Pub Crawl*) so I simply nodded and said hi. Roy on the other hand got all starstruck, grabbed his hand and began shaking it, and professed his never-ending fandom. As we rode up and had a short conversation, Mr. Winkler said he was directing a film in the hotel and if we happened to be near the set, we could catch him in action – presumably from a distance. Roy got off at his floor. I was next. Mr. Winkler continued on.

I got to my room, changed into my bathing suit, grabbed a towel and headed back to the elevator. As I exited on the top floor for the pool, there was a security rope, guard, and sign with a note apologizing to guests for the fact that the pool was closed due to a movie shoot that night. The guard was reciting the message to me when I heard "wait a minute, it's ok, he's with me." It was Henry Winkler! He'd remembered me from the elevator ride a few minutes before and true to his word, told the security guard that he'd invited me to watch the shoot.

He brought me onto the set, which was a chaise longue sitting by the side of the pool. He returned to what he had been doing, going through the scene that was about to be shot with Billy Crystal and JoBeth Williams. My jaw dropped. I was right there, just steps away.

After a few minutes, Mr. Winkler placed me exactly where I should stand, so as to not be in the way of anything, got everything lined up and gave instructions to start shooting. Before they got more than 10 seconds into the scene, Mr. Winkler yelled "cut!" From his position he was looking not only at the lounger with Billy and JoBeth on it, but diagonally across the length of the pool, and to a stairwell barely visible in the movie-set lighting. But clearly visible, and walking directly towards the camera, was my buddy Roy. He must have used the stairs instead of the elevator.

"Hey you!" shouts Mr. Winkler.

Roy stops, realizes something's not quite right. With all the movie lights and people at one end of the pool, and nobody swimming in it, he catches on fast.

"Me? Are you talking to me?" he replies, in his best Fonzie impersonation. Mr. Winkler starts laughing.

As I'm standing right next to him, I tell Mr. Winkler that's my friend Roy, who he'd also met earlier in the elevator. Roy trots over to us and apologizes. By then a manager for the Westin is also by our side and, in a great showing of customer-first attitude, says that there is no need for Roy to apologize. Obviously it was the hotel's fault for not securing that stairwell properly and that it was she who should apologize to us for any embarrassment caused. She hands us her card and asks us to please drop by her office the next day so that she can make it up to us.

We stayed until the scene was successfully shot, bade goodnight to Mr. Winkler and the two stars, and called it a night. The next day we dropped by the manager's office and once again she apologized on behalf of the hotel. Then she proceeded to hand us a mitt full of coupons. A few coupons for dinner for two at any restaurant in the hotel (no dollar limit!) Cash value coupons for use at the gift shop. At least a dozen free drink coupons for use at any hotel bar. We ate and drank very well for the rest of the week.

And the movie? *Memories of Me* (1988) also starred Alan King, who did a marvelous job of it. I've enjoyed watching it a couple of times, especially the pool scene.

About ten years later, it was my turn to be the cause of a "cut!" on a movie set.

I was in Toronto and staying at the Royal York Hotel downtown. I was rushing diagonally across the lobby to get out the main entrance and down the road, likely to see a Jays game, when that three-letter word rang out. Apparently the whole lobby, or at least the part that I had just run through, was being used as a movie set.

I stopped, turned, and immediately recognized Carl Reiner standing beside a big camera. I approached, and he explained that he was in the middle of shooting a scene for his movie, and that I had just run right in front of his two stars as he was shooting. He was pointing to Bette Midler and Dennis Farina, standing right behind me. Gulp! But in a very classy move he suggested I could stand just off to his side and watch them try to shoot the scene again if I wanted to. To heck with the Jays!

This was a much more elaborate shoot than the pool scene. They had set up a fictional check-in desk using the concierge's station. Looking away from that desk (I was standing behind and to its left) the hotel's usual check-in/out desk ran out-of-scene down the left side, and there was enough space for genuine guests to access it. The lobby itself was set up so that Bette and Dennis could approach the movie desk from a distance right up to it. From their point of entry to the movie desk there were a bunch of extras sitting and milling about, all of their movements choreographed in sync with the stars' approach. In the far distance, regular hotel traffic continued, most passersby totally unaware of what was happening at the other end of the lobby.

I don't know how many takes had been shot before I interrupted things, but they only did one more. My most vivid memory is how such a tiny (in real life) person like Bette Midler could cut such a huge presence in real life. Before and after the shoot she was easily THE centre of attention.

That Old Feeling (1997) is a fun movie to watch, especially every scene with Bette!

Cream Pie

Over ten years ago, a competition was held to decide where the National Research Council was going to build a new 75,000 square foot aerospace manufacturing technology centre. Five locations submitted their bids by the deadline. They were reviewed and a recommendation passed up the line. Then word came back down to destroy all copies of all five bids and to wipe out all documentation about the competition (I kept all of mine in a filing cabinet until I left NRC). The winner had been chosen and it was none of those five. The new facility would be located on the campus of the University of Montreal, which was, until then, never considered in the running.

Now I'm sure that it was merely a coincidence that the then-

Rector of the University happened to be good friends with then-Prime Minister Jean Chretien. Such is the nature of how business gets done in Quebec.

In any case, plans were made for a big early-afternoon press conference and reception at which a bunch of dignitaries and officials, including the Prime Minister, would make the announcement. It was to be held on campus in a big atrium / foyer.

That morning I was there to help with preparations. We set up displays and draped off the area. Space was set for camera crews and reporters. A small stage with podium was erected. Everything went off as planned.

About an hour before the actual event, an RCMP officer entered the room with his German Shepherd and the two thoroughly worked the room, and all of its nooks, crannies, and contents. When done, the two went to the centre of the room and stood at ease, together.

Now a few years before our event, Jean Chretien had been hit in the face with a cream pie by a protestor at an event in Prince Edward Island. So I couldn't resist the opportunity presented to me.

I walked casually up to the officer and his dog, both sets of eyes tracking my approach. Stopping at arm's length in front of them, I looked down at the dog, then back up at the officer and asked, "But can he detect cream pies?" I swear the dog understood me because he let out a little whimper, dropped down on his stomach, and placed one paw over his eyes, as if to say "the shame of it all." Even the officer, up until then stiff and all business, had to look down at his canine partner and laugh.

Bank It Off His Left Nut

I used to be an avid golfer. I'd play up to seventy rounds in a calendar year. I'd travel with my golf clubs so as to not miss an opportunity to squeeze in a round. And I'd go on three golf trips with different buddies each year: Vegas in January; Florida in April; and Myrtle Beach in November.

Prior to the Florida trips, that group used to visit Atlanta's Stone

Mountain. Beautiful scenery with two pretty good 18-hole courses located just minutes from the in-park hotel that we stayed at. It was on one of those trips that I came closest to making a hole-in-one – albeit in a very unconventional manner.

One of the regulars on that trip was Rick. Rick's a lawyer. One evening over dinner we somehow got into discussing the legalities of hitting someone with a golf ball. What happens if you nail someone in the group ahead of you? What about someone "illegally" jogging on the course's cart paths? Someone on another fairway even if you yelled "fore!" That sort of thing.

One question was, "what happens if the group ahead of you waves you on, and then you hit one of them?" Rick's opinion was that it was a free shot; that they gave you the right to play that shot, accepted the risk of getting hit, and no fault could be attributed back to the player who hit the ball if someone waving him on got hit. Sounded fair enough to me.

The next day Rick was in the foursome ahead of mine and was just finishing out a par three that has a very elevated tee. The hole played 186 yards from our tees, without factoring in the huge elevation change. My foursome had been waiting patiently up on the tee box while Rick's chipped and chipped and chipped and then putted and putted and putted... until they were finally done. As they were leaving the green, I yelled down, "it's about time!" Rick stops, looks back up at us, gives thought, walks back to the flag, and then positions himself right over the hole in front of the flag and waves us on. Actually it's closer to a "bring it on, take your best shot" gesture.

I was "away" and Robbie, one of my playing partners, wondered if I really should hit. I told him that Rick and I had been over this the night before. Legally at least, I was in the clear. So I teed up a ball, armed with my weapon of choice, and swung away. Robbie, standing to my right, immediately said, "that's looking pretty good" as the ball gained height like a mortar round. That soon became a more emphatic, "that's looking really good" as he followed the ball's flight from our elevated spotter's position. As the ball now hurtled towards its target, Robbie's mind processed the trajectory into an expected landing point, and yelled, "look out!"

By now the white ball, having started up high, but having first climbed higher, was falling almost vertically, and from his position almost directly below, Rick could not have seen it against the overcast sky. But he did hear Robbie's warning and at the last moment attempted to vacate the premises. Too little, too late. As Rick began to run to his right, he opened up his stance, and at that very instant the ball caromed off his left nut and stuck inches from the hole. It must have been but a glancing blow, because Rick managed a few more staggering steps away from the landing zone before realizing he'd been hit. He looked back up at the tee box and, perhaps realizing that three more of us still had to hit, hurried off the green to rejoin his playing partners who were laughing like crazy at this point.

I eventually walked up to my ball and tapped it in for birdie. We later wondered if it would have holed-in had Rick's junk not intercepted it; and whether it would have counted as a hole-in-one had it gone in after the interception. I'm still not sure what the ruling would have been on that, and despite my best efforts, Rick has never volunteered to let me give it another try.

Postscript: As we walked off the green, someone in the foursome behind us made a hole-in-one. Perhaps that day, it was just meant to be.

Nightmares of 256 Supple Street

After my graduation and our marriage, Gen and I moved to Pembroke to start our working careers and family. After a few years we were about to outgrow our rented apartment, with one child in hand and another on the way. It was time to make the move to a house.

We bought a house at 256 Supple Street from an older couple who were downsizing, and who we met at the local pool. They had listed the house a year before and it had not sold. We offered them their asking price, and a deal was done.

The house was built around the year 1900 by a lumber baron, coincidentally with the last name Barron. It was a solid all-brick structure on a good-sized lot. We would be but the fourth owners in its 85-or-so-year history. But it needed work.

By the time we sold it some four and a half years later, I'd only made a dent in a "to-do" list as long as my arm. For years and years after moving to Ottawa, I'd wake up from a "renovation nightmare" about 256 Supple Street. Plumbing, heating, electrical, you name it. The owners of a house a block or so up a neighbouring street had completely gutted and re-done their home and that's what it probably would have taken. But we couldn't afford it, so I tackled things one at a time - learning at least some handyman skills as we went along.

The cosmetics were fairly straightforward. There were layers and layers of wallpaper to be removed from the plaster and lath walls, which then needed serious crack-filling before painting. We vowed to never again wallpaper a wall.

During the wallpaper removal, electrical wires were uncovered where wall and ceiling fixtures once hung. I once made the mistake of assuming that the labels on the breaker panel actually did what the label said. So when I flicked off "living room lights," I was greatly surprised when, standing on an aluminum stepladder digging a pair of old plastered-in wires out of the ceiling with my fingers, I suddenly found myself propelled through the (luckily open) French doors and out into the hallway. I think Gen, who was playing with our kids in the hallway at the time, was equally surprised.

That incident led me to completely map out the house's electrical system. It was no easy task. It seemed that the old knob and tube system was still somehow at least partially connected and running in parallel to the "new" wiring (which was already decades old.) In the master bedroom, there was what could only be described as a "Frankenstein breaker" in a box above the bed. By moving that huge knife switch from one set of contacts to the other ("Throw the switch, Igor, the switch") every wall and overhead light in the house would come on - regardless of whether the actual room switches were on or not. My guess was that it served as a burglar alarm / warning of some kind.

Every year, the sewer system would back up into a pit in the floor of the basement workshop. When we first called the city to have them clean out the line with their Rotorooter gear, they told us not to bother showing them the way - they'd been there many times before!

The house was heated by a gas-fired gravity-based hot water system. At some point in the distant past it had been a coal-fired furnace - which explained the coal room. (In honour of Gen's relatives of similar name, her brother attached a brass plaque reading "Cole Room" to its door.) It also explained the scorched ceiling in the furnace room. Apparently soon after its construction, there had been a coal fire that charred the joists and the underside of the living room floor. It was a magnificent floor, as you would expect from a lumber baron: very thin, and long, strips of imported European Oak. And because of the fire it was amazingly solid: he had laid a whole extra floor on top of the original, after the fire.

That floor almost suffered extensive water damaged one winter. I was away on business when I got a panicky call from Gen. One of the hot water radiators in the living room had sprung a leak and she was having trouble staying ahead of the leak with towels and buckets. I told her to call Harvey, my friend Kirk's dad, and he came over and managed to temporarily stop the leak, which let her keep heating the house. There was a large reservoir / expansion tank for the water heating system on the top floor, and it could have done a lot more leaking before the level in the system got down to the living room's radiator height. When I got home, I called a local plumber who ended up going from room to room replacing the old packing in all the radiator valves.

While adding insulation in the full walk-up attic, I once discovered a trove of old newspapers that had been wedged between some joists to supplement the meager original insulation. Those papers had been delivered to the original owner by mail, judging by the address labels and stamps. I turned them all over to the local museum.

That attic could get blisteringly hot during the summer, even with the dormer windows open, and with the shade from three massive maple trees that sat on the property. A carpenter friend helped to install one of those whirlybird vents on the roof. When we cut through the multiple layers of asphalt shingles and the very thick roof itself, a solid plume of hot air escaped. That addition helped cool the non-air conditioned house at least just a bit, especially when we left the door to the attic open. Of course that meant the occasional bat could make its way down to the living areas.

One very impressive aspect of that home was the size and quality of the lumber used in its construction. No mere two-by-fours, sixes, or eights. No doubt because of the baron.

Those giant old maple trees shaded the house as mentioned, and the one in the back provided a huge limb from which I hung a long length of chain to make a tire swing. We almost lost my son Nick when, while being swung so high that he was easily passing over the neighbour's ten-foot high cedar hedge and over their property, which was another few feet drop below ours, he decided to let go of the chain. It was by sheer luck that he managed to grab it again before ejecting from the tire. Perhaps we weren't the best parents. But those maple trees also shed a lot. Not just leaves. It was not uncommon for big huge branches to come crashing down. I climbed and pruned them as much as possible but there was always the risk an entire tree could come down in a storm.

There was still lots and lots of work to do by the time we sold it to friends in 1989. We'd hired a real estate agent friend who had done the research and suggested a listing price that was not too much higher than what we'd paid. Housing prices in Pembroke had been very static for a very long time. I decided to change that and insisted on a much higher list price. Even though we ended up selling it to friends, we stuck to our guns and only dropped the amount a bit by the time the deal was inked. When our neighbours found out the selling price they all wanted to kiss us: their own properties had just appreciated by tens of thousands of dollars, as our home would be touted as a long-due correction to seriously undervalued real estate properties, at least in that neighbourhood.

We used those gains to buy our present home. And while we've invested a fair amount in it over the years, unlike at 256 Supple Street, never have I woken up in a cold sweat, heart racing, having dreamt about its state of (dis)repair.

Mind The Gap

I've travelled to the UK dozens of times over the years and absolutely love it. However, those travels have taught me there are three things the Brits just don't do very well: electrical, plumbing, and air conditioning – and the last one's just a combination of the first two.

Never was this ever better confirmed than during a period in July a few years back when I happened to be there during all-time record-setting high temperatures steaming up London and environs.

Most of These Stories Are Somewhat True

I was over for the Farnborough Air Show. As was the usual practice, my team and I would stay in London, usually in the Edgeware Road / Paddington Station area. The routine was to travel to Farnborough and back each day for the event as follows: walk to the tube, take the Bakerloo Line to Waterloo Station, take the Southwest Train to Farnborough Main, take the shuttle bus from the train station to the show site, and walk from bus stop to our booth. At the end of the day, repeat in reverse.

On the day of record, the trip out was uneventful, largely because it was still early in the morning. But as the day progressed it got hotter and hotter, reaching 40 degrees Celsius or so. The trade show at Farnborough is a series of tent-like temporary structures erected on a tiered car park. By noon, the air conditioning in those structures was straining to keep up – and losing badly. Think thousands of sweat-soaked people in full business attire. Luckily I had learned years earlier to buck that fashion trend and at least wore light coloured khakis and "dry-tech" golf shirts. Regardless, it still felt hot – dang hot!

On the return trip, the walk from the booth to the bus was sweltering. The only seats left were on the upper deck of the double-decker bus I loaded onto, and it had no A/C. The train platform was packed with twice the number of bodies as usual; it seems that the heat was causing some trains to fail, so there were fewer of them pulling up to the station to take us to London. When one did, we breathed briefly in relief, as it was a relatively new unit with air conditioning. However, once underway the air conditioning failed, and because it was new, it was designed with windows that could not be opened. We baked as we rolled to London – and even more when the train had to stop for 45 minutes in the sun, as the lines ahead were plugged due to failed switches and trains.

By the time we rolled into Waterloo Station, many people were in distress. It was a massive relief to exit the train. But the worst was to come.

You see, there's no air conditioning in the Underground. At least not on the Bakerloo Line. "Air conditioning" on "normal" days consists of hot fetid air passing through open windows and ducts in each car. On that day there was no cooling effect: the air was blast-furnace hot and only made things worse.

How bad was it? Well, on top of hearing the usual "mind the gap" warning one hears at many stops in the London Underground, that day, just after the doors closed but before we pulled away from a station, the conductor came on over the tinny PA and said (in the calmest, coolest "we shall never surrender" British voice): "Ladies and gentlemen. If the person next to you happens to die because of the heat, please do not activate the emergency stop. If you do, we will stop between stations and many more of you will die from the heat. If the person beside you happens to die from the heat, you should instead wait until we arrive at the next station to remove the body. This has been your conductor. Thank you for using London's Underground."

I'm quite sure that, even in my heat-addled state, I did not imagine it!

D'Oh!

For reasons that escape me, I've never watched an episode of The Simpsons. I've seen snippets and found them funny, but was never inclined to invest more time than that. I do know, at least I think I do, that Homer Simpson has some connection to a nuclear power plant.

As mentioned in another story, I started my post-graduation employment at the Chalk River Nuclear Laboratories. The summer before, I was one of eight tour guides and learned all about the industry and facilities and toured many visitors through the labs, including the NRU (National Research Universal) reactor.

NRU is the world's largest research reactor. Back then it was rated at something like 130 MW (thermal – it produced only neutrons for experiments and isotopes – no electricity) and it was, and still is, a massive, and massively impressive piece of engineering.

As summer tour guides, we were encouraged to make contact with staff and to look for post-graduation work. Before the summer was out, I had lined up a job in Operations, as a shift engineer, at the NRU reactor. I graduated and in 1982 began my on-the-job training.

Shift engineers would train in three areas: Rods (fueling and everything that is inserted into and removed from the reactor), Loops (experimental facilities that make use of special self-contained positions within the core, and which have their own separate cooling, monitoring, and safety systems etc.) and Systems (which is basically everything else.) Once checked-out on all three, usually after three to four years, you can become one of the fully-certified Senior Reactor Shift Engineers. Basically, you're then responsible for a crew of 35 people on each shift who are needed to make things work.

I completed my Rods and Loops training. It's always interesting times at NRU. My first Senior when I joined was named Bill. By chance, the next one was named Bill as well. Other than after the time I passed him a hot stock tip (I'm not saying where I got it from) that he passed on to his son, who bet on it and made bundles (the stock shot up from below four dollars to over twenty-eight), the second Bill seemed not to like me all that much.

One evening, he called me over to the control panel. There was a planned shutdown that our shift was to initiate. However, instead of simply dialing back the power and shutting it down (there was actually a knob, called the "demand knob" that did exactly that) Bill decided, as part of my Systems training, to move the reactor control system over from automatic to full manual control, and to have me work that knob as long as possible to keep the reactor at full power. Of course, the completely separate safety systems, dozens of them, would remain ever-vigilant. Basically if I couldn't twist the demand knob back and forth well enough to control things like log and linear power etc., eventually a sensor would send a signal that indicated a trip point was exceeded, and once this was (almost instantaneously) confirmed by other "channels," multiple trips would occur and a number of things would happen to kill the nuclear reaction immediately, all while maintaining cooling to the core. It was no more risky than dialing back the demand knob on automatic, and in fact trips were frequently used to shut down the reactor when such systems needed to be tested and shutdowns were scheduled anyhow.

But like I said, Bill wanted me to sweat it out.

Why? Well, the tradition was that if anyone did something to accidently trip the reactor, you had to buy the beer for the whole crew at the end of the shift. And they were a thirsty bunch. And since my orders were to keep the reactor operating at full power on full manual mode, this would qualify for beer buying if I failed.

What the demand knob does is to send an electrical signal that ultimately controls the voltage provided to a drive motor located at the top of one of 18 control rods. Normally rods 1-15 are fully out of the reactor, and you're controlling on either rod 16 or 17. During a trip, all of those rods' magnetic catches are released and they drop into the core, absorb neutrons, and kill the chain reaction immediately. By controlling on 16 or 17, I mean that the control system is normally sending positive and negative voltages to the rod that's doing the controlling, and moving it ever so slightly more into, or out of, the reactor core, thus controlling the reaction. It's doing this continuously, back and forth, many times a second.

That's way faster than you can do on manual control, demand knob cradled between your index finger and thumb. The secret, as I had learned, was not to make exaggerated movements that would quickly lead to a trip. Slow and steady - focusing on the overall state.

So I take hold of the demand knob in my right hand, Bill calls for an announcement over the PA that Mackwood is about to take the reactor to manual control, and the fun begins. With my left hand I move the demand selector switch from automatic to manual. The safety systems are so sensitive that sometimes just doing that is enough to cause a trip. But it holds firm.

I should add that I knew Bill was looking to set me up for a hefty bar bill, so I had put down a side bet with him that if I managed to last for a certain fairly lengthy period of time, he would cover the bill. Game on!

Bill had already turned the set points on all of the key trips down - meaning that they were less forgiving and would trip easier. It was a safe thing to do. I was not complaining.

I soon got into a rhythm. I don't recall which rod I was on, but it was probably 16. It is in a sweet spot in the reactor where it can more easily control things. Advantage me. Calm and cool were paying off with trip needles barely moving.

Then Bill upped the ante. You see, our side wager said nothing about those trip points. As the clock ticked down to the point where I would win our bet, he started bumping them even tighter. This increased the stress level. I broke into a light sweat. But I held fast, even though I could feel some shaking from my right hand.

Minutes before the time was up, he had tightened things up to the point where there was no way I could make it. Eventually one channel tripped, an element of panic started to creep in, and another (on another system). This happened a couple of more times until another trip on the same system shut things down. D'oh!

The bar bill was quite high, but you know, there are not too many people in the world who can say they have operated the world's largest nuclear research reactor on full manual control.

Quick Clay

My father was not an educated man. I helped him complete high school by correspondence courses when I was still in grade school. But he was a very smart person, well-read and very quick of wit. He did not suffer fools gladly, even very well-educated ones.

Our short street, Howe Street, was for years an unpaved road. As a kid, I'd play in the large mud puddles that would form after a rain. And "trampoline" on its surface when the clay underneath softened up. We kids did not know it at the time, but like many places throughout the Ottawa Valley, our street was built on top of quick clay.

At some point in the '60s, the City of Pembroke decided it was time to pave some of those dirt streets. One day, it was Howe Street's turn. Preparations began and the heavy equipment was brought in and parked, ready for use the next morning. It had been a wet few days prior to this and the road was still spongy. Parked right in front of our house was a great big Cat bulldozer.

Dad approaches the operator and tells him he shouldn't park it there. The operator calls over a supervisor. Dad tells him the same thing. The supervisor calls over the city engineer, who happens to be there at the time. Dad tells him he shouldn't park it there. The engineer then launches into a tirade along the lines of "I'll have you know I'm the greatest engineer known to man. I have multiple degrees from many universities. You cannot possibly know what I know. We're parking this Cat here."

The next morning Dad wanders out to the street with a mug of coffee in his hand. There, huddled together, are the operator, supervisor, and city engineer. The Cat is nowhere to be seen. Actually, that's not right. Turns out they're huddled around the top of the exhaust pipe, which is sticking up an inch or two out of the clay!

Dad takes a loud slurp of his coffee, says nothing, and with a knowing twinkle in his eye, turns around and heads back into the house.

Jack and Bill

In the late eighties, I was in Los Angeles for a conference. Armed with an expense account, I managed to find two customers to accompany me to a Lakers game. As I was leaving the hotel I stopped at the gift shop and bought one of those disposable 24-shot pocket 110 cameras. (Re-read the first sentence: this was the eighties!)

We took our seats, unfortunately near the top of the stadium. (Blame limited budget and hefty scalpers' fees.) Holding my camera in hand, sitting on an aisle seat, I remarked to my guests that I had been hoping to get some closer shots. An usher standing near us overheard and told me this was the "Fabulous Forum" and I could go right down courtside and shoot all the pics I wanted. I just had to shoot, move, shoot, move, etc. So I did. Got some great shots of Magic, Kareem, and others during warm-ups. I used about half the roll.

At the end of the first half, I scrambled back down courtside to snap a bunch of pics of the Laker Girls doing their dance routines. This time I stood in one place, centre court, just ahead of the court-side VIP seats. After a couple of minutes, I look into the little indicator port to see that I've now taken 24 shots, but I crank the dial again, and the film advances. I'm not sure whether it's film, or the leader.

Then I hear a woman's voice. I can't place its location. It seems to be coming from all around me. And it says "Oh my God. It's Jack Nicholson!" I turn to my left and there's Jack standing beside me, looking way cool decked out in black leather jacket and hat. I turn to him and he extends his hand. We shake as he says "Hi. How are ya?" I raise my camera and ask if he minds. He says go ahead. The shutter fires. Jack then walks diagonally across the court to the VIP lounge.

So there I am thanking my lucky stars when I hear that voice again. "Oh my God. It's Bill Murray!" I turn to my right and there he is standing beside me, dressed in cords and a ratty sleeveless sweater. He turns, we shake hands. I quickly crank the film advance and miraculously it clicks into place. I ask if it's ok to take a shot, which he graciously poses for. He then leaves for the VIP lounge.

I look down at the camera's shot counter and it's firmly on 26. I try to crank it but that's it. No more to advance. Days later, I anxiously retrieved my prints from the camera shop. Jack and Bill captured? Priceless!

Interspecies Love

Back in the days (before YouTube) when "America's Funniest Home Videos" was actually popular, I was sure we had the clip of the year.

Over the years, my wife and I have owned many cats, and one dog.

Sadie, the dog, was an amazingly smart, friendly and loving black American cocker. How smart? From the day she set paw in our home she never chewed, or even played with, anything we did not specifically present to her as "Sadie's toy." And over the years, as her collection of toys grew to a big basketful, we gave each and every one of them a different name. We could take any number of them, scatter them around the house and then simply say "Sadie, go get your..." and name one of them. Off she'd go, nose to the ground and return with that, and only that, named toy. She'd present it to us and wait for the praise and ear scritch she knew she deserved.

As we do with all of our animals, Sadie was spayed before she could breed.

We tend to always have two cats at any given time. When one passes away, it's replaced by a new kitten. Sadie was already full-grown when Tuvok, a black male short-hair cat, was brought into the house. Maybe he was separated too soon from his mother, or maybe it was because of their identical black colouring, but Tuvok took to Sadie right away, walking between her legs, rubbing up against her, and cuddling up against her for a nap. Sadie took it all in stride. They seemed to like... no ... love each other.

Tuvok was neutered at six months.

Flash forward a few years and Tuvok was now full grown. One day, as I left the house for work, both he and Sadie were lying on the same carpet together. As I was leaving I told them to "be good." (It's amazing how we talk to our pets!) When I got to my car in the driveway I realized I had left something behind. I returned to the house, opened the door, and my jaw dropped.

There, on the carpet, was Tuvok, the neutered male cat, in "doggystyle" position, with Sadie, the spayed female dog, on top of him, paws on his front shoulders and rear end just a-humping away! As soon as they saw me they stopped, held their positions, and turned their heads in unison to me. I'm not sure if they were thinking "Damn! Busted!" or "Do you mind? A little privacy please!" or even "Don't you ever knock first?" but their looks were enough for me to forget what it was I returned to the house for, say "Sorry," and quietly leave the house. I imagine they started up again when I left.

Nobody in the family believed me when I told them this a few days later, but over the years, they became bolder and bolder in their "lovemaking" and everyone eventually got to see them "at it" at least once. One of my daughters even managed to capture it on video. I'm pretty sure that had we submitted it, this little bit of interspecies love would have taken home a prize or two.

Frog Astaire

A few years ago our backyard had an addition to the usual collection of urban wildlife: a tree frog. My wife called it a sign of a healthy eco-system. I called it a very noisy problem. You see that little critter could sing up a storm. Mostly in the evening, but also at all times of day - and night. Even with windows closed, I found it impossible to sleep when he was singing.

So I set out to catch the little fella. Which is really not all that easy. He'd stop singing if he sensed you were closing in on him. And with the trees and bushes where the sound appeared to be coming from, he was impossible to spot, being naturally camouflaged.

Then one afternoon he started his tune again, but it sounded somehow different. I walked to the corner of the house where it was coming from and he kept it up. He was no longer in the cedars. I looked around the corner and the sound was loud and right in front of me. But no frog in sight. Right there was the electric service, cable connection, phone box... phone box? What would a frog sound like in a fist-sized plastic enclosure? Exactly like what I was hearing.

I carefully pulled the cover off and there, staring at me, was the cutest green frog I'd ever seen, with these big suction cup fingertips. Before he could leap away, I managed to cup him in my hands. I immediately thought of the Warner Brothers cartoon, "One Froggy Evening," and, for some reason, Fred Astaire. "Hello, Frog Astaire," I crooned to it.

Well, cute or not, I needed my sleep so I walked down to the river and released him into a big grove of trees, none the worse for the trip.

I did not see him the rest of the year.

The next summer there was a new noise. This one was very loud and seemed to be coming from somewhere behind our back fence, where there's a bike path and parkland. It was a very haunting and hollow sound, with some echo and reverb. I went through the back gate to check it out.

Earlier that spring, contractors had trenched hundreds of yards of big-diameter conduit throughout the whole bike path corridor (where electrical, phone and cable services ran.) I'm not sure which one this new one was for, since the boxes had not yet been built. There were four-foot high conduit pipes sticking up along the whole stretch behind all of the homes, with one right at the back corner of my property.

As I got close to it, the noise started up again. It came from that pipe, and echoed from one way down behind it, and another way behind me. It was very spooky-sounding. I noticed that the conduit was not capped, and there were a number of "fish" lines coming up and out of it. So I pulled on them and after a few feet, who shows up? Frog Astaire, who gets one look at me and scurries back down into the pipe. So I place a rock over the top. I figure this way he'll re-emerge at some other point and if he starts his singing again it won't be as loud near my bedroom window. I don't hear from him for the rest of the year.

Now I don't know the life expectancy of a tree frog [ok, I just looked it up and it is two to five years in captivity] but the next year he was back and this time he'd brought a friend to the neighbourhood. He was back in our cedars and the other somewhere in a neighbouring yard. Now I had assumed all along that Frog Astaire was a male. The romantic in me assumed that the new addition was his mate. "She" naturally became known as Ginger.

Instead of another relocation, I steeled myself to accept them. And they performed, almost on cue, for a few more evenings, singing together. Then one day they were quiet and I assumed they'd sung, danced, and then eventually been happily on their way to another locale.

Yes Minister(s) !

One of my earliest work-related performance reviews concluded with the overall summary that "Jeff does not suffer fools gladly." It was meant as a compliment and as words of encouragement. I think the boss who wrote those words was the last one that ever "got" me. Every single one after that spent at least some time and effort trying to rehabilitate me. It never stuck.

Another character trait of mine is that I am not automatically respect-ful of people in power, of their status, or perceived superiority. I respect the position, but the person in the position needs to earn respect. In many cases, this flows from the not-suffering-fools-gladly trait.

Over the years, I have come into contact with a variety of Canadian federal politicians, from backbenchers, to junior ministers, to senior ministers, to prime ministers. My earliest recollection of meeting one was during the Miles for Millions Walkathon in 1967. I was only eight years old and would not complete the gruelling 40-mile walk, but partway through the miles I did manage, on a country road somewhere outside of Pembroke, a big black convertible pulled up, stopped, and out came ex-Prime Minister John Diefenbaker. He walked for quite a while with my friends and I, and we chatted each other up. Back then I was really into aerospace and space (the first moon landing being only a couple of years away). I knew about the Canadian Avro Arrow program that had been cancelled by Diefenbaker just before I was born, and I pestered him with questions about why he had done so, until he eventually hopped back into his chauffeured car and sped off, leaving us in a cloud of dust.

Much later in life, when I was part of Team Canada at a variety of international aerospace events (Paris and Farnborough airshows in particular) I would find myself shaking hands and conversing with the ranking government minister(s) touring the Canadian Pavilion and attending the official Canadian reception in the evening. I would always greet them by their first name, not out of disrespect, but because that's how I greet everyone. While this raised some eyebrows amongst the "bees" (the ministerial entourage that's always buzzing around their boss) it usually worked well, judging by the ministers' reactions. With only one exception, they all appreciated the more personal touch, as far as I could tell.

I have very positive memories of an encounter I had with then-Minister of International Trade, Art Eggleton. We first met during his walkabout and he seemed genuinely interested in what folks had to tell him. Later that evening, we found ourselves standing next to each other at a reception at the Canadian High Commission on Grosvenor Square in the Mayfair, and struck up a conversation that lasted at least a couple of bottles of wine. By the end of the evening, we were the only ones left, standing in the foyer, solving the world's problems. For quite some time Art's assistant had been trying to pry him away and into the car idling just outside at the curb, but I kept suggesting that he stay for another glass of wine. She was finally successful and while he got chauffeured back to his hotel, I had to stumble back to mine.

A couple or more years later, I was shaking then-Minister of Industry Allan Rock's hand on a fine Monday morning at Farnborough. I was immediately not impressed by the man. He seemed clearly offended by my first-name greeting and tuned out immediately. Fair enough. I'd test him again later that night. But let me first digress.

Almost a year before that, I was preparing for a trade show in Montreal when Geoff, a counterpart of mine from Industry Canada, called and asked about the event. He then asked if he could share a booth with me. I said I'd be happy to do so, but we'd need to buy more space to accommodate him. He said he had no money left in his budget that fiscal year, but if I would cover his costs, he'd arrange for a transfer of funds the following fiscal year when he again had money in his budget. It worked for me, since I had enough slack in my budget to cover the costs, and since I knew the following year was going to be a little tight anyhow. So I incurred the expense and he attended. The next fiscal year rolled around and I called to ask about the transfer of funds. He said he didn't have them and wouldn't have them, and I'm out of luck. There wasn't much I could do about it – except make a mental note.

So back to Allan Rock and Farnborough. The leader of the bees, and the person in charge of the minister for the event, was none other than Geoff, the guy who had stiffed me. Rock delivered the customary welcoming speech at the Canadian Reception at Canada House that evening. As the crowd eventually started to dwindle, I spotted Geoff and Rock standing alone together across the room. A plot was hatched in microseconds, while I was already halfway across the room to them. As soon as I got to them, I cut into their conversation as follows: "Excuse me, Allan, I have some important news for Geoff. Geoff, I was just up in the hotel room with 'the girls' and there seems to be a problem. They won't accept your government credit card as payment." Then I turned and walked away fast, but not so fast that I missed the looks on both men's faces. Priceless!

While I would continue to meet a variety of ministers at events up to my retirement, the one other that I remember most was Maxime Bernier, then-Minister of Industry. He struck me as a quite a nice guy, albeit not the sharpest pencil in the box. (He would later resign due to a scandal over his ex-girlfriend's ties to the Hell's Angels.) At the end of day two of the Farnborough event, I was standing, as usual, at the Farnborough Main train station, waiting for the next one to Waterloo Station to arrive. Walking down the platform towards me was an unaccompanied Maxime, holding his train ticket, with a puzzled look on his face. We made eye contact as he approached, and he recognized me. (He and I are both tall and could spot each other over the throngs on the platform.) I noticed commotion on the platform on the other side of the tracks. The bees had lost their boss and were buzzing about trying to find him.

I asked him if I could help. He said he did not know where to go. I asked to see his ticket, which was first class, and then, consulting the display to see the expected length of the next train to Waterloo, I pointed much further down the platform (and away from the bees) to a numbered post. "Maxime. Go stand there." I told him that's where the first-class car would most likely be aligned when the next train pulled up, which it was. As the train pulled up, the bees could be seen getting on at its other end. I don't know if they caught up to him on the train or not. Perhaps most memorable about Maxime was that this was the first time I'd told a minister "where to go."

Americans Spying on Americans

Years and years before WikiLeaks and Edward Snowden, I pretty much knew that the US Government was spying on its own people.

I play basketball, year-round, every Wednesday evening at my club, which is a big multi-sport/activity operation. There's a summer and a winter league. Winter league consists of six teams of ten players each and, depending on the year, there can be a healthy turnover in players from one year to the next.

One year we welcomed a black fellow by the name of Dave from Atlanta onto our team. He was a very good player and fit in just great.

While the league is "competitive," quite a few of us also, not incorrectly, call it a beer league. After a game, win or lose, you go "up" to the sports pub for a cold one. On one occasion, Dave joined us. We engaged in the usual chit-chat, and I talked to him about Atlanta and the time I played some great pick-up games downtown when I was there. I asked who he worked with and he said he was with the US military, deployed to a Canadian Forces operation here in Ottawa.

"Cool," I said. "What's your specialty?" I asked. "Communications" was the reply. I asked where he was working out of and he said a place in the south end of Ottawa, which was a pretty short drive to the club. Hmmm. So I asked what road it was on. "Leitrim," was the reply. "Canadian Forces Station Leitrim?" I asked. He nodded yes.

At that point, I put two and two together. I had a vague knowledge that CFS Leitrim did electronic eavesdropping. I drove past it regularly on my way to play hockey on Fridays at a rink just down the road from it. You could see a variety of towers and other antennas about the property as you drove by. I also had read somewhere, correctly or not, that the US was prevented at that time by its own laws from spying on its own citizens from within its own territory.

So I processed all that and said to Dave: "So they've sent you all the way here to spy on Americans back there!" It wasn't a question, so he didn't respond. Actually, I'm sure he would not have responded if it were a question. I didn't press it, but always remembered the conversation. Dave played one season for us until he was transferred somewhere else. I'd completely forgotten about him until last year when the Snowden Affair erupted. While the extent of the information leaked by Snowden was surprising, that the US is spying on its own citizens did not surprise me in the least, thanks to that conversation over beers with Dave many years before.

Crop Patterns

The best man at my wedding was Kirk. We've been friends since childhood. While we lived on opposite sides of town, it seemed like every time we were signed up for some sport or lesson, like hockey, baseball, or swimming, we'd end up on the same team or in the same class. We were in high school together for four years. We worked as summer students together. And except for a year or two here and there, we've lived in the same cities at the same time. He was my first and only choice as best man.

A month after my marriage to Gen, it was his and Annette's turn, and I reciprocated as his best man.

A day or two before the big day, Gen and I had the two of them over to our apartment for a pre-wedding dinner. The wine and beer flowed. At some point, a small argument broke out between the about-to-be-weds and Annette said she was leaving, heading for the parking lot and their white Chevy Malibu. By the time we managed to get outside to try to stop her, she had already gotten behind the wheel, started the car, put it in reverse to back out of the parking spot near the end of the lot, and disappeared.

I don't mean she put it in drive and drove off fast. Nope. Before she could stop reversing and put it in drive, she backed off the edge of the end of the parking lot, which unfortunately had no retaining barrier, and plunged backwards down a steep incline to the farmer's field below. Not a huge drop; maybe six feet or so. But it was deep and steep enough to briefly expose the entire underside of the car.

We rushed over to the edge and saw that the car was now several feet into a field of soon-to-be-harvested hay. Neither Annette, nor the car, were hurt.

Now I claimed to have been drinking less than the others, so I elected myself driver and moved Annette over. Kirk sandwiched her in the middle of the bench seat by hopping in on the passenger's side. Gen, clearly the smartest of the bunch, stayed up in the parking lot. It was dark out, so I turned on the headlights. I said I thought there was a ramp of sorts, not far away, where there was an auto service garage backing onto the field, and off we went.

It's surreal driving at night through a hay field, plowing it down like a giant blunt scythe, while your headlights shine just a foot or two ahead of you. But we could see the approaching back of the garage. I reduced our already slow speed to walking pace as we got close, lined up the car to where I thought the ramp was, and then, clunk! The "ramp" was more like a 45-degree asphalt retaining wall. This was not going to work.

So we backed up and headed off in search of some other way out of that field. We were driving in a pretty random pattern, getting to the edge of the field on occasion to be confronted by a treeline, or rock fence, and heading off again in another direction. Of course, we never thought to just follow the perimeter until an exit was found. After all, the farmer had to get his equipment in somehow to harvest the crop, didn't he?

In the open field, we were traveling at a pretty good speed at times, the hay making a loud swishing sound as we plowed through it. After what seemed like miles and miles of random direction changes, and sometimes driving in circles, an exit was found that led to a road that got us back to the apartment. While the car looked like an overstuffed scarecrow with the amount of hay it had accumulated in its bumper, grille, and wheel wells, it was none the worse for wear.

We retired to the apartment, and eventually the night, any thoughts of driving now put firmly to rest.

The next morning I wandered down to the parking lot, and over to the edge where the journey had started. While the field didn't quite match the intricately-done patterns I had seen on TV, what I saw made me pretty sure that alcohol, and perhaps even the occasional Chevy Malibu, played a far greater part in the appearance of crop circles than ET ever did, because laid out in front of me was one very wicked set of geometric patterns covering an amazingly large part of that field.

8-Tracks, Shotguns and Rifles

I had a childhood friend named Paul. At one time, he had a problem: he was a shoplifter. The bigger problem was that he was darn good at it. My problem was that I helped him, not by stealing or even helping him steal, but by selling a lot of the stuff that he stole.

In my first year of high school, my locker contained a big selection of 8-track tapes and car players that Paul had purloined. I'd sell them to the senior students who were down in the automotive wing hopping up their Dusters and Camaros after class. Now, had the authorities raided said locker, I would have gotten off scot-free because all of those goods had been given to me by the police.

You see, what Paul and I had done months earlier was to take all of it and put it into a couple of very big boxes. We removed all of the labels, so that they could not be identified as having come from a specific store. Then we damaged and dirtied the boxes a bit, and carried the whole lot to the police station and reported that we'd found them under a bridge. After a period of time when nobody claimed them, they were turned back over to us. We'd discovered a way of laundering stolen goods through the police!

On one occasion, I met up with Paul after one of his shopping trips and he showed me a shotgun and two rifles, along with boxes of ammunition, he'd managed to shoplift from a downtown sports store. I told him that laundering those through the police might not work. His intention had been to keep them. Not for use in hold-ups or anything like that. For honest-to-goodness hunting. But he couldn't keep them at home, so they were broken down, and we biked out to his old family property in Westmeath, with the parts concealed in our tent and sleeping bags. We used a canoe to transport them to an island on the Ottawa River where, after firing several rounds for fun, we wrapped them in plastic, put them in a big gun bag, and stuffed them into a hollowed-out log, which we plugged with dirt and leaves.

The following winter, Paul broke his leg while skiing. It was a bad break and he spent several weeks in hospital with his leg in traction. During that time, one of his younger brothers found his cache of cash and some stolen goods in his room. A hospital visit by his Dad was all that it took to extract a confession. I think he only confessed to what was found, but nevertheless the punishment was years of grounding.

One spring years later, we were again in Westmeath and at his old family property. We took a canoe over to the island. There was still ice floating on the river at the time. We trudged through slush and muck and found that old log. It had rotted quite a bit and wasn't hard to break it open to extract the gun bag. Unfortunately (or fortunately), things had not stayed dry and the parts were nothing more than rusted junk. As was our plan anyhow, we tossed it all into the river.

On the return trip, we capsized the canoe and barely made it back to the island. And I do mean barely: we were dressed in winter clothes and had no lifejackets on. Stupid! The old canoe did not float when swamped, and we struggled to tow it with us. When we crawled up the rocks back onto the island, we were already suffering from hypothermia. Paul had a lighter with him and we managed to build a fire to get warm and partially dry our clothes. An hour later we set out again, now paddling with our hands, which soon went numb, and eventually made it back across the river channel to shore.

What with nearly drowning and hypothermia, I figure we pretty much atoned for our short lives of crime as shoplifter and fence.

Maxi-Me

I've met a great bunch of men on the internet and now we get together regularly to enjoy each other's company. Seriously. And some of them open up their homes so that strangers like me can visit, sometimes for days on end, sleeping in their beds, eating their food, and drinking their wine, beer and spirits. Honestly. And a lot of them bring their wives to these get-togethers, and the wives love being there. Truthfully. And some even bring their children, who run and play amongst the adults. Yup. And our leader is a bald-headed Italian rock god by the name of Zing with a penchant for Robert Graham shirts. Huh?

I'll explain.

Years and years ago, a certain type of person, mostly male, started to populate a web site dedicated to audio and video issues. With time, online friendships and some adversarial relationships developed. The former led to some individuals meeting up whenever they'd find themselves in the same locale, and eventually smaller regional gatherings were held, notably by those in the Atlanta area. The latter grew to the point where, for some, that web site was no longer a fun place to hang out. In addition, the site itself was largely ignored by its owners and frustration by the members was mounting.

So a very forward-thinking member of the group, whose online handle is Zing, decided to create a new audio video web-based forum, The Audio Annex, and in August of 2010 the migration to it began. With that change, some very neat things happened. More friendships were born and more get-togethers were held. And one couple, Batman and Mrs. Batman, who had hosted get-togethers (GTG) at their incredible Philly-area home (the "Batcave") in the summers of 2009 and 2010, decided to make it an annual event, open to all Annex members, and even others, to attend.

So it was, in June of 2013, that I found myself embarking on an eight-hour drive from Ottawa to the Batcave for the fifth such annual GTG. On previous visits, I'd flown, but my recent "laid-off" status resulted in a change of habit. It turned out to be a nice drive that gave me plenty of time to think, and scheme, which I'll get to in a moment. First I had a border to cross.

My chosen route took me south from Ottawa to the Thousand Islands crossing north of Syracuse. Traffic is normally fairly light and I've never been more than six cars deep in line. On this occasion I drove straight up to the border agent without having to stop, which also meant that I had no time to pre-think about what I was going to say.

I handed her my passport and said "G'Day" to start the conversation.

"Where are you from?"

"Ottawa, Ontario."

"Where are you going?"

"To a friend's place near Philadelphia."

"What will you be doing there."

"Hanging out in the Batcave mostly."

She now looks up from her computer monitor and at me.

"What is your friend's name?"

"Batman."

Very puzzled look.

"THE Batman?"

"No. His real name is Chris, but I think he believes he is. He has his wife dress in a Robin costume."

Her whole body turns to me and she's now very intent on what I'm about to say.

"And will you be meeting anyone else besides Batman and Robin?"

"Sure. A whole house full of similar people from around the US will be there. It's mostly guys I've met on the internet."

"Have a good time," she says, handing me back my passport, a "knowing" smile on her face. Maybe I should have invited her to join us?

So I resume the trip and get to thinking about that conversation. It really is a neat bunch of folks that I'm about to see again, and no doubt some I've not yet met. And all of this is possible not just because of the willingness and generosity of Bats and his wife to host us, but because Zing had taken the time to create The Audio Annex a few years previous, and ministered to it on a daily basis to ensure it operated as designed. You know, I thought, we'd always said thank you to Bats and Mrs. Bats for hosting these GTGs, but nobody had yet paid tribute to Zing. It was about time.

As I continued to drive, a plan was hatched. Part of the plan involved a shirt that I had packed. A year prior, at the previous Batcave GTG, Zing and I had talked men's clothing: he about Robert Graham shirts, a few of which he sported during that GTG, and me about Kroon sports coats, of which I own several. A Robert Graham is not cheap: typically $200-300. So imagine my surprise to have "discovered" the one and only (at the time) Robert Graham factory outlet store in Orlando earlier that year. And for about $80, after discounts, I now owned my very own Robert Graham shirt, which I planned to wear at the GTG as a tribute to Zing.

But that wasn't enough. I had also packed jeans and shoes that closely matched Zing's "look." Closer. But not close enough. I stand 6'3" tall, not counting my head of hair. Zing's much shorter than that, including his completely bald pate. I had it! The only question was how to pull it off and when.

I decided to do it early on an evening when the most people were in attendance. People come and go over several days, but I figured most folks would be in town by Thursday. So I had the date.

I arrived on the Tuesday. One of the first things I did was to tell Mrs. Bats about my plan. I needed her help and she would be the only person to know most of it. She agreed, but was a bit skeptical as to whether I would go through with it or not.

The next day I picked Razz and MattB up from the airport. Once at the house I enlisted Razz's help. He was not told of the entire plan; he just knew that at an appointed time on Thursday evening he would help Mrs. Bats assemble the crowd at the foot of the main staircase that empties into the great family room and kitchen, and position Zing at the bottom of those stairs, facing the crowd, with instructions to Zing that he not turn around. Razz was then to step back into the crowd, camera at the ready.

It all came off without a hitch. Let me use Zing's own posted words as to what happened on that Thursday.

"The group, as a whole, was scattered throughout the house but most of us - including Babs and I - were on the deck. Suddenly Mrs. Bats came out and said she needed everyone inside for a special presentation. Once she gathered everyone from all nooks and crannies of the house, we were then instructed to gather facing the staircase. While everyone is getting situated to see this presentation, Razz motioned for me to come see him. He starts some chit chat about camera and photography when it was interrupted by the bellowing voice of Jeff upstairs and out of sight. He began his speech by thanking everyone for converging and witnessing this special occasion.

It was at this point I started suspecting what was about to happen. Knowing Bats and Mrs. Bats like I do, I had a feeling they were involved in some sort of "presentation" to commemorate Babs and I having a 20th anniversary this month and I thought they may take advantage of it while the group was all together. Before long, Jeff's speech turned directly toward me when he mentioned starting the Annex and the glue that holds us together. I knew at that instant, it had nothing to do with Babs and I but rather just me. About the time that set in, Razz said to me "I need you to stand right here with your back to the stairs. I'll hold your camera". If I was uncertain about anything, it became very clear who this was all about.

Jeff continued with some very kind and sincere words about me, my sense of fashion, my wardrobe (particularly my collection of Robert Graham shirts) and the birth of the forum for a few minutes. Now I could tell he was coming down the stairs. I had no idea what dastardly trick was about to be pulled on me. I was half expecting a cooler of Gatorade to be dumped on me. Pretty soon I heard him come around the last corner of the steps and the crowd went nuts! When I turned around, there stood Jeff with a shaved head and a Robert Graham shirt (he took a liking to mine last year and recently bought his first one - likely with this event in mind).

I was floored! Honored, humbled and very moved. The fact that he would go through all this effort was nothing short of astonishing to me. By the time the shock, fun, laughter and awe subsided, it was all I could do fight off a tear. I was genuinely touched. The plan, intention, effort and act were all simply fantastic."

I think that one attendee, Heeman, summed it up rather nicely as well: "You could not guess what Mackwood did in a million years...He is one crazy bastard!!!"

Another, PaulyT, was obviously concerned with my well-being when he thought to himself: "Jeff's wife is going to kill him."

What Zing did not know at the time was that Mrs. Bats' participation went far beyond crowd control. About an hour before my descent, she and I retired to the master bedroom. Actually to the master bath of that bedroom, where, trimmer in hand, she sheared off all of my hair. With trepidation at first, but after she was sure that I was up for it, with gusto. I was then left to shave it completely bald and sneak over to my upstairs bedroom to change into my Zing uniform of blue jeans and Robert Graham shirt.

Speaking of which, I had also asked Zing's wife, Babs, to ensure that Zing was dressed that evening in a shirt that most closely matched my one and only Robert Graham.

In the end, except for more than a few inches in height, we looked like twins. Hence my adopted and self-bestowed honorary moniker: "Maxi-Me."

Singapore Satisfaction – Part 1

I'm amazed that, seemingly year after year, Air Canada ends up winning some "best airline" award. I've travelled with them extensively for decades and while they are ok, they are far from "best" in my books. Then again, maybe I shouldn't be so amazed given who their competition is: every other airline in North America. Let's compare and contrast my experience with them on just one trip, versus the performance of Singapore Airlines, one of Air Canada's Star Alliance partners.

I was going to be traveling to Singapore on business and decided it would be a great idea to take Gen along. She'd never been there before. More importantly, our oldest daughter was living and working in Thailand at the time, and Bangkok is just a hedge hop away from Singapore. So I made my plans to include a Bangkok stopover on the return leg, booked us in for a weekend at the Bangkok Hilton, and used points to get Gen a ticket that matched mine.

I needed to be in Singapore on a Sunday, to give a speech at a sizeable gathering of business people. Taking travel time and the International Date Line into consideration, that meant we would start our trip from Ottawa, in the early morning on the Friday. The route had us doing Ottawa to Vancouver, Vancouver to Hong Kong, and Hong Kong to Singapore. The first two legs would be with Air Canada and the last with Singapore Airlines.

Our tickets were for economy class but I was planning to use upgrade points at check-in. At the counter, the agent started the process, but then ... trouble. She told me she could not check me in; there was a problem with my passport. That came as a huge surprise to me since the passport was still valid and would not expire for four months. Gen's was good for another seven months.

I was told that to enter Singapore my passport had to be valid for at least six months after the planned date of departure from Singapore. That was news to me. Was there anything she could do? "No," was the answer and she called for the next person in line. We didn't move.

We tried to find a way to make it work but got nowhere. We refused to budge. I told her to check us through anyhow and I'd take my chances. Couldn't do it, she said, because if the authorities turned me away, Air Canada would be liable for a $10,000 fine. So I pulled out my credit card and told her to pre-authorize $10,000 on it to cover that possibility – just in case. Still no luck.

So we called over a supervisor and she went through the whole thing again with us. Her only suggestion was to go downtown and apply for a passport renewal (on the assumption that we'd be handed it that day) and then come back on Monday, which was the soonest they could re-book us. Yeah, that wasn't happening. She tried to shoo us away as well. It was then that my devious little brain did its thing.

I asked what the passport entry requirements were into Hong Kong. Three months, was the answer. So why the hell don't you issue me my Air Canada boarding passes through Vancouver to Hong Kong? They had no coherent argument against that, so they did. They tagged our bags to Hong Kong and said we'd have to claim them at baggage and then leave the terminal and re-enter and head to Singapore airlines to see if they would issue us boarding cards for the last leg of the trip.

I started running "what if" scenarios in my head on the Ottawa to Vancouver flight. What if we are not allowed to connect to Singapore? Where do we stay in Hong Kong? Where is the Canadian Consulate in Hong Kong and how fast can they issue a temporary passport?

Those sorts of things. During our brief connection time in Vancouver I was able to fire off an email message to a contact at the Canadian Consulate in Singapore, describing my predicament and asking him for advice and help if he could. (It turned out he couldn't.) We boarded our flight to Hong Kong.

Normally I enjoy these long flights, especially when upgraded to business class. I get to catch up on my reading and movie watching and sleep and eat and drink. And that part of the Air Canada experience is almost always a very good one. Their in-flight selection of movies, and especially music, is excellent. In business class the food is very good and the wine selection is great, as far as airlines go. I should have been relaxed and calm but I was a complete nervous wreck.

A few hours out from Hong Kong, I gave Gen the rundown on how things could play out. (She usually lets me do the worrying about such things.) I told her to simply follow my lead and instructions. First stop would be baggage claim as soon as we de-planed. But boy, did things change when we landed.

As soon as we exited the plane, there was a Singapore airlines rep standing there holding a big sign with my name on it. He told me to come with him, that they were expecting us and that everything was going to be ok. He wasn't kidding. He used his security card to whisk us into some staff corridors and we emerged a while later at some semi-hidden Singapore Airlines help desk. There an agent had already printed our boarding passes and handed them to us. She also informed us that they had checked and Air Canada had not bothered to even load our bags onto our first flight out of Ottawa. They (Sing Air) had arranged for them to be sent on later flights but she was afraid that they would get to Singapore at least a day after we would. But not to worry, they would look after us. I'd find out what that meant later.

The rep then took us in tow again and we emerged through some hidden door, right next to the departure gate. The flight was about to close and he escorted us right to our seats on the plane and wished us all the best. He said a colleague of his would greet us at the other end.

Same thing happens in Singapore. A rep leads us from the plane and directly to customs and immigration. He gets us into a special line, asks for our passports, and, after handing them to the agent, says a few words to him, and we get waved forward. The passports get stamped and the agent tells us to enjoy our stay in Singapore. We're in! We thank the rep profusely and we get the impression that he's done nothing but what they do all the time: offer great caring service. (Are you taking notes, Air Canada?)

At the baggage carousel we're approached by another Sing Air rep and she asks if we're the Mackwood's before asking us to come to her office. She's been told to expect us and says that Air Canada messed up with the luggage again but that she would look after us. She presents us with two half-decent sized duffel bags that are loaded with an assortment of generic clothes and a ton of toiletries. She then disappears for a minute and comes back with two envelopes, one for each of us, and asks us to sign for them. Which we do. She then calls us a limo, on them, to take us to our hotel. It's on the way to the hotel that we open the envelopes to find that they each contain $250Sing and a note apologizing for any inconvenience and saying that we hope this small token would help make things at least semi-right.

Remember. Singapore Airlines was blameless in this mess. It was all Air Canada's doing. Would Air Canada have behaved in a similar fashion had the reverse happened? Yeah, right. I could not have been more impressed, and the experience only further reinforced how relatively poorly North American air travelers are treated.

'72 Ski-Doo

1971 and 1972 were banner years for snowfall in the Pembroke, Ontario area. There was roughly 50% more snowfall in each of those two years as in years before and after that period. It was also a great time if you were in the business of selling snowmobiles, as evidenced by an explosion of manufacturers, makes, models, and sales.

During those years, a number of families in my neighbourhood bought machines. There were sleds from Ski-Doo, Arctic Cat, Snowjet, Snow Cruiser, Polaris, Alouette, and Yamaha, to mention only a few of the nearly one hundred manufacturers of the day. (Sales would plummet and almost all of them would go out of business following the 1973 oil crisis.)

My parents bought a 1972 Ski-Doo Olympic 300. It was primitive by today's standards, what with its bogey wheel suspension and 15 horsepower single-cylinder two-stroke engine. No heated seat, handgrips, or footrests. Manual start. But it could break trail through feet of powder and hit just over 50 mph on a hard packed road (at least that's what the police officer said I was doing!)

Neither of my parents were the outdoorsy physically-active types, but for the first two winters they got out once in a while on sunny Saturday or Sunday afternoons, leaving me to look after my much younger brother. Oh the horrors! But at all other times it was pretty much my sled and I treated it as such, making sure it was properly maintained, adjusted and set up.

Almost every evening, after chores and homework were done, I'd meet up at the local outdoor hockey rink with my riding friends. Off we'd go, sometimes for a couple of hours. There were open farmers' fields, and back country roads, hard packed and powder snow, trails through the forest, and miles and miles of hydro line rights-of-way. There were quarries and rivers. We explored them all. We rode until our hands and feet were numb with cold and sometimes until the tips of our noses turned white with frostbite.

Back then gas was cheap: 39 cents per gallon if I remember correctly. Fill up a five gallon can and add a quart of oil, shake, pour, and you were on your way for three dollars, which was still a fair amount of money back then, especially since you'd easily go through that much gas in a full day of riding.

Before racing snowmobiles on open water became a sport (if you could call it that) we inadvertently discovered that you could skim across it. We'd been riding fast up the Ottawa River at night when we hit a 30-foot-wide section. We all made it over and kept going, but decided to take an overland route on the return trip.

There was one big farmer's field that would grow huge snow drifts along one tree line and we'd spend hours "surfing" and punching through them, digging our machines out from time to time. I recall that one farmer did not like us being in his fields and came out to chase us in his tractor. He thought he had boxed us in at one end until one my friends pulled out a set of bolt cutters from under his sled's seat and snapped off the chain that the farmer had used to close the previously open gate we'd entered the field through.

There was a sand quarry quite a way out of town that had these great big curved surfaces formed when the sand was dug out, and we'd spend hours treating them like gigantic banked turns. We learned that you had to get it just right because if you climbed too steeply you'd slow down too much and possibly roll on the way down (boy, could those machines take a beating!), and if you went too shallow, you'd build up so much speed you'd fly off the lip of the banked curve (boy, could they ever take a beating!)

We found one country road that ran straight for a few miles with only a few country houses along it. We'd go tearing down it to see how fast we could go. We had no speedometers, so we measured out a set distance and used my stopwatch to time ourselves between two markers, using a quick bit of math to convert to actual speed. I'm happy to report that my technique was confirmed by police radar to be accurate. Luckily we really weren't speeding, just underage drivers without drivers' licences, and it resulted in nothing more than a warning.

Within a few years, as the fad wore off and the machines got old and broke down, the number of riders in our group dropped off. I can't even remember when Dad sold ours, or who he sold it to. I've never had the urge to ride today's beasts, even though they have more than 10 times the power and most every creature comfort imaginable. Sure they go fast, and ride the trails like they are on rails, but I doubt they can break trail through five feet of snow in the middle of forest like that old '72 Ski-Doo could do.

A Son's Duty

After collecting story ideas over a period of several weeks, I began actual writing on September 1, 2014. Maybe I had already decided in the back of my mind to do this story first, but it was that day, after a nice long swim, that I sat down to do it. It might not be slotted first in the book, but it is the most important one to me. It's not a funny story; just one that I really wanted to tell.

And so I shall...

My father, Steve Mackwood, passed away in December of 1993, after a long battle with cancer. His eventual death was therefore not sudden, not a surprise, and to a large extent a relief of sorts.

Prior to his death, during one of those rare moments when the morphine was not rendering him incoherent, he and I talked. I managed to tell him how much I loved him, and how I felt that he had been the perfect father. I told him that when he eventually passed away, I would stand up at his funeral and deliver a eulogy that fully expressed those feelings. He told me he wished he could be alive to hear it. We laughed at that.

After he died, things, as they do, became hectic. Mom was doing a great job with all the funeral-related preparations, but there was a lot to do in a very short period of time. One evening, she was on the phone to the parish priest who would be saying the mass for Dad, and I was there beside her. We had talked about the eulogy and she thought it would be a great idea. While she was talking I whispered to her, "Don't forget to tell the priest that I'll be delivering a eulogy." She did, and then she went silent.

Apparently, such a thing was not allowed either in his church, or in any church in the diocese, and he informed Mom that I could not deliver a eulogy. At that point, she cupped the phone and told me the news. My immediate response was, "Tell him we'll take our business elsewhere!"

Now while Mom rarely put up with "guff" from anyone, she also never ever questioned the Catholic Church, and certainly would never argue with a priest. So she said, "Yes Father, we understand."

Well I certainly did not, but I held it in check and the service went ahead without a eulogy. And my dislike of the Catholic Church grew.

Flash forward to 2010 and Mom is not at all well. She barely survived heart surgery (actually a post-surgery infection – the surgeon did amazing work) earlier that year, and she was transferred back to Pembroke and put under the care of her family doctor. For reasons unknown to us, and the nursing staff, he decided to take her off anti-coagulants which led, a few days later, to massive pulmonary embolisms and strokes. She was never the same, mentally and physically, and eventually passed away early in 2011.

But prior to that we went over her funeral arrangements in detail. We talked about me giving the eulogy. We both remembered many years prior, and what had happened with Dad. She wanted me to stand up in front of the church, "My Church" as she called it, and deliver it.

She felt very strongly about "her" church. When Mom and Dad bought their first (and only) house back in the '50s, there was no Catholic church in that part of town. They, and many other families, contributed a big percentage of their very limited income to make it happen. And they kept giving – and gave even more every time Father John would get up and tell the congregation to do so.

After her passing, and prior to the funeral, I called the parish priest. A few times in fact, one day as I was driving from Ottawa to Pembroke. He informed me that the Bishop forbade such eulogies by anyone but a priest, and while he did not agree with the Bishop he would never question his decision. I asked him to let me talk to him myself. He said he would not help me do so. I related the story of my Dad's passing, how I was denied back then, and how Mom and I had decided that I would not let that happen for her. He then told me that my Mom would never agree to such a thing. Now I was past being civil!

I informed him that whether he agreed or not, at some point in the service I would rise, walk to the altar, and deliver the eulogy to my Mom. He told me that he would then be forced to tell those assembled how wrong it was that I had just done so, and that it would forever shame the memory of my Mom. We hung up on each other.

I'm not sure who called whom, but about a half-hour later we spoke again and reached an agreement. He would stand up during the service and say I had planned to deliver a eulogy, but because it was against the Bishop's policy, he told me I could not. He would then explain that instead I would say some words about my Mom during the "social" in the church basement following the service. In return I would not storm the altar as threatened. We agreed. We had a deal.

At the very end of the service the priest thanked everyone for coming and invited everyone to attend the gathering in a church basement across town, as his was under renovation, during which time I would say some words about my Mom. He made no mention of the eulogy nor the ban. He basically reneged on his end of the deal. He never had the guts to look me in the eye as he did so, even though my glare could have set the main crucifix on fire.

Well, during the social I did rise to deliver my eulogy. The priest briefly introduced me and then scampered from the room as soon as I began to speak. I gave that eulogy with my youngest daughter, Allie, at my side. While it was "prepared" in advance, I had no script. I drew from the faces of those in the crowd the inspiration needed. I had a few points that I wanted to make but let my connection to Mom, and hers to the audience, direct what I was saying.

And the eulogy that was "banned by the Bishop" and chased the priest from the room? By chance, my oldest daughter Natasja, happened to record it all. I'd like to share it with you. Word for word, this is a loving son doing his duty in such times of grief.

"Thank you, Father.

I don't need a microphone, but I just want to check: can everyone at the back hear me?

Thank you.

Unfortunately, I've had quite a lot of time to prepare these remarks because, as many of you know, Mom was not well for quite some time.

We had a number of close calls where we put calls out to family and friends and said "now's the time, if you want to say goodbye, now would be the time to do it."

But Mom kept fighting. Over, and over, and over again. Throughout 2010 she made it through the entire year. She had a great Christmas. Many of us had a chance to see her, to talk to her, to know that she understood us at that time. And to say our goodbyes. Maybe not knowing that it was the last time we'd get to say goodbye, but for many of us that's what it turned out to be.

Finally her, her body which had been through so much... when I was thinking about perhaps what, if someone asked "what charity could we give to" I didn't have a list long enough, if I were just to look at the things Mom herself had been through. Heart and stroke. Cancer. Crohn's and colitis. You could name it but, through it all, she kept going, she kept going, she kept going.

Finally she couldn't go any more. She died very peacefully, and I know many of you in her last week were in to see her and I thank you very much for doing that; I know that she thanks you for doing that.

When I went in a few days before she passed away, Gen and I were up; it was a Sunday evening. And Mom had been medicated, but she was sort of talking. Not fully awake. She was sort of saying a few words, and Gen had gone out to get a little glass of water or something to wet her lips, and I leaned over to see if I could tell what Mom was saying, and I realized then what it was. She was saying her Hail Marys, saying her Our Fathers, over and over again. That's because she was such a strong person of faith and her faith was so important to her. But she knew. She knew it was time.

Many years ago, I attended the funeral for my father-in-law, Bert Milliken, and the oldest son, Scot, delivered a wonderful eulogy to his father. And that was one of the things that I was thinking about, in preparation for today, was Scot. I thought back to that time, and what a terrific job you did, and I draw inspiration from you.

I have my daughter beside me. We have a bit of a competition going. Who is going to cry first? I've won, but, a little story, as I continue for a moment talking about Mom, when we attended my father Stephen, when he passed away, some of us managed to be there, at his bedside when he took his last breath, and I managed to be there with my three children at the time – Allie being the youngest. She was my rock. She is now.

I'd also like to mention Uncle Nick Haramis. You know there's a natural order to things. Children bury the parents, older siblings are buried by younger siblings. That order's been out of whack for Uncle Nick. I really feel for you. But I'd also really much like to acknowledge you, and thank you for being here today, for being her honourary pallbearer.

Mom had a heart of gold. She was special to everyone. She gave so much of herself to the community. She was involved with people. But there's one thing that really, I think, really was her, and that was her as a nurse, as a caregiver throughout her life, her association with the hospital. When my brother Wayne and I were looking for a photo to choose to put with the notice, and to use throughout these last few days, we came across the one of her from her graduation as an RN. And that so much defined her, and who she was.

As I was going through her effects, I came across the booklet from her graduating ceremony, and there was a relatively small class; I think 9, 10, maybe 11 nurses graduated that year, and they had listed quite a number of awards throughout that ceremony. As I went through the awards, hoping to see if Mom had received any, it was hard to find some that Mom had not.

And that continued through her life, not with formal awards, but with formal, or informal recognition from all of the people who she touched, who she came across. The number of people that I met in the day and a half, and throughout my life who came and told me specifically that Mom was there when they were born, or Mom was there when their child was born. Or in my case she was there when my children were born. She was there to welcome people into the world, and she always there at events like this to say goodbye to people. She cared that much for them.

I told people of a story. I was horseback riding in the Rockies a number of years ago. And there was a guide with us. And he had no one else to talk to because the other 20 people riding horses were all Japanese and couldn't speak English – or French. And so he rode up beside me and we were chatting, and he said "So where are you from?" and I said Pembroke. And he says "Well I was born in Pembroke." Neat. I said "Are you Catholic or are you something else?" He said "I was Catholic." I said "Then you might have been born in the Pembroke General Hospital." He said "Yes I was." I said "Did your mother ever tell you what time of day you were born?" He said "It was the middle of the night." A thought occurred to me. "Did your mother ever tell you who your nurse was?" He said "Yeah. She had such a beautiful name. It was Amelia." "That's my Mom."

And that's just one example of the number of times that Mom has touched people.

I don't want to keep you from your sandwiches and coffee and treats but I would like to thank everyone. Friends. Relatives. Neighbours. Co-workers. Acquaintances. And her great-grandson [who had just let out a shout]. For being here and for sharing in this which, this really is a happy time now. Mom is at peace. She wanted this. It was her time. We're going to miss her. But we're happy for her.

Thank you for coming."

Risky Business

I'm pretty sure that the 1983 film *Risky Business* was the first time I'd ever laid eyes on anything so beautiful. The magnificent curves and oh so lovely derriere. An element of danger in the look. A seduction. I was hooked. I wanted it.

No I'm not talking about Rebecca De Mornay, or, should I have swung that way, Tom Cruise, but rather the Porsche 928 that falls into Lake Michigan.

Years later, as I was commuting home in my Toyota Sienna minivan, I had what Gen called my mid-life crisis. I decided to buy a Porsche, and not just any Porsche: a 1988 928 S4. Sporting a 5.0l V8 with double overhead cams, that year's version of the 928 was one of the fastest production cars made. I named mine "Dietrich," after the movie star, for its feminine graces, throaty voice, and German origins.

I bought Dietrich used for a fraction of what she originally sold for. She had sat in storage for a number of years and while her mileage was relatively low, unfortunately maintenance issues were a bigger problem than expected, probably because she had been left to sit for too long. I traded her in for an Audi after driving her for five years, the kicker being when she needed a new rad, and the part alone was going to be $2,800! But before I sold her, I had a lot of fun driving her.

Despite a couple of close driving calls (see *Honda Meet Datsun* and *Slow Motion Rollover*) I'm a pretty safe driver, and I stayed ticket and accident-free while with Dietrich. Mind you there was one time, while coming back from Montreal, that I could have earned a pretty hefty ticket.

I was on Highway 40 heading west and had just left the Island of Montreal when a Porsche 911 pulled up behind me, signalled and passed me on the left. I kept pace at just over 120 kph. At that speed you're not likely to get a ticket since it's pretty much what everyone drives. When we hit the split where you can either go left to Toronto or right to Ottawa, we both went right, and our speed increased to about 140 kph. That speed would definitely attract attention, and usually there are lots of QPP cruisers along that stretch of road.

It was a bright, sunny, dry day, and traffic was extremely light: maybe one vehicle every 500 metres or so. The 911 and I took turns taking the lead in the left lane. Not racing; just enjoying the company of another Porsche.

By the time we crossed the border into Ontario we were way above the limit but, while I know it's no excuse, it's still nothing for either of those cars. The other driver pulled up on my left and I looked over to see him pointing his index finger upwards; let's pick it up. We did. Dietrich's exhaust tone was now singing ever so sweetly. Traffic was still practically non-existent and we took turns leading in the left lane and flashing our high beams from far back whenever we were approaching anyone ahead.

I can only describe the feeling of Dietrich at speed as amazing. Her aerodynamic shape generated high downforces that pinned the car firmly to the road. Even though you never really notice any of the gentle sweeping turns on that highway, at higher speeds you do. And she felt like she was riding on rails through them.

At one point we passed two OPP cruisers parked on the connecting road between the two sides of the divided highway. There's usually a cruiser there and this time there were two. Either we were going too fast for them to notice, or they saw us and decided they'd never catch us, because after we rounded the next gentle turn to the right and headed down a long straight section they were nowhere in sight.

By the time we were approaching Ottawa's limits there were a few more cars on the road so we backed off and blended back in with traffic, eventually taking different exits. When I got home I was shocked at how little time it had taken to make the trip. So shocked that I vowed to myself to never again entertain such risky business, even when paired with such a fine piece of work as Dietrich.

Double-Barrel or Doberman?

While I grew up in a small city, it really played like a much smaller rural town. Although my Dad didn't, many of my friends' parents hunted. Shotguns and rifles could be found in most homes. Families had hunting camps and as kids we were always keen to see fresh sets of deer and moose antlers lashed to car roofs in the fall.

As soon as we were able, we took the hunters' safety course, and got our certificate. We'd started with BB and pellet guns, but many progressed to .22 rifles and shotguns (mostly .410-bore and 20-gauge.) It was not at all unusual to see a group of a dozen of us kids, mostly pre-teens, walking down the street, armed to the teeth, heading to "the bush" to hunt partridge. Nobody called the police, and when the police did happen to be driving by their reaction was to wave and wish us good hunting. Nowadays they'd call in a SWAT team or drone strikes!

All this to establish that I'm not some gun-fearing liberal commie.

But the "culture" that I grew up in was exclusively a hunting one. Guns were never for self- or home defence. Heck, most of the time our doors were left open and unlocked. So I never had any appreciation for America's gun culture. None at all. But I got a quick indoctrination in the '80s while on my first visit to an American friend's place.

I'd known him for a number of years. He was one of the funniest people I'd ever met: fast with the quip and always with a joke at the ready. Although he did not look the part, he was also a martial artist and had a side-business teaching people self-defence. On a trip to San Fran I took the Cal Train south to Menlo Park to stay at his large townhome for a weekend.

He gave me the usual friend-visiting-friend-for-the-first-time tour of his multi-level home. On first blush it looked like your typical bachelor pad: big master bedroom, guest bedroom, office, living and dining rooms, kitchen and multiple baths. That was on the face of it.

We started the tour on the top floor in the master bedroom. He opened his closet to reveal a collection of swords, knives, throwing "stars", batons, and other items that would have made a Ninja envious. I sort of expected that, given his martial artistry. But then he pointed out the two sawed-off double-barreled 12-gauge shotguns amongst the collection. "Not for bird hunting," he said. And the under-the-mattress 9mm pistol, clip ready to be pushed in. "I've told the cleaning lady about this one so that when she changes the sheets..."

The guest room, where I was to sleep, seemed even more secure, what with Uzi and MAC-10 fully automatic submachine guns and spare clips at the ready. Just in case one didn't want to wake the neighbours, both were equipped with silencers that were longer than they were. Apparently the MAC-10 would make a neat metallic clinking sound when fired with silencer on. I wondered if you could get a silencer for a sawed-off shotgun?

And so it went, from room after room. Handguns were hidden everywhere, never more than a few steps away. I guess you never knew who might be stupid enough to break in. Luckily nobody did and I never had to empty a clip or two during my stay.

A number of years later, my friend got married and he and his wife moved to San Jose. I guess a condition of the marriage was that the guns had to go. At least that's how it seemed when I visited. That's not to say that home defence was not still de rigueur; it's just that all the guns had been traded in for two German Shepherds, a female and a male, and a male Doberman.

Now Shepherds I knew. I love the breed. Dobermans were new to me; new with the exception of having seen *The Doberman Gang* movie. Based on the film alone, I had to admit being a bit afraid of the breed. The Shepherds were big, as Shepherds go, but this Doberman was huge, as big as a Great Dane. All three dogs were exceptionally well-trained, paradoxically both as protector/attack dogs and as companion dogs. They were absolutely amazing animals.

The male Shepherd took to me immediately. He was a wonderful suck and loved to be petted and have his ears and tummy rubbed. The female a little less so. And the Doberman? Skittish, apprehensive, and seemingly always concerned. As I was, when my friend and his wife said they needed to pop out for a while and hoped I could mind the house while they were gone. I'd noticed that my friend's home entertainment system needed to be set up differently and properly calibrated, so I said fine, I'd pass the time doing so. The dogs were ordered to a separate room and after a while it looked like they had all stretched out to take a nap.

To put things straight, I needed to crawl behind my friend's great big cabinet that held his TV, receiver, and other gear. I was back there, pretzel-like, flashlight in mouth, hands stripping the ends of some speaker wire, when I heard a growling sound. I looked down and could just make out the Doberman's huge snout, inches from my feet and ankles that were protruding from the back of the cabinet. My guess was that he had fallen asleep, woke up, and forgot he had "company." I was an intruder and he was trained to deal with such low-lifes.

Now I did not know what that training entailed. Was I to be

cornered and held until the masters arrived, or was I to become dog food? I called his name. More growling. Other soothing words only brought more and louder growling. I briefly wondered if my friend might have saved one sawed-off shotgun and hidden it behind the cabinet. I stayed put for an hour or so, moving as little as possible so as to not cause more growling, even though I knew he was lying but inches from my feet, until the couple arrived home. The Doberman left me to greet them. I had finished the wiring and was crawling out when they all came into the room. The Doberman never growled at me again that weekend and we each became much more accustomed to the other.

As we were playing fetch in the dogs' training yard (formerly a fenced-in tennis court), and as I watched him run after the ball, a magnificent animal hurdling obstacles in his path, a thought crossed my mind: I much preferred Dobermans to sawed-off double-barreled shotguns.

Swimming –
The Hot and the Cold of It

I'd like to tell you about two very memorable, and different, places where I have gone swimming.

To date, I have only been to Copenhagen once. It's a gorgeous city with some of the tallest, blondest, and most beautiful people you will ever see.

I'm not sure why, but part way through the week when I visited there, I had not yet managed to get in a swim. Maybe it was because I was having a heck of a time finding a pool. From a Google search, there seemed to be one along the river, so I packed a swim bag and set out to find it. The closest subway stop was quite a distance from the expected location and by the time I found it I'd worked up a bit of a sweat.

I'd not seen anything like it before. It appeared to be a very big barge-like structure moored to the side of the river / big canal. It had a wide expanse of decked areas, a diving pool, a kids' pool, and a swimming pool. The diving and swimming pools were actually openings in the barge to the river. Same water.

There was no price of admission: free to all. I approached a lifeguard and asked where the change rooms were. That evoked a very puzzled look. After some thought, he pointed to a public toilet structure some distance away in the park beside the barge. So I went up and changed, thinking that this was a strange arrangement. When I returned to the pool I noticed that, besides myself, there was only me, a few lifeguards, and two old guys in sight – the old guys doing some slow heads-up breaststroke in the pool.

The water level in the pool was some distance below the deck level; so much so that I could not perform my customary dipping of a toe in the water to check out the temperature. I pulled on my goggles and jumped in. Cold! Really really cold! That's what I thought to myself as my lungs clamped tight and my skin registered the pain of what felt like a billion ice daggers. I managed a few pitiful strokes before I concluded that my lungs were never going to allow me to take a breath. I somehow got myself to a nearby ladder and onto the deck where I urged my body to absorb as much of the sun's heat as possible, as fast as it could.

Laying out a towel, I found a sheltered spot on the warm deck and soon recovered from the shock. That's when I learned why there were no change rooms at the facility. Two absolutely stunning stacked Scandinavian Amazons took up a spot on the deck near me, stripped naked, and pulled on bathing suits. One of the old guys finally got out of the water and, like the women before him, stripped naked, towelled himself off, got dressed and left. After an hour or so, I decided I'd had enough sunbathing and, instead of heading back into the park to change in the toilets, decided to do as the locals do. However, I was a bit more modest about it and decided to stand at the barge's railing facing the water, before dropping suit. Which happened to be at the very instant a tour boat passed by, loaded with Asian tourists, not 25 metres away. I smiled for the cameras.

On the other side of the world from chilly Copenhagen is hot and humid Singapore. The last time I was there, the spectacular Marina Bay Sands hotel had recently opened. It's the one with the huge boat-shaped structure perched high atop three towers. And incorporated into that structure is the most impressive infinity pool ever. Having seen pictures of it before I knew I had to swim there, like a salmon needs to swim upstream to spawn; however I was not a guest, and likely will never be, given the cost.

So I did some research and found out there were regular tours offered, where one could ride the elevator with the group, to the top, to enjoy the view, but not the pool which was for hotel guests only. I decided to "wing it" and see what I might be able to pull off. Now I must confess the task was made easier by the fact I had met someone

earlier in the week who had stayed there for one night, and gave me his now-expired key card. It would never open anything, but it would prove to be a valuable prop.

All of the hotel elevators require key card access. So what I did was to show up at the hotel already dressed for the pool: shorts over bathing suit, sleeveless shirt, and sandals. Sunglasses completed the look. I hopped on an elevator with a load of tourists and rode it with the guide to the top. As everyone exited, they passed by a security guard and then a locked entrance to the pool deck. I separated myself from the pack of tourists, waved my expired key at the guard, and he buzzed me through the gate. If you look like you belong, you belong!

The pool was amazing. The sights from the top were breathtaking. I figured that since I was already there, I might as well get in a full work-out, so I swam laps for well over an hour. Unlike Copenhagen, the water was warm. Also unlike Copenhagen, the guests did not change poolside. It left me wondering what the reaction would have been, had the two Scandinavian Amazons been there on vacation, oblivious to local custom.

Corporal Punishment

For reasons unknown, my English-speaking-only parents decided to enrol me in a French-only school. I like to believe they were truly enlightened thinkers who saw the value in learning Canada's other official language. It was a decision to which I can trace a large part of how my working career played out. The ability to speak French got me my first significant summer job, which led to my first post-graduation job, which led to everything else.

Then again, maybe they just wanted to stir things up a bit.

I ended up spending nine years (kindergarten and grades one to eight) at the Catholic Ecole St. Jeanne D'Arc in Pembroke. I was taught by one great teacher (unfortunately for one year only), many fair to middling ones, and some truly poor ones. It appeared as if the only real qualifications necessary were that the teacher be a francophone and have completed some level of high school. I was not the best-behaved student by a long shot, and on many occasions heard teachers mutter the words "maudit Anglophone" (darn English speaker) when referring to me.

The saving grace was that, despite what was surely an inferior learning environment, it was populated by some absolutely terrific students. Yes, many came from dirt-poor families. Yes, many had, like me, behavioural issues. But on the whole, this was one great group of kids, many of whom became very close friends.

The small school had very little in the way of sports facilities. But we ran and played at recesses and lunch like crazy. Give us a ball of any kind and we'd make a game out of it. Softball. Soccer. Broomball. Football. We played them all with wild abandon. We were a rough-and-tumble lot, and torn clothes and cuts and bruises were our badges of honour. It was no accident that my small cohort of grade 8 graduates would go on to disproportionately populate the sports teams of the much larger high schools we went to. Many would also excel academically.

Those years in that school were also the years when it was open season on "bad" behaviour. Corporal punishment was allowed. And at Ecole St. Jeanne D'Arc it was taken to new levels. It was only later on in life that I connected the dots and recognized the true significance of attending a school named after a Catholic who was burned alive at the stake.

Allow me to digress with an observation or two about the differences between French and English Canadians. When an Anglophone curses, it almost always involves some reference to a sexual act. "F***-You" and "MotherF***er" being two examples. When the Canadian francophone curses it can still be sexual, but they take it to an even "higher" level by referencing the Catholic Church, and more specifically its sacraments and symbols. "Hostie, calisse, calvaire, tabarnack," and "sacrifice" are but a few examples.

So when it came to corporal punishment, at least back then in that Canadian French Catholic school, it should come as no surprise that many of the "techniques" related back to Catholicism and Christianity. Sure there was the ubiquitous "strap". I recall having had it first administered it to me by a sado-masochistic principal with deep-rooted sexual issues. He administered it with orgasmic relish. But that was a stochastic thing; the pain would pass reasonably quickly.

And, somewhat like the school's namesake who presumably did a slow roast at the stake, we were usually deemed to be in need of a more prolonged bout of suffering, at the hands of our punishers. So rather than being ordered to, for example, bear the shame of having to "sit" in a corner, we would have to kneel in the corner – an obvious reference to religious submission – on the hard floor. Those whose knees could take it and needed some extra pain would be forced to kneel on their thumbs or palms – shades of crucifixion! Or on their knees with arms extended in the sign of a cross, and if the arms wavered, a wooden pointer across the back served as a reminder to keep them up. After an hour or two like that, I think we would have welcomed a good waterboarding instead!

Of course we all did something to "deserve" some form of punishment, but while nowadays it would mean the loss of some privileges, back then it was corporal punishment at its worst. And there wasn't really anything us kids could do about it. Well, I do remember one very small act of rebellion on my part.

In grade 7 or 8, I'd probably done something wrong during one class because as we were leaving the classroom for recess one day, our male teacher grabbed me by my shirt and attempted to lift me off my feet. I was a "husky" kid back then, and pretty strong for my age. That teacher was short and I probably outweighed him. So I in turn grabbed him by the front of his thick tweed coat, lifted him up, and managed to hook the back of his coat collar to a coat hook on the back wall. And there he hung, until a passing teacher saw him and helped him down.

This earned me a suspension, and probably a near-expulsion, from school. I don't think I ever again resorted to physicality to show defiance to authority. And while I would, on a few occasions, administer a "spanking" to my kids in later years, memories of my days in grade school were always in mind when I did, and served to limit its application.

Broken Noses

Which came first: the chicken or the egg? How about the bigger-than-usual nose or the broken nose? An apt question given the size of my nose and the number of times it's been broken.

At my parents' 25th wedding anniversary party, a big bash held in their hometown of Renfrew, Ontario, I was accompanied by my then-fiancée, Gen. At one point, I was asked to come to the mic and say a few words about Mom and Dad. But I also took the opportunity to bring Gen closer to the family, with words that went something like this.

"Gen, I know you've had a big burning question on your mind ever since we met. Well, this evening, as you sit amongst many of my family members, I am prepared to answer that question. I know you want to know how in the world I ever ended up with a nose this big [pointing to my schnoz]. Here's your answer [now opening my arms wide and looking around the hall.]" My aunts, uncles, and cousins couldn't help but get a good self-deprecating laugh out of that.

Okay, so maybe genetics has had a hand in my nose. But I think I've helped it along the way.

In the summer just before I was to start high school, my friends and I were out gallivanting through "the bush," a good-sized forest not more than a ten-minute walk from our neighbourhood. We'd brought our guns along and had spent some time plinking tin cans and the odd crow. We stuck mostly to the trail that meandered through a good part of the acreage, but we'd occasionally beaver our way through the brush. You had to do that to get to Fort Cow Poop, which was a structure built many years before by the now-older boys of the neighbourhood. It had been added to, and demolished, and rebuilt many times using whatever old logs (and freshly-felled trees) that could be found. That day it consisted of a tree fort structure at least twelve feet off the ground, and you climbed up to it on pieces of wood nailed to the tree's trunk.

After we'd had our fill of plinking from that perch, we unloaded our guns and headed down to the ground. I was down below, directly underneath the fort, when Phil yelled "catch" just after dropping his 410 shotgun my way. I looked up just in time to catch it with the bridge of my nose. That smarts!

In grade 9 gym class, we were wrestling when some big bruiser decided to demonstrate a take-down on me, planting my face nose-first into the mat. It was nicely broken and bleeding profusely when "Daddy" Wags, a gym teacher and former football player back when their helmets had no faceguards, reset it on the spot. The pain diminished immediately, and I learned an important lesson: when broken, grab nose immediately and reset, which I've done every time since.

Basketball in the face: reset. Elbow in face while playing basketball: reset. Child's head butt to nose: reset. Too many times to remember (except for the basketball to the face during the period when I was writing this book, which resulted in a concussion on top of the broken nose!). Oh, the nose will show a purple bruise along the now well-established break line for a week or two, the eyes will blacken a bit, and the nose itself will swell up and settle back down to a size just slightly bigger than before the break. But I now see my honker as a sign of experience, if not accrued wisdom. At least that's what I tell myself whenever I get a glance at it in a mirror.

Stroke One – Having a Sharon Stone

In October of 1999, just past the age of 40, I suffered my first stroke.

I knew something was wrong as soon as it hit. I was up on a step-ladder on a bright beautiful fall day, cleaning dead leaves out of my eavestrough above the front door, when I was hit with a blinding headache. I managed to get down off the ladder, open the door, and croak "Gen" – who managed to get to me in time to soften the descent to the ceramic tiles in the front hall.

I knew something was really wrong when she started asking me questions and all I could do was make pathetic gurgling sounds.

Sue, an ER nurse from across the street, must have seen what was happening, because she was hovering over me with Gen. "Could be a stroke," and "get him to hospital," were among the words I remember the two nurses saying to each other.

So I was buckled into the front seat of the car and Gen sped to the Ottawa General. By then I was feeling extremely weak and disoriented, but had found the ability to mumble actual words – some of which might have been coherent.

Gen pulled up to the emergency entrance, grabbed a wheelchair and rolled me inside and up to the triage nurse's desk. After a quick looking-over, and despite my symptoms, I was wheeled off to one side of a crowded room to await my turn at the registration desk. I think

Gen went and parked the car at that point. By the time she came back a few minutes later, I was feeling worse. I'm not talking "gee, I'm feeling kinda crummy" worse; I could honestly feel myself about to shut down completely, stop breathing, and die. I managed to lift my head, and when Gen bent down to me, whisper the words "going sour" in her ear.

Somehow I knew that phrase would convey all that was needed to a sharp cookie like Gen, because at this point the world began to move ever-so-fast, as she grabbed the handles of the wheelchair and headed into the heart of the ER unit. As the triage nurse scrambled to keep up, I recall Gen yelling "Where's an open room and get a team here stat!"

I was put on a table and surrounded by all manner of professionals. I was examined, poked, prodded, had IV lines started and blood drawn, monitors attached, and in what seemed like the blink of an eye was having a CT scan of my head done. Again in what seemed like seconds I was back on the table and the lead doctor was breaking the news to Gen and I. I had suffered a form of stroke: a subarachnoid hemorrhage (SAH).

A SAH is where a blood vessel blows and spills into a part of the centre of your brain. Apparently about half of all cases are fatal, and if you happen to survive you are usually left with any number of "deficits." But I got off very lucky. It turned out that mine was most likely a blown vein, rather than an artery, and it sealed itself off quickly. I spent a day or two in ICU, and another couple of days in hospital recovering. There were new (and expensive) drugs that had just recently been developed to greatly reduce the likelihood of the initial bleed leading to ischemic strokes. The massive headache I suffered for the first few days eventually faded away (with the help of morphine!) and it took several weeks of healing before I was back to my old self.

Almost exactly two years to the day after I had mine, Sharon Stone, the actress, had a SAH of her own. Having heard about it, I wrote her a letter of encouragement based on my own experience. I never did hear back from her. A North Carolina medical association has come up with the phrase "Sharon Stone Syndrome" to describe what they believe happened to her.

And that's why I've sometimes been heard to say I've had a

Sharon Stone, although because mine came first, I hope she's been telling people she's had a Jeff Mackwood.

The 21-Year-Old Springbank

I love single malt scotch. I used to keep a half-dozen bottles or so under my desk at work, to be sipped from only after quitting time on Friday afternoons, of course. I enjoy it so much that I get nervous if I have less than 40 bottles in my home cabinet at any given time. That's not to say I drink a lot of it; rather I savour it occasionally, and probably drink less than half a bottle a year. That's why I can make a really great bottle of single malt last a very long time.

Like the 21-year-old Springbank that I first acquired a long time ago. I was at a private business reception when one of the hosts, herself a big fan of single malts, took me aside and poured me a wee dram of the stuff from a bottle she kept out of sight – ostensibly to avoid the horror of some unknowing boob filling a tumbler and topping it off with Coke. I was immediately taken in by its complex taste. So much so that I spent the next few weeks eventually tracking down a bottle for myself. It wasn't cheap, but I managed to make it last quite a few years (in rotation with other single malts in my collection.)

It's a good thing I did, because a 21-year-old Springbank became, during that period, a bit of a holy grail. For whatever reason, it was nearly impossible to find a bottle, and the distillery was not issuing new releases of the stuff. Perhaps it was the glowing reviews that had pointed people in its direction, like this one I just retrieved from masterofmalt.com: "It's a spectacular dram that offers unbelievable complexity."

I was in Amsterdam on business just after my bottle was finally finished. I happened across a liquor store with a massive single malt selection in its lower level. I was slowly perusing the numerous single-malt-laden shelves when I caught sight of the edge of a label on a bottle tucked behind others not like it. Could it be? It was! A dust-covered bottle that had apparently sat where it wasn't supposed to for years. I plucked it off the shelf and held tight to "my Precious."

The manager looked a little surprised when I presented the bottle at the cash. He was a single malt lover himself and did not know they had that one bottle of 21-year-old Springbank in stock. I was all too happy to pay the rather steep price for it. Then the manager hit me with an even bigger surprise: that evening, in their boardroom, 12 lucky people would be joining him and a Springbank representative in a tasting of six of their single malts, the youngest being the 21-year-old! And it turned out they had one seat left at the table, for some very reasonable price.

This brought a tear to my eye. Not a tear of joy but one of deep sadness. You see, I had made arrangements for dinner with a client and there was no way I could cancel, or be at two places at once. (Had there been two seats available, we would have been doing a liquid dinner!) So I had to decline. But at least I now had a bottle of the 21-year-old.

When I arrived home, it was placed in the featured spot in my cabinet. All was right with the world. Then Gen decided to paint a bunch of rooms. So the cabinet's contents (dozens and dozens of bottles) were moved downstairs to safety while furniture was shuffled this way and that and, over a period of a couple of weeks, I painted all of those rooms. Painting completed, I hauled the bottles back up and carefully placed them back where they belonged, except that the 21-year-old Springbank was nowhere to be seen. I looked high and low for weeks, but it was never found. Its disappearance became one of those great mysteries in life.

I of course asked (and then questioned, and then grilled) each and every family member about its possible whereabouts, to no avail. By now it was impossible to find any 21-year-old Springbank anywhere. Gen noticed that the liquor stores were, by then, selling much younger bottles of Springbank and brought one home. But while a good single malt, it was not the 21-year-old. I eventually made my way through the entire grieving process and got on with life.

Then, years later, my son Nick handed me an envelope and said happy birthday, Dad – even though it was still a week before the date. The envelope had been opened, but inside was a letter from Canada Post telling me they had confiscated a bottle of 30-year-old Springbank that had been illegally destined for me, by mail, from the US. I was confused. Nick explained he had gone online and paid $500 US for it

113

as a special gift to me; it was something he had wanted to do for years. It didn't take a genius to figure out what the genesis for this generosity was. It turns out that, years previous, he and his best friend at the time had grabbed a bottle from the basement during the painting period. Not knowing better, and luck being what it is, of all of the bottles to make off with, it had been the 21-year-old Springbank. He was now trying to make amends.

I'm sure that when the idea came to him, and he found and ordered the bottle from some shop somewhere south of the 49th, he never planned for its rescue to become a month-long all-consuming odyssey on my part, but it did.

You see that letter from Canada Post did not only say that the bottle had been intercepted, it also clearly stated that as punishment for having so badly violated postal law, the bottle and contents were to be disposed of on the last day of July. There was no recourse mentioned, just the cold hard fact that it was a goner.

So I called them. I got verbally what I'd seen in writing. I could not do anything to save the bottle. More calls. Could I have it shipped to me by bonded courier? Yes, but the bottle was at a secure Canada Post facility that was not accessible by such couriers, and Canada Post offered no such service itself. They could only mail items from that facility and it was illegal to mail it to me. Catch 22! Could I travel to said facility, pay a fine, and retrieve the bottle myself? Nope. The secure facility was not accessible to the public. This went on for days, and weeks, the bottle stuck on death row, until finally the execution date came.

So I made what I considered the final appeal. I asked yet another Canada Post rep if there was any hope and she said not. Then, in complete frustration, I said I wanted the corpse back after the execution. Huh? I asked if it was illegal to mail an empty bottle. Pause on the other end. No, but why did I ask? Because, I said, I knew that someone in that facility was just going to take that valuable bottle of single malt home with them and claim that it was destroyed, and I at least wanted the bottle back. I was told to hold.

A long time later, I was transferred to someone else. I repeated my entire month of woe to her, and my last-ditch request to at least have the empty bottle mailed to me. She then asked why I did not simply have the full bottle mailed to me. I told her I was told, numerous times, that this was not possible. Well, she said, only if it's mailed to Canada, the US, or one South American country (Brazil, I think). Everywhere else was perfectly legit. Nobody had ever mentioned that option.

I asked her if she could please hold and then I made a panicky call to a Canadian friend in the UK and asked for her home address. I would explain why later. I got back on the line with Canada Post and arrangements were made to ship the bottle to my friend. It wasn't as easy as that, a temporary stay of execution was granted, and we eventually found a way for me to pay the required fine, fees, and postage to see the bottle on its way to the UK.

I had chosen this particular friend, of all the possible destinations, mostly out of panic, but also because I was pretty sure she would be traveling back to Montreal for Christmas that year. She was, and agreed to bring the bottle with her. She did, and we met at a nice restaurant over dinner (on me) where she presented the bottle, unopened. (A tough thing for her to do, as she's a fan of single malts as well.)

That bottle has since assumed its rightful place front and centre in my cabinet. I can happily report that the 30-year-old is an amazing single malt, obviously related to its younger sibling. It has been consumed sparingly over the subsequent years until there is now but one stiff drink left. I am saving it until some extremely special occasion warrants its consumption. Perhaps the first publication of this book?

Low-Hanging Exit Sign

In the early '80s, I was fairly active politically, at least at a local / riding level. My uncle was well-connected within the Liberal Party of Canada and the local riding association, and when I expressed an interest in getting involved he was very happy to help. At a riding association meeting soon thereafter I was chosen, with his assistance, to be one of the riding's representatives at the upcoming leadership race. My pledge was to choose the person who I thought would make the best Prime Minister for Canada; in other words, I was going down as an uncommitted delegate.

I was really looking forward to the experience, but never suspected the most memorable moment of the convention would be my encounter with an exit sign.

At the convention, I went to as many sessions as possible, asked plenty of questions (including many that were important to our riding) of the candidates, and eventually decided who I would support on the first, and then the second ballot. My chosen candidate lost.

That evening there was a big celebratory party, which Gen attended with me. The beer was flowing and a good time was had by all (except maybe the losing candidates.) As things were winding down, Gen and I left to catch a cab back to her parents' place, where we were staying. But we somehow got lost in the side and back corridors of the Ottawa Convention Centre. We eventually came to a set of emergency exit doors up a short flight of stairs and down a corridor. I must have missed the warning sign saying an alarm would sound if the doors were opened, because I did, and it did. Really loudly. I did what any responsible inebriated person would do in that situation: I yelled "run" and took off at sprint speed back down the corridor, Gen struggling to keep up. (I don't have to run fast, just faster than you. Old joke.)

Well, she did catch me in short order, but not in any way due to her fleetness of foot. Rather it was because I decided to launch myself off the top of the short flight of stairs in the hopes of simply dropping to the level below still at full speed. Would not have been a problem had it not been for the exit sign hanging from the ceiling right over said stairs. Caught the leading edge right across the top of my head and sheared it off; the sign from the ceiling, not my head from my body – although the immediate pain and shock had me thinking so. Amazingly, my feet continued to spin in mid-air; I was a pretty good long-jumper in my day and I held the form beautifully. Only it was a concrete floor at the bottom of the stairs that I fell into, not a pit of sand.

When I came to...

Gen had caught up and could not stop herself from laughing. (Never aim for sympathy from a nurse, especially if you marry one, and certainly not when you've just creased your skull and blood is running down your face.) I don't know if it was the shock, her laughing, or the booze, but I was plenty peeved. So much so that the adrenalin got me back into running mode and out of the building. I lost Gen but I somehow managed to get back to her parents' place. Gen bit her tongue the next day, and for several after that. But it still cracks her up to think back to when she saw me give that exit sign one heck of a beating with my head.

And while that memory is also etched permanently in my head (luckily the crease is not – see *Maxi-Me*) strangely enough, I have no recollection of the name of the person I voted for on those two ballots.

Incoming!

I've been hit in the head quite a few times in my life (explains a lot!) but never as hard by another human being as the time I'm about to tell you about.

As a university student, I spent one summer working as a labourer at CFB Petawawa. My initial assignment was with the lawn crew but two weeks of walking behind oil-burning smoke-belching old lawnmowers was making me sick, so I asked to be moved to another group. I then spent most of the rest of the summer with the masons. Mixing "mud," hauling bricks, building and taking down scaffolding. It was good hard work and I actually learned a fair amount about bricklaying.

Then one day I twisted my back when a full wheelbarrow of mud almost tipped over on me, and instead of letting it go I yanked hard to keep it upright. I had to take the next day (a Friday) off and when I returned the following Monday I found my spot with the crew of masons had already been re-assigned to someone else and I was now in a small pool of labourers to be assigned daily to carpenters, electricians, etc.

So I loaded sheets of plywood onto trucks, carried a ladder around, watched paint dry, that sort of thing. One day I got assigned to an electrician. We called up a truck, loaded in his ladder and some tools, and headed out to the edge of one section of the base where a contingent of SAS from the UK was training with their Canadian counterparts.

It seemed that a few light bulbs were out and some outlets didn't work in their temporary mess hall. There was nobody around to greet us but the Sergeant Major. He was a huge man, easily 6'7" tall. Massive barrel-shaped chest. Flaming red hair with a matching handlebar mustache. A mass of humanity, with a huge smile from ear-to-ear. He reminded me a lot of Marvel Comics' "Dum Dum" Dugan, a member of Nick Fury's team. He pointed out the problems and an hour or so later the electrician had everything working just fine. As a reward, the Sergeant Major asked if we'd like a beer. But of course!

So he positions himself behind a makeshift bar at one end of the mess hall, with us on the other side. He announces that the bar is now open, and looks at me. There's a pause of sorts. He then repeats again that the bar is open. Again the pause. Then the lights go out. Mine, not the ones we've just repaired. He has caught me with a massive blow to the head with a fist the size of a pumpkin. Barely saw it coming and certainly not fast enough to duck. When I come to... I'm many yards away from the bar, face down on the floor. The Sergeant Major helps me to my feet and when my shaky legs are good enough to keep me upright, admonishes me: "you'll remove your hat when you're in my bar."

You see the mess hall that we'd been working in was really just one step up from a big tent. It looked nothing like a bar. The structure at one end I'd been standing at before the howitzer hit me looked nothing like a bar. But when the Sergeant Major said "the bar is open" it became a bar. And at that point I was expected to remove my yellow hard hat, which I failed to do. Apparently the Sergeant Major was just being helpful when he removed it for me, along with (almost) my head, albeit in a very unconventional manner.

So helmet off (it was way off in a corner somewhere) I again stood before the bar where, with a huge welcoming smile on his face, the Sergeant Major asked, "now what will ye have?"

The Kilts

Some time ago, in a Paris café, a plot was hatched. Alcohol was involved. The plotters were my work colleague Ibrahim, a black Muslim of Ethiopian origin, Brent, a white American friend and frequent "wingman," from the outskirts of Atlanta, Georgia, and myself. A blood oath was taken (actually I think someone spilled a glass of red wine). One year from that day, at a big reception in Glasgow, Scotland, the three of us would show up in formal Scottish dress.

One thing all three of us shared was absolutely no current connection to Scotland, nor, as far as we could tell for two of us, Scottish ancestry. Certainly not in Ibrahim's case. Even though my family name may mislead you in that direction, it's actually a fabricated name from the 1800s and is pure Polish in the original. Brent's surname is a common Scottish one, but you likely have to go back many generations to find a direct link to the old country. We also shared a common love of entertaining those in our company. Actually Ibrahim, as you'll see, is a quiet guy who usually does not want to draw attention to himself, but as I said, alcohol was involved, the great un-inhibitor!

As the year went by, we would remind each other of the commitment. I started doing some research into the various tartans. There were none for "Clan Mackwood" nor for "Clan Ibrahim" – although we suggested that a traditional "black" tartan would look fantastic on him. I contacted some clothing rental shops in Glasgow for some suggestions. Apparently there were a few that are unassigned to a particular clan, and which can be worn by anyone. (Actually, I was told you could wear any tartan you'd like and nobody would take offence.)

As the date approached, Brent went silent. But I knew he was still "in" and just looking to surprise everyone. Ibrahim was pretty much out; the booze apparently wore off at some point. However, he remained very supportive of Brent and me. I now had a shop all picked out. And on my first day in Glasgow I paid them a visit.

They had for rent all the items of clothing and paraphernalia needed for a formal event. Everything from the kilt itself, to the shirt (the one item you get to keep), the tie, the waistcoat, the sporran (man purse), the sgian dugh (small knife/dagger), to shoes and socks. I may have forgotten an item or two, but tightie-whities are not mentioned on their list.

I made arrangements to pick it all up in the morning of the day of the reception and when I did the first thing that struck me was that the kilt was darn heavy. They took me through a dress rehearsal and it took some time to get it just right. But the end result was impressive, so much so that I was tempted to wear it for the rest of the day. But that would spoil the surprise.

So later that day and back at my hotel I struggled a bit to get it all back on just right. There were printed instructions, but there's nothing like having a salesperson to help you out. Ibrahim and I were planning to meet in the lobby of the hotel, along with two female co-workers. I went down early and asked the youngish male desk staff if anything about my dress looks out of order. They said it looks fine, but they'd never worn anything like it themselves. Ibrahim arrived in the lobby, in business suit and tie, at the same time as the ladies. We hopped into a cab.

Now wearing a kilt takes a bit of thinking and effort when one is in mixed company. Women are used to the challenges of dresses and skirts. I've never worn a kilt, and certainly not one in the "traditional" manner. So I'm taking care to not offend anyone. That part goes ok until we arrive at the reception, which is being held in a big museum. The cab pulls up to the curb and I decide that, while the others can get out curbside, I'll hop out on the side facing away from the museum, and the crowd at the front entrance. It's while I am in full "splits" position, one leg fully out of the cab and the other still in, that I notice the shocked expression on the face of the young lady standing on the other side of the entrance road taking pictures of the museum and arriving guests. I stand fully erect (meaning I'm now out of the cab), look back at the museum, and say, "beautiful sight, isn't it?" She nods her head but I'm not sure she's convinced.

Inside the museum, the reception was in full swing with easily a thousand guests milling about. Across the main hall it was easy to spot Brent, sporting a very natty green(ish) tartan. It was also easy to pick him out of the crowd because, with the exception of the two of us, nobody else, not even the locals, was similarly dressed. Not a third kilt to be seen anywhere. Which made the event all that more fun.

You see we became an attraction. Everyone wanted their pictures taken with us. In front of the museum displays, on the main stairway, with their group, with their spouse, you name it. Most folks thought we were actors / locals hired to give the event a certain authenticity. I even tried to fake the accent, but ended up sounding more like Mike Myers' Fat Bastard than say, Sean Connery.

At one point there was a huge group of Chinese student delegates who all wanted their pictures taken with us. Individually. After we'd accommodated them all, I noticed that amongst their group were two female students who had not come forth, who had been instead assigned the task of taking photos of their male colleagues with us. Perhaps they were shy, but Brent and I soon coaxed them out the pack and I purposely had the guys take lots of pictures of them with us. The girls loved it.

Of course, several women asked if I was wearing anything under my kilt. My standard reply was that it was a time-honoured tradition to not say. (This from a first-time kilt-wearer!) Brent, however, was not so discreet. Maybe it's an Atlanta thing, but he was all too happy to lift kilt to reveal ... diaper-like undies with "Obama's Baby" lettered on them.

It was a hoot. So much so that I was very close to having a kilt made for myself, and purchasing the rest of the outfit to go with it. Perhaps if I'm ever over that way again...

The Thinkers

I have spent a lot of time at receptions during my career. Most of them were interesting and valuable from a business perspective. Still others, depending on their location, were a lot of fun personally. Receptions at museums, after-hours and closed to the public, where attendees could stroll through the galleries, were always a highlight.

Usually the museums relaxed their usual rules about taking pictures (if they had such restrictions) and in many cases they allowed you to get closer to the exhibits. And, of course, unlike during public hours, guests could wander about with drink in hand.

The lure of one such Paris reception was the Rodin Museum. The museum occupies a mansion built from 1727 to 1732. It features over seven acres of grounds with some very impressive gardens. In one of them, very close to the museum entrance and just around the side, one finds a casting of Rodin's the *Thinker*.

It was raining the evening of the reception, so not much was happening outdoors. In attendance with me were my buddy Brent from Atlanta, and my colleague Michele from Montreal. During a break in the drizzle, we wandered out to see the *Thinker*. I know it was a very uncouth move, but we'd been well-plied with champagne by this point, so it seemed like a very natural thing for Brent and me to climb up the plinth and pose with the large bronze statue while Rebecca, Brent's partner, snapped a few photos. I think Michele was a little put out that she couldn't join us, heels and evening dress being unsuitable for climbing.

But she wasn't put out for long because inside the museum was a much smaller casting of the *Thinker*, *le petit penseur*, and Michele and I posed with it for several really neat pictures, mimicking the statue's thoughtful bearing. We were able to snuggle right up to it, which caught the attention of one of the museum staff members. When we were all done, she approached and politely informed us that it was not possible for us to get so close to, and to touch the exhibit, especially not that one. In all her time with the museum, she apparently had never seen anyone photographed with it in the way we were. We politely accepted her admonishment; she was just doing her job.

However, when we were leaving the museum as the reception was winding down, she again approached us, explained that she was a part-time art student, and discreetly asked if we could email her copies of the photos, which she would use as part of her studies. It took no thought on my part to do so. I never did touch base with her to see what use she made of them, but I hope that she received a good grade for whatever assignment they formed part of.

The 155-Pound Subwoofer

I'm a bit of a home theatre nut (ok, more than a bit), and after one trip to the Batcave (see *Maxi-Me*) things got a little bit nuttier. "Batman" (the owner of the house in which sits the Batcave – a custom-built home theatre) had yet again swapped out some gear, and this time it was the addition of a very big subwoofer (an SVS PB13 Ultra for the aficionados out there). After spending some time listening to it (More like feeling it. Or being felt-up by it.), I knew I had to have one.

I also knew that Gen would have some reservations about adding yet another sub (there were already a few in the room), she being the type of person who would prefer a bass-free world. And by "reservations" I mean "throw a fit."

A quandary.

The solution was that old classic: better to beg forgiveness than to ask permission.

So I made arrangements for the Canadian SVS distributor to ship me one and have it delivered at a specific date and time when I knew Gen would be away from the house for a couple of hours. It arrived in a large double cardboard box, lashed to a large wooden pallet, with a total shipping weight of 175 pounds. The delivery driver was able to dolly it to my front door but that was it. I was on my own.

First I removed both front doors to make more room and then cleared the hallway leading to the basement steps. The pallet had been placed in the front door alcove. The sub's box lined up with the doorsill and I was able to slide it off and down the hall to the stairs. The box just fit with some pretty severe gesticulations to make the 90 degree turn down the steps, after I'd removed the handrails. I probably should have left them on, because at one point, as I led the crate down the steps, I really could have used something to slow my descent aside from the wall at the bottom. Luckily, the crate was okay, although I probably left an impression in the Gyproc.

I unboxed the sub at the foot of the stairs and eventually shuffled the 155-pound beast into the home theatre and its chosen spot in the back left corner. An existing sub in that location was hoisted on top. I broke down the shipping box and loaded it into my car with the wooden pallet. After I re-attached the handrails and doors, I carted off the packing materials for disposal. Then I returned, wired the new sub into my system, and calibrated it. I had just shut everything down and gotten upstairs when Gen got home.

"What'd you do today?" she asked.

"Not much" I said, trying not to wince from what was probably a set of bruised ribs.

There's usually very little ambient light in the theatre when we are watching a movie. It had to be a year later. The lights happened to be on when Gen was getting seated for a movie. She looked over and noticed the SVS for the first time. "Is that new?"

A short pause.

"Nope – it's been like that for a long time."

Roll movie.

The Best Darn Margaritas in the World

I have embarked on a lifelong quest: to find the place that makes the best margarita in the world. Actually that's not entirely true. I've already found it. Now I'm trying to find a place that even comes close to being as good as the one I've already found.

How good is it? Well, according to Gen, good enough to piss your pants over. Good enough to run carefree into the Med at midnight. Good enough to get me up dancing, shirtless, in a gay club. Good enough for Gen to warn me to never write about "those margaritas" in this book.

I consider that a challenge.

You see my buddy Bruce, his wife Annie, Gen and I were vacationing together in a town called Sitges, which is about a 30-minute train ride down the coast from Barcelona. It's an amazing place with great weather, beaches, shopping, food, and nightlife. It hosts numerous festivals throughout the year. It's also one of the world's top gay and lesbian tourist destinations.

The main stretch of beach is really nine interlocked beaches separated by rock walls and piers. It stretches from downtown out to a resort development and golf course. We rented a villa at about the mid-point of this stretch, about a ten-minute walk along a terrific wide boardwalk (actually interlocked stone) that runs along the seawall, longer if you walk along the shoreline.

The four of us headed into downtown one early evening. Bruce and I were going to have a few beers, the ladies were going to shop, and then we'd meet for dinner, which typically one does not do before

9pm. For reasons unknown, by the time we got downtown I had a hankering for a margarita. The girls split to shop and Bruce and I started looking for a place that made them. This turned out to be a difficult task. Bar after bar said they did not. Some locals pointed to a nightclub that did, but it only opened well past midnight. Facing defeat, we stopped at a little place on a pedestrian-only street, and plunked our behinds on the plain dark blue benches outside its front door. A perfect location for people watching.

The bartender / waiter appeared. We were about to order a couple of cold beers when I, by chance, asked if he could make a margarita. "Si," was the reply. Make it two. Soon thereafter, he came back with two whiskey-style tumblers, rims salted, a little ice, filled with the most incredible-tasting margaritas. I have no idea what tequila he used. Nor what else he mixed in. They were perfectly limed, strong, and delicious. Definitely not the resort-style watered-down crushed-ice slurp-fests you find the world over. We took our time savouring them, paid, and then headed off to find the wives.

Bruce and I were both "feeling it." Which is very unusual since we'd normally be a six-pack of beer down before we felt that way. Definitely not light on the tequila!

After a bit of shopping, it was time for dinner, which as I recall was probably the least impressive but still good meal of our trip. After dinner, we suggested to the wives that we return to the bar for more of those margaritas. Bruce opted for beer, but Gen and Annie joined me in having margaritas. They were as good as the first ones. The street was now bustling and the place immediately beside us raised its steel-shuttered door. The music started up. It was a small nightclub with a bar, almost no seating, and a dance floor. After a couple of margaritas, the girls were up dancing. I eventually joined them. I was pretty sure the girls and I were the only "straights" on the dance floor, but the other patrons did not seem to mind at all. Bruce held down our blue bench seats and cheered us on.

After four of those great margaritas and a long time up dancing, I figured it was time to go native, peeled off my sweat-soaked shirt, and continued dancing. I think Annie took photos. But we eventually ran out of steam, and although the partying could typically run through to sunrise, we headed back to the villa.

It was then I realized how strong those margaritas were. You see, just as we got to the seawall sidewalk, a very tipsy Gen said she had to pee, and did. Sensing that she now needed to clean up, she yelled out that she was going for a swim, bolted down a set of stairs to the beaches and began running to the surf, with me in hot pursuit. It was a moonless night and very little light from the street was hitting the water. You could hear the surf pounding the sand, but couldn't really see it. I caught her at the water's edge and managed to save... just her purse and its contents as she then plunged/dove into a big wave. Gen was never in any real danger; even drunk she's a better swimmer than 99% of the world's population. She emerged soon after, soaking wet, and proclaimed herself "all clean."

We walked the beach to the villa and were soon fast asleep. Gen woke up the next day feeling a little off, and tried to get me to promise to never speak of the previous night's happenings. Needless to say, I did not agree. We did agree that those margaritas packed a punch. More importantly, they really were the best-darn-tasting margaritas in the world.

I've returned to Sitges a couple more times over the years, and stopped at the blue bench bar for margaritas. It was no fluke: they were just as great on those occasions as the first. I've tried, and tried, and tried to find a place, any place, the world over, that can match them. The search has become a bit of a Holy Grail quest; perhaps I should just let the legend stand as it is.

The Perv

Whether it's in high school, university, work, or some other environment, I'm sure most of us have known a member of the community who creeps us out and sets our "beware" radar on alert. In my three years in residence at university, one person had that effect more than others. I'll call him the Perv.

It was nothing overt. It was how he looked at people and interacted, or not, with them. Women felt the least comfortable.

And it was little "incidents." Like how, when we were can-mates (meaning our rooms shared an adjoining bathroom) he would "accidentally" always manage to walk in on any female guests of mine who happened to be using the shower at the time. It was more than an annoyance.

In third year, we were again can-mates, but this time instead of two double rooms sharing, it was two singles – just he and I. The other thing these rooms shared was a telephone that sat in an opening between rooms, with a lockable door at each end. Gen and I suspected, or better yet, sensed, that he was eavesdropping on us by opening his side and sticking his head in as far as he could.

And one night she was positive she'd heard something – a suppressed sneeze or something. So I came up with a rather drastic plan of action.

We very quietly got out of bed. In the near-pitch dark, I grabbed one of my hockey sticks, positioning myself near the cubbyhole to allow me to quickly extend the butt end, at full-force, through the opening. Gen took hold of the cubbyhole door at our end, and with a barely audible "now," opened it. I thrust the stick through the opening with all my weight behind it.

Now when coming up with this plan, I assumed one or two things: either the Perv was not in the cubbyhole, in which case I might break the latch/lock on his cubbyhole door, or he would be there, in which case the butt end, which I tried to keep right where his forehead would likely be, would knock a lesson into him.

Turns out the latter was true, although, as we'll see, the lesson might not have been fully learned.

I could feel the butt hit something solid, movable, but not wood. My thrust continued to full extension, and pushed whatever was at the end of the stick out and into the other room. There was no cry, but a bit of a crumpling sound. I closed the door at my end, put away the stick, and got back into bed.

The next day the Perv was not seen. His door never opened. He did not appear at the floor's usual cafeteria table. Same thing the next day. But the day after that, he showed up at dinner, with a dressing on his forehead. I had not told anyone else about what I had done (yes, in hindsight that was a little irresponsible of me, especially if the body had started to smell!) and people did not usually initiate conversation with the Perv, so nothing was said about it. With time, the bandage was removed, and the bruise underneath faded from sight. We never again felt his presence in the cubbyhole, nor were guests walked in on, so perhaps, I thought, the lesson had been driven home after all.

Some years later, I found out it had not. I happened upon a newspaper article. A man had been caught taking pictures in the women's change room in the sports complex. He had been sneaking in through the emergency exit at the back, taking pictures and then running away if seen. This had apparently been going on for some time. The culprit? The Perv.

Pembroke Pub Crawls

It's a pity, but as far as I can tell from extensive Google searching, nobody has yet published a historical summary of the numerous pubs, bars, men's rooms, taverns and lounges that once, and in some cases still do, populate my hometown of Pembroke, Ontario. Because if there was one great pastime when coming of age in Pembroke (or sometime before it if you had fake ID), it was the main street pub crawl.

I was able to frequent a few establishments by the time I was 14, and all of them by 16. The legal drinking age back then was 18. Pembroke's Main Street, and immediate side streets, contained a compact collection of drinking establishments of all kinds.

Not including licensed restaurants, in my formative years (1973-1978) you could start at the west end of Main Street with the Pembroke Hotel, and work your way east by way of the Hillsborough Hotel, Copeland Hotel, Windsor Tavern, and Mackay Tavern. Sober, you could make that walk in five minutes or so.

The Pembroke Hotel had a men's room (obviously for men only) on the lower level, and a lounge one floor up. Both were good-sized rooms. Downstairs had a shuffleboard table and two pool tables. Best of all there, you could buy quarts of beer. Dad and I spent quite a few nights in there playing pool and drinking beer and it was probably one of the first licensed establishments I ever drank in. All of the old-timers knew Dad. He'd spent his younger years hustling pool through the Ottawa Valley and that included trips from his home town of

Renfrew to Pembroke. Even though I was 14 at the time, I was with Dad and was served. After that, I could go back on my own without any questions asked. Upstairs featured live entertainment and over the years I saw some great bar bands. One of the most memorable acts was an appearance by "Gloves" McGinty, whose shtick was to play the piano with the keys completely covered by a cloth. And boy could he play. It was honestly a night to remember. The Pembroke Hotel eventually burned down.

The Hillsborough Hotel, also known as the Hug and Slug, sat a block off Main Street. It also had a men's room and a lounge. You could get a really good cheeseburger platter in the lounge, washed down with 64-ounce jugs of beer. It was a favourite stop for me and some of my friends before Friday night high school dances. Of course you ordered a jug each - parallel, not series, drinking please! You could also get food in the men's room, but it was limited to pickled eggs and pickled wieners. Oh, and chuck wagons as well (disgusting ham and cheese sandwich-like things that were heated in their cellophane wrapper). "Ozzie" the bartender had trouble getting the tongs into the pickled egg jar so he'd reach in with a hand and pull one out, put it into the tongs, and then place it on the plate for you. Classy! Someone once tried to burn down the Hillsborough.

The Copeland hotel had a lounge and a tavern by the time it burned down in 1976. The band playing there that week was told to remove their instruments when they were done playing, earlier on the night of the fire. (Are you sensing a common theme yet?) My strongest memory of the Copeland was how huge the two bouncers were (I think one had played football for the Ottawa Rough Riders) and how easily they evicted a drunk through the front doors just as I was about to enter. And I mean actually through the front doors. Luckily they were made of glass, so I saw him coming and had time to jump out of the way of the body and flying glass. One of the bouncers noticed that he'd cut his own hand on said glass and proceeded to pummel the unconscious drunk on the sidewalk for having done that to him. Tough love towards sobriety, I guess.

The Windsor Tavern is still in business, as far as I can tell. It's also a block off Main Street. We didn't go very often because it was all country music all the time back then (and might still be), but it had a nice big room and some of the bands were pretty good.

The Mackay Tavern was a favoured hangout of military service-men stationed up the highway at Base Petawawa. Back then the Airborne Regiment still existed (prior to being disbanded for some serious issues brought to light during its deployment to Somalia). It was also the scene of several conflicts between civilians and soldiers. Prior to the Airborne's arrival, a fight was a fight like any other: a couple of guys would go at it, get thrown out, and possibly resume the fight in the parking lot. When you were at the Mackay and a fight broke out, if you heard someone yell "Airborne" you learned quick to either bolt for an exit (with or without your unfinished beer) or dive for cover under one of the sturdy tables, because all hell was about to break loose. Rumour has it that after one such battle, a member of the Regiment tossed a live grenade off the Pembroke Street Bridge on his way back to base. I tend to believe it.

So after your crawl from one end of Pembroke's Main street to the other, and assuming you visited both the lounges and men's rooms, you would have drunk at least eight beers, and it's almost a certainty that some of those were quarts or jugs. If you were still game after that, you'd hitch a ride "over the bridge" to Quebec, hitting Moorehead's (torched – there's that theme again), and the Chez Charles along the way to your end goal of Chapeau, Quebec, where you would find Keon's and finally Fred's (The Chapeau Hotel – also now burned down.)

The latter was an incredible historic landmark and deserves a book of its own. So too does its owner and namesake Fred Meilleur, who passed away in 2009. He was a huge man with a head way too small for his body. But he had a great big heart. He acted as bouncer in the bar and if he removed you for bad behaviour he always seemed to do it nicely. As long as you were well-behaved he'd serve you, even if you were probably underage. (You knew he knew you were underage when he'd come up to you and suggest that you leave and go stand on the sidewalk on the other side of the road, which you did just in time to watch the place get raided by the QPP. Fred always had advance warning!) I spent the night of my 18th birthday asleep across from Fred's, the sidewalk as my pillow. 18 beers on your 18th was the tradition.

From the earliest of times that I can remember, right through to a few years before his death, it was a family tradition to go to Fred's for dinner. Fred would serve you personally and knew everybody's name.

You could get massive steaks and pork tenderloin for outrageously low prices. You had to order your baked potato in advance – but the mashed potatoes and gravy were fabulous if you didn't. The pies were incredible. Fred had an excellent selection of wines and very low mark-ups on the bottles. And the dining room's walls were adorned with all sorts of memorabilia and taxidermied animals.

As well as a great place to drink when all the bars in Pembroke had closed, Fred's was also where you could hear some fantastic bar bands, many of whom played their own original music. I will never forget hearing Triad, with Neil O'Connor on guitar, Jack Clouthier on drums, and if I'm not mistaken, Ray Heney on bass. I still have a near-pristine vinyl copy of Neil's excellent album *Inlaws/Outlaws* (1977) on which Jack and Ray, as well as others, play.

When I was "growing up," a true Pembroke Pub crawl always ended at Fred's.

Proud Father

At the risk of having my daughters accuse me of favouritism, I'd like to tell you a bit about my son and the great sense of pride I feel about him.

My son struggled in grade- and high school. He's a smart guy, but has difficulty concentrating on tasks at hand in a classroom environment. It took him an extra year or so to complete high school, and when he did it took him more than a while to move on to the next step.

He's made the odd misstep, but most pale in comparison to my own screw-ups. Sure he may have purloined my best bottle of single malt (see *The 21-Year-Old Springbank*) but his one foray into potential criminality brings nothing but laughter upon recollection. As we did for all of our kids, we opened up a children's bank account for him. Into it went birthday money and the like. My son took notice of how deposits were made at the ATM. One day he decided to experiment. He put his card into the machine and deposited an empty envelope, to which he gave a value of $0.01. He then saw that his balance had gone up by $0.01. He then did the same thing with $1.00 and then $10 and... he made it all the way to $10,000 before the system booted him out. This resulted in a call from the bank manager and a suspension of his banking privileges. The bank manager could not understand why I was laughing about it, but I was.

He has our family's love of water, and like the rest of us became a lifeguard and instructor. He did very well as part of the city's lifeguard team at provincial championships. He swam competitively for a few years and his times dropped quite a bit during that period. The one characteristic that seemed to shine through was how comfortable he is in the water. And as we were to find out, how good he is under the water.

He decided to get his SCUBA licence and passed without difficulty. Through that activity he met the owner of Logs End, an amazing little local company that salvages old growth forest logs from the bottom of local rivers that were used to float logs to market over a hundred years ago. Billions of trees were cut and a small percentage of them (which still means a huge number) sank and were buried in the dark, cold, almost oxygen-free silt at the bottom – perfectly preserved. Logs End takes these salvaged logs and turns them into some of the most gorgeous wood flooring you'll ever see.

It's a pretty straightforward process. Logs End "owns" the salvage rights to hundreds of miles of river. Dive crews tackle a small section at a time, and working in sometimes pitch-black conditions, they feel around the bottom for logs, measure (by feel) to determine which ones are economically salvageable, and then lasso the end with a rope and marker float. A salvage barge comes by later to haul out the roped logs, which are offloaded to trucks heading to the mill.

The owner offered to check my son out to see if he'd make a good diver, so my son and I drove an hour upstream on the Quebec side of the Ottawa River to meet with the owner, and his primary diver. That diver happened to be an off-duty police officer, and the head of the Ottawa Police Dive Unit. I felt good about having him dive with my son this first time.

We motored off on the dive boat and eventually came to a fairly large bay. The two divers suited and tanked up and off they went together. I helped to feed out the rope and floats, which were in 25-foot linked sections. You could trace the movement of the divers by both their air bubbles and the floats that would pop up to the surface, indicating a roped log. They were working in 10-20 feet of water.

After quite a while, the police diver surfaced. He was low on air. We chatted about my son and he said he was "a natural." He said he'd never had a "newbie" stay down longer than he did; that the excitement always has them going through their tank very much faster than him. Nick was down for another 10 minutes and when he surfaced he wanted to swap tanks right away and head back down.

He'd finally discovered something he knew he really wanted to do. He dove for Logs End for a year while attempting to get accepted into college. It took him two rounds of applications but he finally was accepted into a commercial diving program. Only twenty-four of the forty-five in his class who started the demanding program ended up graduating; my son was one of them. He returned to Ottawa and dove a bit more for Logs End and then for a true commercial diving company, but it was mostly part-time seasonal work. At my urging he headed to the west coast to a position that came open and he's been out there ever since.

He's done the usual commercial diving work (underwater structures, ship inspections, etc.), as well as sea urchin fishing (which requires commercial divers.) He's a volunteer with the Royal Canadian Marine Search and Rescue, and he's now a fully-trained Coxswain with them.

He's engaged to a most wonderful girl.

He recently went back to school (on full scholarship) and got his welding qualification. For a kid who struggled in school, who did not know what he wanted to do in life, he continues to make me one heck of a proud father.

Great Pyramid of Giza

I don't have a bucket list per se, but I know several things that would be on it if I did. Visiting the Great Pyramid of Giza had always been at the top of that non-list, so in 2009 when I was planning my first, and what so far has been only trip, to the Middle East and back, I could not help but notice that Cairo was smack-dab on the line my flight would take into London Heathrow on the way back. So I broke it up into two flight segments and arranged a full weekend stopover.

As I did back then, I was traveling with my golf clubs. I'd managed to get in a round in Dubai, and for Cairo I'd booked myself into the Hilton Pyramids Golf Course. With a name like that, how could I resist!

As one should always do, I had arranged for a driver to meet me at the airport upon arrival in Cairo. We made the drive through the city in the dark. I was struck by how impoverished things looked on that trip. Your average car typically had no functioning lights, but then again many of the cars did not function at all, judging by the numbers of derelict vehicles that lined the highway. Many of the buildings that we passed were unfinished but occupied hulks, clearly without electricity or even windows.

Tourist-wise, things seemed very slow, at least judging by the lack of guests at the hotel. I was met at the front door by both a bellhop and an armed guard. The desk clerk knew my name before I even mentioned it (could I have been the only expected guest?) He said that as a Platinum Member I was being upgraded to a nicer room. He escorted me there personally. It was on the ground floor and would be best described as a luxury suite: living and dining rooms, bedrooms, and a porch that sat in its own private grassy yard. There was a guard hut (with the requisite armed guard on duty 24/7) at the back corner and when I asked where that led, he said to the golf course. He wasn't kidding; the starter's stand and first tee were right there.

I played two rounds in two days. It was a very good course. At the far end, you could catch a glimpse of the Great Pyramids in the distance. Mind you, they are so big you can see them from quite a ways away. On my first round, there was nobody but me and a foursome of Swedes that I caught up to on the back nine. On the second round, I started off playing in thick dense morning fog, something I never would have expected in the middle of the desert. Luckily I'd played the day before and remembered the general layout of each hole, and I was hitting the ball straight, because the ball would disappear within 20 yards. I would drive the distance I expected it to be, and there it was. While I had shot a 94 in sunshine the first day, I shot an 82 that foggy day.

I dedicated one full day to touring the Pyramids, hiring the same driver as well as a licensed guide. He was a younger chap, fluent in English (and other languages) with a degree in history. He knew the system well and we headed over to the pyramids at the crack of dawn to get in line for the very limited number of passes issued daily for entrance into the Great Pyramid itself. We got there well before the busloads of tourists and I was among the first to have a ticket in hand. We walked around the site and my guide gave an excellent lesson on its history. He then delivered me to the entrance. I would be without his help while inside. The public entrance is actually through a tunnel carved out by grave robbers. This is not for the claustrophobic; it's a long tight steep fit, with seemingly no fresh air. You eventually link up with the "real" passage and make your way up through the Grand Gallery to the King's Chamber. I really can't adequately describe how magnificent this massive construction is. I was simply in awe at the skill it must have taken to pull the whole thing off, thousands of years ago.

The return trip through the passages was much more difficult. By now, there were people like me trying to descend through the same steep, mostly dark, small passage while others were coming up. I was behind a very big woman who took up most of the space all by herself. On one occasion she became stuck and we had to wait quite a while for her to stop panicking, free herself, and resume the trek downward. I honestly don't know what Plan B would have been had she not been able to get unstuck. There were no staff or officials to be seen inside and it would have been up to us tourists to work it out.

It was a relief to finally see daylight again and the private tour of the site with my guide resumed. We hiked away from the three pyramids to take some distance shots. We spent time in the museum at the base of the pyramids that houses a boat discovered preserved under the stone floor that surrounds the pyramids, and we finished up with some quality time with the Sphinx. It was almost too much to take in.

After that, it was the obligatory visits to a series of merchants. My guide was well-connected with owners of stores selling papyrus paintings (I bought two); Egyptian cotton (I bought a scarf); and (mostly gold) jewelry (I took a pass). I made arrangements with the driver to take me back that night for the sound and light show which, while dated and a bit hokey, was pretty darn impressive.

It was with regret that my weekend ended and I was back on the highway heading to the airport. During the day, traffic moves at a snail's pace, but that gives you a chance to buy some lovely parting gifts (and bagels) from the many vendors who line the road and approach your car as you pass by.

I was feeling pretty good overall up until I went to check in for my London flight with Egypt-Air. It seemed that even though I had a ticket and confirmed seat, my seat was no longer available. I was told it had been given to someone else of more importance. I asked who and was told a Muslim. There had been a pilgrimage of sorts in town and a shortage of seats to handle them all when they were leaving. The airline's policy was to ditch any infidels and give their seats to card-carrying Muslims. Other than a weak apology, I was given nothing to compensate for the several-hour wait for the next available flight. Next time I'm going with Atheist-Air!

Coliseum

I love the Ottawa River. Except for a few months here and there, I have lived my entire life within a mile of its shoreline. If I were to stop typing this tale right now and bolt out my front door, I could be on its banks within minutes. It is hundreds of miles long and by the time it passes by Montreal and into the St. Lawrence it is a very significant waterway. It supports a number of hydro dams and was the economic backbone of the Ottawa Valley for over a hundred years. And one of the really neat things about it is that it has some great whitewater rafting within an hour's drive of Ottawa.

Decades ago, some pretty smart entrepreneurs formed whitewater rafting companies and grew businesses that would, at their peaks, see tens of thousands of people rafting down the great Ottawa River every year. I've done the day trip four times in my life. But it's been quite a number of years since my last trip, probably because I got more than my money's worth that day.

Back then you'd run several sets of rapids, and depending on the river's level, each set's character could change. There are sections of calm flat water, and sections where you can hop out and do some body surfing. You'd be in a 12-person rubber raft, plus a guide. Your only real task was to paddle hard whenever the guide told you to. He'd do all the steering.

It seemed like every time I rafted, the guide in my boat turned out to be not only someone I knew, but someone who I had taught to swim, or coached, back in my lifeguarding / instructing / coaching days. I'd always bring along a pair of swim goggles to wear, and have a Speedo on under my shorts, and, contrary to rafting company policy, would always be allowed to hop overboard and swim a mile or so of flat water alongside the raft. Did I mention how much I love that river?

My last trip was no different, with Billy at the back guiding us. Our busload of rafters for the day was put into five rafts, and after the usual safety briefings and paddling lesson, headed off. Billy told me it would be a bit of a wild trip this time because the water level was bringing out the best (i.e. fiercest) in each set. He wasn't lying!

I took up a spot at the back left, just in front of Billy.

The first rapid is a place where the entire river passes through a very narrow gap. It basically turns itself sideways ninety degrees and becomes very deep and very narrow. As the huge volume of water accelerates through the gap there's a drop, and then as it slows down when the gap opens up, there's a hydraulic jump that you punch through. That day it was huge. When we hit, several of the rafters were flipped backwards through the raft, and one was launched over my head and off the back, just missing Billy. I threw my paddle into the raft and, reaching back and over the side, caught the back of her lifejacket and hauled her into the raft like I was landing a twenty-pound pike. It all happened so fast she didn't have time to be afraid. She was back in her place as soon as we cleared that section.

And so it went for most of the trip, although nobody else went overboard, at least not from our raft.

There is one legendary rapid called Coliseum, and it's the last one of the day. It has a central wave called the Big Kahuna, and that day it was massive. Even well upstream, we could hear its roar. Earlier in the day, the tour company had thought about using a different channel, thinking Coliseum was simply too big. They decided to give it a try anyhow. But now there was some indecision on the part of the guides who were lining up in the still-water eddies above that section. It felt sort-of like a very crowded airport with loads of planes on taxiways waiting for takeoff.

There was a group of rafts from another company ahead of us and they decided they'd try it first. One after another, they would take off down the channel, paddling with great effort, lining up perfectly with the central wave of the mighty Coliseum, and one after the other, Coliseum would pick them up and seemingly shake their occupants from their rafts. Now nobody was in any real danger (shaken, not stirred as it were), as there are always plenty of safety kayaks around to retrieve people and get them back into their rafts. But it's still better to skip the shake-and-save treatment.

When it came time for our grouping of five rafts, I suggested to Billy that our raft go first. We made a change to the lineup and put all the "lightweights" to the back of the raft and my buddy Kirk and I at the very front. Our job would be to pull our way over the top of Big Kahuna before the raft stalled and was flipped. So off we went. I've got to say the experience was both terrifying and exhilarating. Terrifying when we dropped down into the hole in front of Big Kahuna and could see nothing but a huge vertical wall of water in front of us (not to mention the deafening roar – or was that screams from the rear passengers?), and exhilaration as we crested the top and Kirk and I leaned as far forward as we could, pulling the raft safely over the top.

No upending. Nobody overboard.

Our raft immediately headed for the shore to our right. Kirk and I hopped out and ran back upstream on a path along the river's edge. You see, there was a second part to our group's plan. The other boats waited for Kirk and me to be the dead weight and horsepower in each of their front ends. Each of those five rides on Coliseum was as amazing as the first: the hole, the wall, the crest, and safely over. Not one lost occupant. But by the end we were drained.

Our guides said they'd never seen Coliseum as big as that day. After having tackled it five times, I figured I'd had more than my share of it. I have not done it again ever since... but I am tempted!

Cold, Darn Cold!

I recently completed Chicago's Big Shoulders 5k open water swim. It's held in Lake Michigan, where weather and water conditions vary tremendously from year to year. By all accounts, the conditions in 2014 were the worst ever, and they left me with a newfound appreciation of the dangers of hypothermia. And caused me to remember a race from long ago.

There were plenty of places to swim, besides the community pool, if you were a kid growing up in Pembroke, Ontario.

There are numerous public and private beaches along the Ottawa River. Petawawa Point, with its "Danger, Deep Hole" sign was one of them. Pembroke's Riverside Park was another. If you rode your bike out to Cotnam Island, you crossed a short bridge that was a perfect launch point for a jump into the river. And on your way to Westmeath you could stop at the always nearly deserted White Sands Beach, where you could walk out hundreds of metres and still only be up to your chest.

And there was "the Quarry" which was exactly that: a big rock quarry filled in with water. It was fenced and the gate was locked, but that never stopped dozens of kids from hitting its cold clear water. The older kids would build a diving board out of scrap lumber. We'd ride logs we found floating around. We'd bring our snorkeling gear and spend hours exploring its depths. And it was at the quarry that I first saw someone swim training.

There was a family near my house whose children were all excellent swimmers. They all had beautiful technique and could ply the water with little effort. I lifeguarded with Mark, and his older sister Ava was our boss. But years before that older brother Gord's training in the quarry was my first exposure to the family and its swimming talents. The quarry was 100m or so wide and Gord would spend what seemed like hours swimming across and back.

Flash forward many years. Gen and I were about to embark on the second annual Kiwanis cross-river fundraising swim. You would start at the marina on the Pembroke side, and swim across to the "red barn" on the Quebec side, touch the dock, and return. It was two kilometres each way. I knew Gen was a faster swimmer than me, so I had resigned myself to a second-place finish. When the swimmers were marshalled and announced, I quickly changed my estimate to third place, as Gord was to be one of them. He looked to be in great shape and apparently was now an accomplished triathlete. However, like most triathletes, he had little or no body fat. And back then nobody wore wetsuits while swimming.

Now the evening before, Gen and I had been down at the waterfront to check out conditions. The water was calm and relatively warm. Ideal. The morning of the swim, things could not have been any more different. Apparently the large hydro dam miles upstream had released a huge amount of water, and that water was very cold. It had made its way downstream and now the river was frigid – at best. In addition, the wind was howling and the river was covered in whitecaps. Nevertheless the race was started. It was a very tough slog.

I soon lost sight of Gen, but for the first kilometre or so, I kept Gord just a bit ahead of me. Eventually he pulled away and I lost sight of him. However, as I touched the dock on the far side, I saw him on the dock, wrapped in blankets and shivering. He did not look well.

The conditions seemed even worse on the return trip. I was getting hammered with waves and several times found myself retching and unable to breathe. On one occasion, I actually passed beneath the surface and had to force myself back to the top. That was when I decided to quit and began waving my arms for help. But there was nobody in sight. You see, the organizers had assumed everyone would swim as a pack, and all they needed was one boat in the lead and one in the rear. They failed to realize that over such a long distance swimmers would get strung out with hundreds of metres between them. Gen was somewhere way ahead with the lead boat. And way behind me somewhere were other swimmers and the chase boat.

So I had a choice: swim or die. I swam. I finished second. I don't know that I saw Gord after the race. I think he was taken away for medical treatment.

Flash forward again to 2014. It was the Big Shoulders race. The water was very cold and the chop and swells were high. As my wave of swimmers entered the water, we all looked at each and you could see the apprehension on each other's faces. Being "older" swimmers we were no fools, so we only waded in to our waists, not chests like the previous waves of swimmers. The starter's boat had to back up for us. As the countdown for our wave hit 30 seconds, there was a look of panic in the crowd. But we plunged forth at the gun – and the shock hit!

I had trouble breathing and the skin all over my body registered the pain of the cold. By the first turn of the triangular course, the pain had gone away – replaced by complete numbness. Between the first and second turns, the swells were murderous, especially as we approached the second turn. The only saving grace was a patch of less-cold (I refuse to say warmer) water that gave us hope. After the turn, I recalled the organizer's joking remarks about being able to body-surf the back stretch. The engineer in me knew that the waves closer to the wall would be biggest and most regular so I went wide around the turn, went into sprint mode, and caught wave after wave. At one point, I was moving faster than people jogging along the path above me! Then the less-cold water disappeared and I began to shiver as I swam – something I had never experienced before.

I contemplated quitting as I came close to the beach, and the turn that would take me again around the two-and-a-half-kilometre triangle, to complete the five-kilometre race. But I somehow found myself wedged between other swimmers and made the turn with them. The second lap was no better than the first. There seemed to be far fewer swimmers around me. There also seemed to be fewer safety boats in sight after the first turn. It was only afterwards that I learned many of them were busy hauling swimmers back to the beach.

I again body-surfed the back stretch as much as possible. However, I had lost all feeling in my arms and legs, so I think I might have been doing more flopping than swimming. And it was a good thing I couldn't feel my legs, because I knew that both calves were cramped up rock solid – normally a very painful thing.

I swam to the beach and somehow managed to get up and stumble through the finish gate with a time of 1:38:47, met by other team members. I toweled off, put on my sweats, sat down, and began to shake uncontrollably. My jaw was clenched tight. I was unaware of my surroundings. And at that moment, I remembered back to my days as a kid at the quarry, seeing Gord swimming in its waters, and then seeing him, defeated by the cold, shivering on that dock. Up until then I had never appreciated what hypothermia was really like.

The Scotch Night

In the mid-'90s, I attended an aviation conference in Chicago. It was to celebrate the 50th anniversary of the original Chicago Conference, which established the International Civil Aviation Authority. It was organized by Ed, a buddy of mine, who was a publisher at *Aviation Week*. It was highly successful, drawing something like 750 attendees when only 350 were expected when the plan was first hatched.

On the last day of the event, after things had wrapped up, I was heading across the lobby of the Chicago Hilton and Towers, where the event had been held, when Ed's loud voice called to me from across the other side. He was standing with a couple of Hilton managers, they in their Hilton jackets. Ed told me that because the event had been so successful, and so profitable for the hotel, they were treating him to whatever dinner and drinks he wanted from the hotel's bars and restaurants. They'd have no problem if I joined them. Who could resist an offer like that?

It did not take long for us to decide that we would start at the hotel's main bar, lobby level. Ed and I had been there earlier in the week and it had an exceptional selection of single malt scotches. The four of us ponied up to a high table and stools. We asked for the scotch menu. As I was looking it over, I asked one of the managers if everything, and anything, would be on the house. "No problem, sir," was the answer.

Ed quickly came up with the idea to explore the regions of Scotland through the selection of malts, so we set off on our journey. We were initially somewhat reserved in our selections. Sure we stepped up from our regular Talisker and Oban, usually $6-8 a glass, to more expensive ($60-80 a glass) varieties. After we'd "done the country" once, we started again, this time with $100-300-a-glass selections. These were exceptional scotches, the likes of which I had never before tasted. At some point we ordered dinner. I'm sure our filets were accompanied by a nice bottle of wine. But then it was back to the malts.

By the end of the night we'd had our fill. When the cheque came for the lead manager to sign, I caught a look at the bottom line: $6,000 and change! Given that the managers had refrained from drinking alcohol, and our dinners were not more than $50 each, almost all of that tally was for single malt.

Excellent!

I helped the managers manoeuvre Ed to the bank of elevators and up to his room. I bade them farewell and wove to my own. I woke up the next day feeling a bit "off" but it was more than worth it. I had tasted single malts I would never have been able to even sniff on my own ticket.

Paintings – The Self-Portrait

A year or two after meeting Kurt E. Schon (see *Paintings – The Lessons*), I happened to be in San Francisco on business. After a day at a conference, I met up with Chuck, a buddy of mine, and we went to Fisherman's Wharf for dinner and a few drinks.

As we were walking off the rather big seafood meals, we passed a storefront with a couple of hostesses standing outside the front door, taking invitations from very well-dressed folks, handing them a flute of champagne, and ushering them inside. We were dressed in our suits and ties, and liked champagne as much as anyone else, so we stopped and got in line.

I honestly don't know how we managed to talk our way in, but we did, two-fisting our first round of bubbly.

We were inside an art gallery. It had just opened and was apparently featuring a single artist. There was quite the crowd inside. We mingled. And we drank more bubbly. And we mingled some more.

The paintings were far from the 18th and 19th century ones that Kurt had shown me. Quite frankly I was not that impressed. They seemed to be nothing more than oddly thrown-together shapes and colours, on a variety of sizes of canvas. But the champagne was first rate. The more I drank, the more I stopped to stare at a given piece.

At one point, I found myself all alone in front of one painting when someone came up behind me and asked what I thought of it. I figured what the heck, might as well pretend I know something about art, so I started waxing poetic, throwing random bits of psycho-babble together, and was almost embarrassed by how thick I was laying it on. The champagne was helping tremendously.

Now the painting was truly meaningless to me. I really had no idea what it was supposed to be. But then the proverbial light bulb went off. I don't know how, but I correctly guessed that the woman standing beside me was the artist AND the reason she was particularly interested in my opinion of this particular painting was that it was her self-portrait. I did not tell her that I so suspected. Instead, I ratcheted up the old gift-of-the-gab and went on about how the artist was obviously feeling some deep emotional pain, yada yada yada, and used this obvious self-portrait as some kind of cathartic experience. All of it pure nonsense – but bang on the money.

I had just made a new best friend. It seems nobody had understood that painting like I had, and everything I'd said about it was true. She revealed herself as the artist and for the rest of the evening, until the gallery closed, she walked me around the room and introduced me to every guest she could. Chuck looked on in amazement: I was showing an artistic and cultured side that he never knew I had. He and I both!

Boeing, Boeing, Gone!

I had a chance to properly bookend my career, with a notable success on each end. Instead, my employer, the National Research Council of Canada, would crush that final achievement in a blizzard of executive incompetence, and I would become its jetsam. But aside from that final act, it was a good run.

As told in *Opportunity From Tragedy*, I had a major success early in my career that led to me eventually joining NRC in 1989. I was interviewed by the executive VP of NRC at the time. He told me he would only agree to hire me if I committed to shaking things up, to making

NRC change its business ways. Within five years, that VP was long gone, and I was bloodied and bruised from running into brick walls. I decided to be much more focused (on aerospace only) and far less outspoken on the overall state of NRC and the things it needed to do.

That served me in good stead and coincided with a push to make the aerospace lab at NRC much more revenue-focused. Thanks to many factors, including the marketing efforts I had already initiated, revenues increased by a factor of 10 over a five-year period. They would continue to grow year-over-year. Staff levels more than doubled by the time I left in 2013.

I had a lot of success throughout my tenure at NRC Aerospace, and received awards and accolades. But as I approached retirement, I felt more and more that it was all too easy, that doing deal after deal, to all of my clients' satisfaction, had now become automatic. I wanted one more career-defining deal, to bookend my working life, before I retired.

That opportunity presented itself when I met with our client relationship manager (CRM) for Boeing. Boeing had long been an NRC client, but almost exclusively on a standard testing, or fee-for-service basis. It brought in good money, mostly in the form of wind tunnel testing, but not the sort of strategic long-term forward-looking collaborations we'd been successfully launching with other major aerospace companies. Boeing was effectively the last, and biggest, aerospace company with whom we did not have such a relationship.

The CRM and I spent a fair bit of time brainstorming what such a relationship and deal might look like, and we borrowed what we felt were the best elements we'd done with others. From that emerged a starting point and strategy that we discussed with our management team and colleagues, and which they wholeheartedly endorsed. I took on the role of lead negotiator.

I began by selling Boeing on the broad concepts. It would be a long time before I even presented them with a draft agreement (which I already had in hand). Instead, the early meetings dealt with a number of generic issues, at both a philosophical and practical level. For example, I had developed some very neat ways of looking at, and dealing with, intellectual property matters, and I brought my Boeing counterparts on board with them. Eventually I presented them with the draft agreement, and even though it took many months (which is not at all unusual) of conference calls with their contracts and legal people to get the wording just right, we ended up with a version that was what the CRM and I had initially envisioned and which was completely acceptable to Boeing.

We "shook" on it and they sent me signed copies for NRC's execution.

Now let me tell you something. In my entire career, where I had taken the lead in putting a deal together, not once had my bosses ever refused to sign off once the client had done so. Not once had it ever been sent back for revisions. I'd always taken care, throughout the process, of keeping senior managers, finance, legal, everybody who needed to be, fully informed and on board. I always worked within my mandate and always delivered good, if not great, deals in the end. Executive sign-off always went something like this: "That's a Jeff Mackwood deal, where do I sign?" There are a lot of things that I can't do, this sort of deal making is not one of them. My clients knew when we shook on a deal, it was a done deal.

The Boeing deal arrived for signature at what would turn out to be a horrible time within NRC.

Ordinarily such a deal could be, and was, signed off by the manager in charge of the aerospace sector. But what we frequently did was to escalate the signing up to a VP, and even the President's level, for visibility. Call it good press within the organization. In many cases, for major deals, we worked with the client to jointly promote its signing. The timing was right to announce the Boeing deal at an upcoming major international aerospace event, as we had done with others in the past.

So the manager of aerospace sent the deal to the VP, with a recommendation that he sign it. That VP was really a "temp" occupying the position until a competition was completed for the position. So he decided to sit on it and wait for his replacement to come on board. Actually, if that's all he had done, things might have worked out better. Instead he had an assistant review the agreement. Now she knew as much about such things as I know about rare Latvian coinage, which is to say nothing. So she referred it to a "contracts" person in Corporate NRC who had no knowledge of the case, and probably less knowledge about this type of deal. Together they crafted a list of "concerns" that was laughable at best. My legal counsel and I then spent time addressing (and shooting down) every one of those concerns in a note back to the temporary VP. He then left the file for the new VP.

We figured the new guy would be happy to sign off on such a great deal, to cement a big success only days into his tenure, to revel in the spotlight. Wrong! Instead, he decided he wanted to make his mark by showing all of us NRCers how smart and clever he was, how much he knew about everything, and, conversely, what little ignorant people we were.

Armed with the silly comments now on file, and ignoring the cogent rebuttal of said comments, he proceeded to rattle off a list of concerns that were essentially a demand that the negotiations be re-opened with Boeing and major changes made to the entire agreement. I was in Chicago on business when the CRM forwarded them to me. I felt ill. I did not sleep that night, working instead on a way to salvage the deal. I knew Boeing would never agree to what the VP was demanding. More importantly, they never should agree to it. I know I wouldn't have if I were in their shoes.

An internal conference call was held. The VP and I had never met, nor even spoken, up until that point. He had a number of people in his office with him for the call. The CRM was there as well. I took the lead in defending the deal as signed by Boeing. After the meeting, the CRM told me I had done a masterful job of diplomatically skewering all his demands, of pointing out how wrong and silly they were, and in laying out the consequences of proceeding per his demands. But the VP stood firm and none of the other people in the room, some of whom knew better, spoke out in support of the deal as constructed.

I was removed from the file. Boeing was told the deal was now re-opened and they would be dealing with someone else. Basically I had been "burned" and my handshake was now worthless. The new negotiating team took a year to eventually negotiate a contract that represented a very small part of the original deal, and which did nothing more than to allow standard fee-for-service work to continue. They never did come to terms on the real meat of the deal: the establishment of a long-term strategic arrangement for collaborative R&D. Boeing was none too pleased. And neither were the NRC staff who had been eagerly awaiting the deal so that they could launch new projects.

Over a year later, and after a few more run-ins with him, that same VP signed my layoff notice. I had to laugh at how much easier it was to get him to sign that piece of paper. By then, even though I was missing a bookend, I was very happy he had.

Paris Shower Stall

I've been to Paris many times, but have only ever stayed at one place while I was there: Le Grand Hotel de Champagne. It's a lovely three-star smack dab in the centre of Paris, in the No. 1, a few blocks from The Louvre in one direction and not much further to Notre Dame in the other. Great access to the Metro and the RER (trains). So much for the non-paid advertisement.

For many visits I requested the same room: 202. Like all rooms in the hotel it is small, but right next to the exceptionally small elevator, so that moving bags up from the lobby is more convenient, plus it has windows that open onto the narrow street, rather than onto the inner courtyard that is not much more than a noisy fetid-air utilities shaft.

The room might be small but it is cozy and quiet. However, it has a small bathroom and an even-tinier shower stall. After one incident, I learned to exercise extreme caution while using it.

The hotel had plenty of hot and cold running water. The first time I used the shower, I got in, pulled the thick cold plastic curtain closed behind me, and stood facing the shower, with its hardware lined up just inches in front of my privates, which was coincidentally, where the shower head was also pointing. I pulled the on-off handle towards me and my nether parts were immediately assaulted by a hard jet of hot water. My body's reaction was to push itself back, which then put my bare butt in contact with the cold shower curtain. This then caused my hips to push forward thus whacking my scrotum on the shower handle. Which then caused me to push my hips back until my butt hit the curtain again, which then...

I was doing the "pelvic thrust" right out of the *Rocky Horror Picture Show*'s "Time Warp"! And yes, it was really driving me insane! So much so that to avoid permanent damage to my tender bits I had to eventually launch myself backwards out of the stall and into the bathroom wall and onto the floor, shower curtain torn from its rings and partially wrapped around me, in order to escape.

When I recovered... I had to laugh. And make a mental note to turn the water on and check it before entering the shower stall, carefully.

The Last High - Thai Sticks

It wasn't until entering university that I first tried "illegal" drugs. Alcohol had been, and would always be my "drug" of choice, but in the late '70s, in a university dorm, you could not *not* try pot. And I liked it, a lot.

I know I have an "addictive" personality. If you can try something and it feels good, I'll want to keep doing it. And in some cases crave it. Alcohol, drugs, gambling, fast cars, you name it. However in recognizing this facet of who I am, I've also learned to control it; to control the cravings. I can drink in moderation, or quit for long periods of time. I can go into a casino with only $10 to "waste" on the slots and not drop a penny more. I can resist the urge to buy another motorcycle or sports car. But not so drugs.

By my third year of university, I was using dope more and more. Not yet to pothead status, but enough that I was occasionally missing classes and spinning Led Zeppelin high instead. And I had no desire to quit. My marks were slipping but that did not seem to matter much to me. Luckily, I progressed to Thai Sticks, or to be more precise a single Thai Stick.

I could never be sure what was in it (likely pot, hash oil, and opium) but I got higher than I had ever been, and lower as well. It was like a bad "hippie" movie: flashes and swirls of colours; voices talking and sometimes yelling; dizziness; paranoia; and a deep feeling of apprehension. I lost three days of classes to my trip and its recurring "flashbacks."

When I was finally settled down and clear-headed I vowed right then and there to never again do drugs. It's been offered many times since, but I have never accepted. I've sat in Amsterdam "coffee shops" and had a soft drink and that's all. I don't preach abstinence, and never will. But I practice it.

Which is why I always chuckle to myself when someone responds to some offbeat suggestion of mine with the classic "are you high?" remark. Nope, been there, took the trip, don't ever want to travel there again.

Good Relations

I was once a session chair and speaker at a conference on "procurement" in Toronto. As session chair, I got to give my presentation after the others had done theirs. I noticed how a theme of "the importance of good relations" had emerged, so at the start of my own talk ("Negotiating and Managing Intellectual Property Issues in Contracts") I ad-libbed a bit of a tale based on recent experience, which touched on the theme and would get the crowd engaged.

It went something like this.

One beautiful summer Sunday morning, I was driving back to Ottawa, from an overnight visit in Pembroke with my Mom. Back then, it was a bit of a tradition for me to make pancakes for the family for Sunday breakfast, so I was inclined to make the usual ninety-minute-plus drive as short as possible.

The weather helped. That it was early in the morning and hardly anybody was on Highway 17 at the time helped even more. Driving my 1988 Porsche 928 S4 helped a lot.

Whenever the highway opened up, I'd do the same with the Porsche. On one stretch, just west of the first turn-off to Renfrew, I was traveling pretty fast when a police cruiser, coming towards me but hidden by a gentle hill in the road, suddenly appeared. He immediately "lit up" and a fraction of a second later, we passed each other.

Before we had done so, I laid on the brakes - hard. The Porsche may have had very good acceleration, amazing top speed, and one-"G" cornering ability, but what always impressed me most was how fast the brakes could shed speed when you needed them to. In the brief instant between me seeing him, him lighting up, and us passing, I had already scrubbed away almost all of it to the point where just after we passed I gently pulled off the side of the road, just before the hill. I waited.

In my rear-view mirror I saw him brake hard, turn even harder, and hit the gas. No sooner had he done so, than he realized I was sitting right there waiting for him. So he braked hard and pulled up behind me. I got my licence and registration ready and dropped the window.

Up to it eventually walked one very big police officer.

"Good morning, officer. Nice day, isn't it?"

"Yes, sir. Registration and insurance, please."

"It would be such a shame to spoil such a nice day."

"Sir, do you know how fast you were doing?"

"I may have been going a little fast officer. You see, I was thinking about the pancake breakfast I'll be making for my kids when I get back to Ottawa on this fine day."

"A little fast? Sir, this is going to cost you quite a bit in terms of fine and demerit points."

"Gee, officer that would be a shame. To spoil such a great day after spending a wonderful time with my Mom in Pembroke."

"Sir, you were going very fast."

At this point I notice his name badge. His family name is Polish. Time to change the approach.

"You know officer, my Mom was from Renfrew and my Dad, who passed away a number of years ago, was as well. We have all sorts of relatives in the area. We're probably related."

To that he puts both hands on the car door and bends down to look at me better and to start a conversation about family history. It seems that his family went back as far as mine in the area and when we're a minute into rattling off family names and connections he stops and says "Hey! He's a second cousin of mine too."

"No kidding. Please say hello to him for me the next time you see him."

"I will," he says and straightens back up.

He goes back to his cruiser and soon comes back with my licence and registration, as well as a ticket, which he hands me. He apologizes, and then explains.

"Jeff, I have to give you a ticket because I called it in as soon as I pulled you over. However, I've written it up as 15 kilometres per hour over the limit. It's a $53 fine and two demerit points. That's as low as I can go. Sorry."

I happily took the ticket, shook his hand, and resumed my trip home, convinced more than ever about the importance of good relations.

The conference attendees liked the story. Whether it was because of the story, the presentation that followed, or both, the attendees must have rated me very high, because for years afterwards the conference organizers kept asking me to come back and speak again, which, for whatever reasons, I never did. However, as of just a few years ago, some of their conference brochures were still offering a videotaped copy of my presentation to conference attendees, as part of their registration.

How Much For That Guy in the Window?

My first trip to Hamburg, Germany, was in late winter / early spring of 2003. I returned a year later.

Travel guides describe the city as being "cold." At the time, I thought it was as apt a description of its citizens as its weather. Whether it was the taxi drivers, or the waiters, I found them to be way on the other side of "reserved." Perhaps for that reason, and perhaps because I was traveling solo on those two occasions, I tended to hunker down in my hotel, not explore the city, and generally be sullen.

Well, talk about wrong impressions. In 2005, Bruce, my by-then regular tradeshow booth-mate, joined me. We ventured away from the hotel, and my eyes were opened to what a truly wonderful and fun city Hamburg is.

In 2006, Bruce and I were joined by Steve, who was just starting out on tradeshow duty.

Early in the week we met up with Mark, an American sales guy from a big exhibiting company. Bruce and I had first met him a year or so previously at one of their receptions and, like us, he had a great sense of fun. Steve fit right in.

Part way through the week we were befriended by Maite, a Spanish female researcher working for Boeing in one of their European offices.

On the second day of the show, Maite dropped by the booth and asked us what we were up to that evening. Now we four guys had already decided we were going to visit the Reeperbahn that night. Mark had been there before and would play guide to us three newbies. Maite asked if she could join us, and even after describing what we expected it to be, she was game to join us.

We took a cab to the area and walked the couple of blocks to the actual red-light street. Plastered on the massive entrance to the street were signs warning that no women were allowed past that point (with the exception, of course, of the working girls.) Apparently it's tradition for the girls to throw rocks at any women who wander down the street. Tough crowd!

Ever the gentleman, Mark volunteered to take Maite to an Irish pub a couple of blocks away, where we would meet them after walking the street.

The street was as expected: window after storefront window of working girls in various state of undress, advertising their wares, and attempting to lure customers in. We walked to the end and back – wallets firmly stuck in our pockets. We then joined Mark and Maite at the pub.

It was nearly empty. A couple of Aussies came and went. We had some issues with a group of British football fans, but nothing came of it. Just the five of us and the bartender. Maite had a camera and a number of typical "friends in a pub" pictures were taken. She then asked about the actual street – which we described to her. She said she was disappointed that she did not get to at least see it, and felt it a shame that women were excluded.

Then the proverbial light bulb went off over my head. I noticed that the pub had four ground floor dormer windows, two on each side of the door, facing the street. I took Maite by the arm, and told her to come with me. Walking her out the front door and a bit of a distance up the street to the left, I told her to wait there for two minutes and then walk slowly back to the pub, stopping to look into each of the four windows.

I raced back into the pub and told the guys to get "undressed" – leaving the detail of what that meant to each of them. In practice it

meant down to boxers and briefs, although I briefly toyed with the idea of going *au naturel*. Then we climbed into the windows, one in each, and waited for Maite to walk by, which she took her time doing.

When she did, she was greeted by four semi-naked men, one after the other, showing their stuff and grinning ear-to-ear. Now when that figurative light bulb went off earlier, I had not thought of two things: Maite had a camera (equipped with a real flash) in hand and was very willing to use it (and months later, send us copies); and our "display" would attract a large crowd of women to the front of the pub, all of them cheering and applauding.

They all wanted to know "how much for that guy in the window?"

The Amber Necklace

While visiting Venice with Gen a number of years ago, we happened upon a small shop with a great selection of amber. I'd never really appreciated the range of colours of amber, until we were shown a necklace that showed eight different types.

What caught my attention the most about it was how the colours reminded me of my Mom, and the dresses she typically wore. So we bought it for her. She loved it and it looked great on her.

Flash forward a few years. Unfortunately, Mom was now in a home, pretty much confined to a bed or a wheelchair. We had just sold her house and were holding a big yard sale of all of the remaining contents. Mom was the queen of yard sales. Every Saturday morning she used to hop in the car, and with a purse full of nickels, dimes and quarters, and perhaps even a loonie or toonie, visit as many yard sales as she could. You could tell she was sad to be missing her own sale. Well, not completely missing it.

You see, prior to the sale we'd separated out personal items to be kept, including jewelry. Mom had spent a lot of time over the years as an active buyer of the shopping channel's wares, including hundreds of watches, and tons of costume jewelry. Not knowing what to ultimately do with it all, we'd simply taken it over and stored it temporarily in Mom's closet at the home.

Now the home had rules about how much jewelry, costume or real, could be kept in a room – for good reason. Not be left completely left out of her own yard sale, Mom enlisted the help of a resident or two and held her own room sale. Before staff caught on, she had sold dozens and dozens of items (for small change) and then started to simply give it away. When one cleaning-staff member passed by the supervisor's office with her pockets bulging with loot, the jig was up. The supervisor rounded up as much of it as had not yet walked out of the building and called us.

I went over to the home right away. I understood completely how Mom must have felt: it was her stuff and she was free to do with it as she pleased. She was unable to be at her house as we sold its contents. The supervisor explained the rules and how they were in place to protect the more vulnerable residents who might be taken advantage of. I could see both sides and it was agreed that, for the next few days, Mom would have a box of selected costume jewelry that she could give away as she pleased. She had a lot of fun handing out costume watches, rings and necklaces.

Necklaces! Did the amber necklace's stones not look, at least a bit, like some of those colourful glass ones that Mom was giving away? In a slight panic, we searched through the boxes and luckily came across it, as well as a number of pieces of real gold and diamond jewelry, which we put into a separate jewelry box.

When Mom passed away, most of those pieces were passed down to her grandchildren. However, I still have a few of them, including the amber necklace. I can still picture her wearing it, the colours suiting her perfectly. It means too much to me to let it go.

The Boyfriend Killer

As soon as my oldest daughter reached "dating" age, I tried to cultivate an image of a father who would allow no shenanigans from any of her suitors. Upon first meeting them I'd try to find a way to be casually holding Mr. Aluminum Baseball Bat at the time. Most of the relationships survived that first encounter, but one of them didn't. In fact, I don't think we ever set eyes on one another.

When our kids were younger, I set up a couple of computer workstations down in the basement. They were kitted-out with printers and a scanner and other stuff so that they could do homework and projects, and surf the Web. In that same area of the basement, I had also set up an early version of a home theatre, prophetically equipped with both a couch and a loveseat.

One afternoon, I came home from work earlier than usual. The day before, I had handed down some punishment to my son: he was not allowed to "play" on the computers downstairs until after he had done all of his homework, upstairs in his bedroom, and after I had gotten home and first checked it over. I heard some noise coming from the basement and immediately assumed it was my son, already violating his parole conditions.

So I opened the basement door and yelled at the top of my lungs: "What the hell is going on down there?! Get the hell out of that basement!" and slammed the door. Then I headed upstairs to get out of my work clothes, satisfied I'd probably instilled the fear of death in him. This was confirmed by the sound of him running up the stairs, bursting through the basement door, and heading right out the front door. I was impressed. He must have done the whole trajectory in only five or six strides.

Then I noticed my son looking at me from his bedroom, and my youngest daughter doing the same. Soon afterwards I hear more footsteps and my oldest daughter comes into view. "Daddy!" she says, tears running down her cheeks. "He was just about to kiss me!"

It turns out she had just started seeing a new boy, and decided to bring him home after school. Upon hearing my yell of admonishment, as lips were just about to touch, he apparently turned three shades of white and tore off up the stairs as fast as his legs could save him.

I still don't know who he was. I don't think our paths ever crossed again, as that was his first and last date with my daughter. On the upside, that incident, more than any involving Mr. Bat, firmly established my reputation as the boyfriend killer.

A Crasher's Tale – Part 2

My second greatest crash is set in Paris, France.

I was over, again with a team, to cover the Paris Airshow. Like the Vegas event, and in fact like most such events, half your waking day is usually spent at the show site, and the other half working the receptions in the evenings. Usually the big companies (and governments) do theirs on the Monday and Tuesday of the week, and by Wednesday, things are getting smaller and more intimate. That's not to say they're cheap. In fact, some of the exclusive ones are not to be missed.

A week or so prior to the show I was talking to Tony, a good friend of mine, and member of our Paris team that year. He told me about a discussion he'd had with a university professor (call him "Dr. Keith") in the UK, who was working on some manufacturing technologies that were of interest to us. Dr. Keith had asked Tony if he would be in Paris – which, as it turned out, Tony would. Tony suggested that they get together for dinner later in the week, say on the Wednesday. Dr. Keith said he couldn't that night, as he would be on a yacht on the Seine for a very exclusive party put on by some regional economic development agency in the UK. Tony thought no more about it until he mentioned it to me.

So... armed only with the knowledge that an event on a yacht would be happening one evening, I searched for and found that agency's number and called them. Here's how the call went:

> "Economic development agency."
>
> "Yes, hello. My name is Jeff Mackwood, I'm calling from Canada, my number is XXX, my email address is YYY, and my assistant has told me you have invited me to your event on the Seine. I'd just like to let you know that I've had her cancel all of my other planned engagements for that evening and am now very pleased to accept your invitation."
>
> "Thank you, Mr. Mackwood. We look forward to hosting you."

I repeated my contact info and hung up.

Then I waited for the inevitable return phone call, which went something like this:

"Hello, Mr. Mackwood"

"Yes?"

"We spoke a few minutes ago about our event. It seems there is a problem."

"Yes?"

"You see Mr. Mackwood, I can't seem to find a record of us ever having sent you an invitation."

"I fail to see how this is a problem."

"Well, Mr. Mackwood, it means that you will not be able to attend."

"Oh that is a problem. Especially since Dr. Keith and I have spoken and he is now very much looking forward to meeting with me at this event to discuss matters of mutual economic interest. And not only that, I also indicated to Dr. Keith that I would have Tony, a colleague of mine and someone who has been in serious discussions with Dr. Keith, along with me at your event as my plus one, something I forgot to mention when we spoke earlier. Please see that he's added to the guest list."

After a lengthy pause...

"Yes, Mr. Mackwood."

"And please email me the complete information on your event. My assistant has left for the day and I can't seem to find it in her office. Thank you."

End of call.

Sometimes the bold approach works.

The day of the event arrives and it's a gorgeous, hot, sunny day in Paris and environs. I leave the show a little early to get back to the hotel and then walk over to the yacht, which happens to be moored behind Notre Dame. I'm the first person to board and take a lounger on the top deck after being handed a glass of champagne. Does life get any better?

There's a coach bus hired to bring attendees from the show directly to the yacht. It pulls up at the street above the Seine and the first person to exit is Tony, who pops open an umbrella to shade

himself from the sun, and marches, a la tour guide, other attendees behind, down the inclined roadway to the boat. I could almost imagine some military band accompanying him, perhaps playing the Monty Python theme.

The guests board, hors-d'oeuvres are served, the champagne flows, and eventually the yacht casts off and heads down the Seine. It's not a big crowd, about 80 people in total, and the mood is very relaxed as the boat makes way. Eventually we're called to the dining area and are seated to a five-course, five-star meal. We've also been seated at Dr. Keith's table and part-way through the evening we learn that it's his birthday. Once again ignoring the rule to lay low, I rise and get everyone's attention. I announce and toast Dr. Keith's birthday to great applause and more flowing champagne. Tony and I become the life of the party.

Later that evening, as dinner is over and things have quieted down, Tony and I have retired to loungers on the upper deck. We convince (via a nice tip) a steward to bring us each a fine Cuban cigar and a bottle of very nice port. As we're enjoying them, the yacht passes by the Eiffel Tower, which at that very moment is putting on its flashing light show. A wonderful evening!

Actually it was a wonderful evening for another couple of characters as well. The next day we read in the papers that at that very moment, Tom Cruise was beneath the Eiffel Tower proposing to Katie Holmes. I think we had the better time!

The Robert Grahams

Perhaps because it drives Gen so crazy, I've been wearing "Charlie Sheen" bowling shirts for several years now. I've got a few dozen of the things and wear them for just about any occasion. They're comfortable, and stylish – at least in my books.

I've also got a sizeable selection of Kroon sports coats. These are great looking, good quality, and highly functional articles of clothing. Gen convinced me to buy my first Kroon when we were visiting Montpelier, Vermont for a weekend. I paid full price for that one but have since found many more at great discounts from a variety of online sources.

I have a good friend who's into men's fashion and his kryptonite is Robert Graham shirts. These are amazingly good-looking shirts, with great designs and a wide palette of colours. As mentioned in *Maxi-Me*, it was only because of him that I bought my first Robert

Graham shirt – at a price considerably lower than what he had been paying. He was a little miffed by that.

In the Spring of 2014, Gen and I were again in Florida and made time to hit the Orlando outlet shops. I headed straight for the Robert Graham store. I had a goal: to stock up on a sizeable number of their shirts – enough to last a lifetime – at a great discount. In the back of my mind was the notion that since I was now retired I might not find myself traveling and therefore might never get another chance to do so.

We went on a Tuesday because Tuesday's are seniors' days, meaning an extra 10% off. (Senior is defined as anyone over 50 at those outlets.) The store was empty except for the salesman and me, so I got the chance to try on dozens and dozens of shirts. I had three criteria for choosing a particular shirt: obviously the look and fit came first, the bottom-line discounted price (including multiple purchase discounts) next, and the initial full retail price (typically $250 and more per shirt) was last. I figured I'd use my entire duty-free allowance of roughly $800 (for re-entry into Canada) on those shirts, and I wanted to maximize the number of great-looking, high-quality pieces.

Through careful selection, and the additional seniors' discount, I was able to buy thirteen of them within my duty free limit. That worked out to just over $61 per shirt. I was happy and had to share my happiness with my friend. So I texted him the good news. "I hate you. You are no longer welcome to visit," was his response.

I knew it was in jest, but you know, I wouldn't have found fault with him had it not been. I did send him another text saying the salesman had told me another Robert Graham outlet store was supposedly about to open much closer to his home town. "Okay. I still hate you, but you are now welcome to spend the night." And Gen and I did, on our drive back to Canada.

The Sea of Tits

My first visit to Munich, Germany was in the month of May during a spell of gorgeous weather. The beer gardens were packed, and the locals flocked to the parks to soak up the rays. My buddy Bruce and I decided to do both.

We were staying at the Hilton Munich Park, which sits right next to the huge *Englischer Garten* (English Garden). It has a large manmade lake, artificial streams, meadows, and nearly a thousand acres of space.

We got into shorts and sandals, grabbed blankets from our hotel rooms, and headed over. First stop was the beer garden where the drink du jour was *radler* – a shandy made with half beer (in this case the in-season *maibock*) and carbonated lemonade. A couple of large steins each hit the spot. Then it was off to a big open field to enjoy the sun. We spread out our blankets, took off our shirts and soaked it all in. The grass was long, thick, and green. Wildflowers poked up between the blades of grass. And all around us, as far as the eye could see, were hundreds and hundreds of topless Teutonic wonders. A veritable sea of tits flowing with the grass and the wildflowers.

It was the perfect setting to drift off into a dreamy state of bliss, aided by the beers.

Sometime later, I was awakened in mid-dream by Bruce. Apparently he had not drifted off like I had. He had decided to explore the park. Now he had returned to get me, all excited. I needed to come with him to the other end of the park. There, he assured me, not only was it topless, but "they" were all completely nude. Hundreds of them.

The remnants of the dream drifted away and I set off with him on the journey to Nudeland. It was quite the hike. We passed by another beer garden along the way, and stopped for a quick fill-up. As we continued our trek, the end of the park could be seen and if you looked closely you could see that, yes, a lot more body parts were on display.

As we got very close, we could see that there was a very clear demarcation line between nude and topless. The line was a narrow and shallow stream that separated that tip of the park from the rest of it, with short footbridges at each end to allow foot traffic from one side to the other – although with a short run you could easily hop the stream without getting wet. It was also apparent, as we approached, that people on the other side were being much "friendlier" with each other than on the side we were approaching from. A lot of bodies were coiled together, and given the sun and heat of the day, it wasn't for mutual warmth.

Bruce was all excited (not that way!) and told me he surely had not been imagining things when he'd been down this way earlier. But something was striking me as a little odd. There seemed to be another difference that I just couldn't put my finger on. Until, as we walked along the path by the edge of the stream, on the "topless" side, we came upon two older gentlemen standing in the stream washing off each other's private parts.

I turned to Bruce and asked if he'd gotten this close to the stream and this end of the park before going back to get me, or whether he'd determined it was all nude from more of a distance. From a distance, he said. Oh. Then I guess he had not noticed that all of the couples on the nude side were man-on-man and woman-on-woman?

Not that there is anything at all wrong with it, but clearly it was not what Bruce had expected, at least not judging by the look on his face as reality set in. He was all too happy to have us return to the other end of the park, to our blankets, and to the more comforting, for us, sea of tits.

You're Still An A-Hole Watson!

The other day it was 2014 municipal election time in the Province of Ontario. In Ottawa, the incumbent mayor, Jim Watson, was re-elected with an overwhelming majority of the vote. Clearly the electorate likes him, and I admit that he does a pretty good job of things. However I still hold a deep-seated grudge against him and have taken the opportunity to let him know it, from time to time.

If you've ever been at a sporting event (football, baseball, basketball, hockey) in Ottawa, and at some point during the game Jim Watson was introduced or shown on the big screen, and soon thereafter was heard a booming voice from on high yelling, "You're still an Asshole, Watson," that was almost certainly me. Whether it was back when he was a lowly city councillor, or his first period as mayor, or when he was a provincial Member of Parliament and cabinet minister, or during his most-recent period as mayor. I found it hard to resist.

The reason goes back to the start of my third year in university.

When we returned from summer break, those of us who'd been on the same residence floor the year before learned that one of our res-mates would not be returning. Peter, a biology major, had taken his own life weeks before. We were heartbroken. He was a great guy and had occupied the room next to mine. He played and partied with us, and he took photos for the residence newspaper and yearbook. I still have prints of photos he took of me and others when we were all costumed-up for trick-or-treating. We did not know why he took his life, but we knew he would be greatly missed.

So a few of us proposed to purchase and have installed a commemorative plaque at the end of the floor's hallway. It would probably still be there today, decades later, had it not been for Jim Watson. You see, for reasons that I could never understand, Jim objected to us wanting to commemorate "some guy who killed himself." He opposed it strongly and, already the politician, convinced the floor newbies to go along with him. The plaque idea died.

I told Jim Watson at the time that he was an asshole. And that's why I've publicly bellowed out a reminder to that effect many times since. I'm pretty sure that he doesn't know it's been me all of these years; at least not until he reads this story.

Obituary

Unlike Gen, I almost never read the obits. I rely on her to bring the ones for people who we might have known to my attention. She never would have done so when Claude Lafrance's appeared in July of 2014, but I couldn't help but see the article in *The Ottawa Citizen* that covered his amazing life, and death.

I'd known Claude for a number of years as a result of us both being in the aerospace business. We had served together on the Board of Directors of Aerospace North America, and I was struck by what a true gentleman he was. We never spoke of his past accomplishments, and as I sat reading his obituary I learned that they were numerous and far more than just impressive.

His RCAF flying career, including action in the Korean War, was extensive, and probably explained why I'd never seen Claude even come close to losing his cool, even during a pretty acrimonious discussion during one Board meeting.

But what I'll remember the most about Claude was the time, soon after 9/11, when we ended up travelling together to the same event. At some point during the multi-flight trip we were passing through security together, with me in the lead. There were armed soldiers everywhere and you could feel the tension. There was no "please and thank you," just barked commands. There also did not seem to be any profiling of passengers. Just complete randomness on top of chaos.

I passed through relatively unscathed, with just an extra pat-down or two. Claude, on the other hand, was chosen for one of the more detailed searches. Keep in mind that this is a Caucasian grey-haired man in his mid-seventies, extremely distinguished-looking in his business suit, with a pleasant smile on his face. He was stripped down to his undershirt, frisked several times, had all of his possessions emptied onto a table and inspected. He was questioned at length and in the end simply told to gather his stuff and move on.

Throughout it all, he remained completely unfazed. "It is what it is," he said to me once he'd put himself and his stuff back together. That poise left an enduring impression on me. His obituary called him "the epitome of a true gentleman." Too bad there's no word that means "more than the epitome" because Claude Lafrance was it.

Lucky's Lake Swim

One of the most interesting and fun open water swims has to be Lucky's Lake Swim. It's held every day of the week except for Sundays, all year long, at Lucky Meisenheimer's estate on Lake Cane in Orlando, Florida. From 2008 to 2010, I managed to do the swim seven times. I was tempted to stop after my first.

Lake Cane is typical of any body of water in that part of Florida: full of wildlife. That includes the possibility of gators. In fact, Lucky plays that part up quite well. The first-timer badge that you get for completing the one-kilometre swim (across and back) has a gator's head in its centre, with the words "enter the food chain." There's an alligator cast in metal lying in the water where you enter. And, at least when I swam, Lucky carried a knife in a pull buoy tucked between his legs "just in case." But there's never been a problem – at least not to date.

During the week, the swim starts at 6:30am. When I did my first swim it was still pitch black outside. And foggy. So foggy you could not see more than 50 feet ahead. But the water conditions were great: calm with a slight chill – just the way I like it. There were only a half-dozen or so swimmers and Lucky arrived at the dock last. He gave his usual quick safety talk and then, seeing as I was the only newbie that morning, had two special tips for me: head in that direction (pointing into the darkness to our left) and swim to the beach with a dock and a single light at the end of the attached boathouse (none of which was visible due to the fog); and do not swim in that direction (pointing to our right, again into darkness) because that's where the swamp is, and who knows what you might find, or might find you. Before I could change my mind, Lucky pushed off.

At first, I tried to follow him, but he is faster than me and I quickly lost sight of him. The swim is only 500 metres in each direction, assuming you stay in a straight line. Even with good visibility, I need to correct my course many times during a typical swim. Five hundred metres should have taken me about seven-and-a-half minutes to complete. After about 15 minutes, I realized I must be off course. I stopped and floated in what was probably the middle of the lake. Still dark and still foggy. I swam some more and started to run through a lot of weeds. I think I was in the swamp.

Again, it's pitch black. You can hear. You can feel. But you can see nothing; not even the hand in front of your face. So I pick another course and set out again. After another 15 minutes, it starts to lighten up and I can make out shapes along the shoreline. I eventually come to what I'm sure is the beach. I turn back towards Lucky's place. By then I can clearly see his two big spotlights beckoning me back.

By the time I get back, the rising sun has broken through the fog. Encouraged, I set out for another crossing and back, this time without difficulty. I can see the other end of the lake and far shoreline where I had swum along the first time. Once back safe and sound, it was up to

Lucky's house, where I was given my log sheet and first-crossing badge. I also got to sign the huge white wall of his house, as thousands had done before me. It was only later that I started to think about how fortunate I had been that morning.

But a few months later, when I found myself again in Orlando, I returned for a Saturday morning crossing. There were many more swimmers – probably 60 or so. I was talking to one newbie who was more than a little concerned about wildlife. (The cast gator wasn't helping!) But she started the swim anyhow, with a friend. I did two crossings that day and most memorable was the huge water snake that slid by my face as I was breathing on my right side. I felt several feet of cool slitheriness as it passed across my cheek and mouth. Yikes. I stopped to watch it swimming away from me, head up as though nothing had happened. My heart rate was now slightly elevated!

I finished that crossing ahead of the newbie I'd been talking to earlier. As she stood in the water at the end, I asked how it had gone. She said okay. I mentioned my encounter with the snake. Had she had seen it? For some reason she got angry at me, saying I should not be inventing stories to scare people like her. In one of life's great coincidences, it was exactly then that another snake, probably slightly smaller than the one I'd seen, swam by right behind her. When I tried to point it out, she got even angrier. Then her friend told her to look, and she did.

I'd never seen anyone walk on water before then!

Bavarian Beer Tour

At a conference in Munich one spring, my colleagues and I knew we'd have a whole day to kill at the end of the week, before we were to fly back home. So a plot was hatched mid-week. Throughout our stay, the Hilton was undergoing a huge renovation. There had been noise and dust everywhere, so we figured we'd take a road trip and get away from it for a day.

I called my assistant and asked her to book a five-series BMW sedan, as there would be five of us taking the trip: Jim, the designated driver, my regular travel buddy Bruce, Catherine and her husband Bernard, and myself. Jim, the only one not staying at the same hotel as us, would pick up the car from a place across from his hotel and meet us at the Hilton at 7am on Friday.

After an early breakfast, the four of us gathered at the appointed hour at the Hilton's front entrance, and Jim pulled up in a 500-series Mercedes! Seems that they were all out of Bimmers. I hop in the front as co-pilot, and the others in back.

Bernard was the most forward-thinking of the bunch, because he'd brought along a big paper shopping bag filled with bottles of beer. Apparently, his research had told him that it was perfectly legal to drink beer in a car in Germany, so long as the driver didn't. Jim was a lifelong teetotaler.

It wasn't long before we were on the autobahn. Jim decided to see what the big Mercedes could do and we were soon moving at warp speed. Of course, we only veered into the left lane to pass, but even at the speed we were going we weren't catching up to many other vehicles. Just the opposite, as a number of supercars went screaming past us. Other than on my superbike and in my Porsche, I've never gone that fast in a motor vehicle. How fast? When I get to a certain speed (150 mph) my eyes start to water. Not from the wind. Rather it's a natural fear-of-dying response – at least natural for me. And my eyes were watering that fine Bavarian morning.

It seemed like only a few beers and little time before we were pulling off the autobahn and taking smaller roads to our first destination: Neuschwanstein Castle. This nineteenth-century palace was built by King Ludwig II of Bavaria and was the inspiration for the look of the famous Disney Castle. The setting is amazing: built into hills overlooking the valley below. We parked at the bottom and started the walk to the top.

Of course, we had to stop part-way up the road for a mid-morning meal of beer and venison stew. We then toured the amazing castle and surroundings and headed for our next destination: Ludwig II's Linderhof Palace. But along the way we took a wrong turn and ended up crossing the border into Austria. Not a problem; it gave us an opportunity to have lunch and more beers at a roadside restaurant. We eventually arrived at the palace, marvelling at its fountains and pools and lavish furnishings and trappings. Old Ludwig sure had great taste!

Back in the Mercedes and cruising along country roads, we came to a nice-looking village. Time for dinner, and more beers. We'd been eating typical Bavarian fare all day and there was no sense changing now. Sausages, stews, potatoes, schnitzel and strudel. Yum! By then, we'd run out of Bernard's bagged beer, so we found a store, stocked up and headed back to the hotel.

We rolled up to the Hilton at 7 pm, bellies still full and feeling more than a bit tipsy. The entrance was bustling with limos and folks arriving in formal wear as far as the eye could see. As I got out of the car, Ingrid the desk clerk, who'd been looking after us all week, was there to hold my door. "Nice car," she said. I gave her a one-minute précis of our day's adventure. "Well," she said, "I hope you've saved room for our party." Party?

She explained that after months of renovations, the hotel was having its grand re-opening party. Everyone who was anyone in Munich had been invited. Three hundred models were hired to mingle with the guests. Bands and orchestras were brought in. Every single ballroom, meeting room, lobby, bar and restaurant would be filled with music, and free drink and food. As hotel guests, we were automatically invited. Had we not seen the invitations slipped under our doors that morning? Apparently we'd left before they were delivered.

We got ourselves cleaned up and presentable again and spent the rest of the night indulging in one amazing bash. I found a bartender who retrieved a bottle of single malt from storage and kept it handy behind his bar, just for me. Each room had a theme: musically and food-wise. My two favourites were the seafood room, where shrimps were piled higher than me and chefs shucked raw oysters all night long, to be served with fine champagne. And then there was the main ballroom where an orchestra played while guests helped themselves from a moat at the bottom of a 20-foot-high volcano down from which poured liquid chocolate, to be drizzled on an assortment of fresh fruit.

It was all very excessive, but seemed quite apropos in light of our earlier visits to Ludwig's palaces. My only regret was being stuffed so much on the road trip, I could not indulge as much as I might have back at the hotel.

The Idiot Vote

Not counting student groups and the like, I've only ever run for elected office once in my life. And while I'm somewhat loath to say never again, that experience has certainly not convinced me I want more of the same.

I was born and raised in Pembroke, and returned there to start my post-education career and to begin a family. I felt a need to return something to the community. I had been involved in helping with other candidates' campaigns, and served on the city's planning board, so I decided it was time to put my own name forward and stand for office, for one of the city councillor positions.

I ran my campaign on the cheap, because cheap was all I could afford. My campaign platform was based on providing an economic environment that would allow young people to establish themselves in the city, rather than having to leave for greener pastures elsewhere. I had buttons and pamphlets made and with Gen's help, canvassed door-to-door.

The all-candidates' meeting was a big event, with would-be mayors and councillors all sharing the same stage. I put a lot of work into my speech, dedicating a significant portion of it to addressing the issues of the francophone community, in French. I was the only candidate to do so, which was surprising to me given that at least one candidate was a francophone himself and 30% of the electorate was francophone. I received more than my fair share of questions from the audience (in both languages) and received very positive feedback from the crowd afterwards.

On election night, my Dad and I were at city hall to watch the results get posted. In the end, I received just over 800 votes. It would have taken 1,600 or so to be elected to one of the eight positions. I was the next closest candidate. On the face of it one might have said it was a good start – something to build on for the next one. I was half way there! But I looked in the other direction – down the list to see who was behind me.

The next closest candidate had just over 400 votes and there were two more with a couple of hundred or so. This left me extremely discouraged. While I know this might not sound right, the fact was that those candidates that I "beat" were complete idiots. They had nothing to offer and it showed. However, they had gathered a sizeable number of votes. So to my mind, if I subtracted their numbers from mine, I figured I had just barely beaten the idiot vote.

As that realization was sinking in, Dad could see how hurt I was. At that moment the local Hydro Commissioner stopped by and offered his "advice": "Next time, don't speak f'ing French and you might stand a chance."

I don't know who was more surprised in the instant after that: the Commish who saw my right roundhouse about to connect with his jaw; me for having launched the aforementioned haymaker; or Dad for being on the ball and fast enough to deflect it enough that I missed connecting by a fraction of an inch. Nobody else in that crowded hall saw it.

That's when I concluded that elected office was not for me. It left a bad enough taste that, when it came time to make a final decision whether to accept a job in Ottawa and move away from Pembroke, almost certainly forever, it was on the list of pros and cons to consider. I accepted the job, memories of the idiot vote etched forever in my mind.

Stroke Two – I Smell Curry

In *Stroke One – Having a Sharon Stone*, I talked about my experience with having a hemorrhagic stroke – a brain bleed. One of the concerns with that type of stroke is that the blood that has leaked into the brain can lead to the much-more-common ischemic stroke. The drugs I took during my recovery helped to prevent this from happening.

A few days after the initial stroke, I was taken to an operating room where I had a cerebral angiogram done. In this procedure, a doctor inserts a catheter into the femoral artery (down in your groin) and threads it up to the carotid artery in your neck. A dye is released that shows the details of all of the blood vessels in the brain as X-rays are taken. Sounds simple.

However, before the procedure you have to sign a waiver

acknowledging you have been told and understand the risks, which include a lot of things up to and including death. The catheter could break, or it could dislodge some plaque from the inside of a blood vessel, both of which could lead to trouble, as could a negative reaction to the dye.

But mine went off without a hitch. There's a warm, bordering on hot, feeling inside your head when the dye is released, but it fades away fast. The images showed that things were looking good, that the initial bleed had sealed itself, and that there were no other visible anomalies.

A bonus was that I talked the doc into doing a side trip with the catheter to near the heart to look for any plaque and he said everything looked good.

Flash forward several weeks. It's a Friday. I'm back in that same operating room, and having signed the same waiver, I'm about to have a routine follow-up angiogram done. But this time it is far from hitch-free. Before the dye is even released, my blood pressure crashes. Just before I lose consciousness, I hear a code being called. The room fills with multiple docs, nurses, respiratory techs etc. I wake up in a recovery room way past the time when I should have already left the hospital had everything gone okay.

They got me walking slowly up and down the hall, and on multiple occasions I experienced amazing olfactory hallucinations: I swore I could smell the strongest, most delicious, curry!

After a few hours, the smells stopped and I was cleared to check out. Gen took me home and put me to bed. She was told to wake me up a few times during the night to make sure everything was okay. The first time she did, she leaned over and asked if everything was okay. To which I replied: "Who are you? Where am I? Who am I?" and a bunch of questions like that. Other than being able to speak, I had absolutely no memories of anything. None at all.

After she questioned me a little longer, she took me back to the hospital where they ran tests on me. Basic memory quizzes like, "I want you to remember the colour red," and a few seconds later, "What colour were you supposed to remember?" to which I replied, "huh?"

This went on for several hours. Then, all of a sudden, a single memory popped into my head. I don't remember what it was, but Gen confirmed it to be a true memory that I should have. A minute or so later, another one popped into my head. And when I say popped, I liken it to a kernel of corn popping. Then another. And another. And another. Until this built into a torrent of memories flooding back into my consciousness. Slamming into my head. It was a rush like no other. And when the popping stopped, my memories had returned.

The theory is that somehow that angiogram led to an ischemic stroke, which led to the memory loss, from which I very luckily made a full recovery.

Actually, that's not true. You see, it's pretty much impossible to know you've lost a memory if you don't know you've lost it. Over subsequent years, I would frequently have people approach me who, prior to 1999, I knew quite well, and who had shared experiences with me. And I remembered none of it. For years and years I faked it, not wanting to admit to having memory "deficits." But later on I confided in family, and then friends, and now with the world.

The process of identifying story ideas (based on my memories) going back to my earliest childhood has been incredibly therapeutic. While not quite like popcorn, totally unexpectedly I have been able to retrieve recollections of events that I had completely forgotten since 1999. In some cases, it has taken the memories of others to trigger my own; in other cases, like visiting Chicago in 2014, being in a certain place has done the trick.

While I was never terrified at the time that the memory loss happened, I think I have at least a sense of the confusion and frustration that patients with illnesses like Alzheimer's must feel. A small bonus to having my second stroke.

Now if only I could find an Indian restaurant with curry dishes as good as what I imagined!

Fight or Flight

I'm not a violent person. I've rarely been involved in a fight of any kind, and would far prefer a peaceful solution to any conflict. But I'm not a pacifist. It's just that I have a "digital" temper: it's either a "0" (fully off) or "1" (fully engaged). And it takes either a lot of prodding to move me to a "1" – or a special set of circumstances where I automatically do so.

I've often told my wife that if there's ever a crazed gunman on the loose in a public place, I'd be the one person running hard towards him. I don't know exactly why, but I've always known I'm wired that way. I can't run away if I can stop others from being hurt or killed.

Perhaps the genesis for this was the 1989 École Polytechnique massacre in Montreal of female students by a lone gunman (who I refuse to even name). Images of those murdered women are forever engraved in my mind. The massacre horrified me and made me very angry. But what upset me even more was that, early in the killing rampage, the gunman entered a room and ordered all of the men to leave. To a person they did, leaving the women behind to be gunned down. I could not understand how they could have done that. How could one, or two, or more of them, not storm the shooter? Yes, risking their lives, but more importantly, and almost certainly, saving many more by taking him down?

I've never been in that situation, so I can't for certain say how I would react. But on many other occasions I've experienced an automated "fight" rather than "flight" response, so I'm pretty sure what would happen.

On a trip to San Francisco, a few years prior to the Poly killings, I took a city bus from my hotel to a record store across town and back. On the way back, I boarded the bus and noticed there was only the driver and one passenger aboard. A quick glance at the passenger, who was sitting in the front right seat, told me he was very ill with what was likely AIDS. When recounting this story, I've often referred to him as "an old gay guy" but while, in that locale in that year, in that condition, he almost certainly was one of the very unfortunate members of the gay community to become infected, I'm now pretty sure it was the ravages of the disease that made him look much older than he was. In any case, he was emaciated and looked very frail. I'll refer to him as the passenger.

I took a seat two back from his.

At the next stop, what I would describe as two punks got on. One sat immediately behind the passenger and directly in front of me, and the other in the seat opposite the passenger, directly behind the driver.

As soon as the bus pulled away from the curb, I noticed the punk ahead of me pull a knife from his right coat pocket and start to move it towards the passenger while his left hand reached around into the passenger's jacket, likely going for his wallet. At the same time, he moved his head forward, saying something to his intended victim, which I could not make out over the bus noise.

Whether the right move or not, I immediately went to a "1" – full fight mode. It was pure instinct and not, in all honesty, a calculated conscious decision. As the punk's knife hand moved towards the passenger I got up, leaned forward, grabbed the back of the punk's head and with all the force I could muster drove his face into the metal handrail across the back of the seat in front of him. You could hear his nose and likely other things break. He collapsed in a heap.

His partner started to get up. I rose to my full 6'3" height and yelled (more like an enraged growl) to not even try it. Then I told the bus driver to pull over, which he did, and opened the door. The punk's partner fled the bus and kept running. I grabbed the limp punk by the jacket collar, dragged him off the bus, and flopped him facedown onto the sidewalk. I don't think this improved his looks one bit!

I got back on the bus and the driver pulled away.

Adrenalin rush over, I dropped to a "0" again and asked the passenger if he was okay. He was shaking like a leaf – and I was starting to as well. He told me that just before I had dealt with him, the punk whispered in his ear that he was going to kill him if he moved. He thanked me for what I had done. Through it all, the bus driver never said a thing. The bus started to fill up and several stops later, I got off in front of my hotel. Still trembling, I headed to the bar.

A few years after Poly, I was in Washington D.C. It was a Thursday evening and there was a bar downtown that I was told had a great happy-hour special and would eventually be jam-packed, as it always was on Thursdays.

As was my custom, I exchanged pleasantries with the two bouncers at the door as I entered. I'd "bounced" for four years during my university days in order to pay some of the bills, and knew it was always a good thing to make friends with the doormen. I found a seat at the bar, and struck up a conversation with the bartender, who was working that end.

Into my second beer, a fellow took the empty seat beside me. My Spidey senses started tingling. The crowd was uniformly done up in business attire, but this fellow was sporting grubby beyond-casual, and smelled the part as well. Now I know that it's not right to judge a book by its cover, but this one told a story of potential trouble.

He orders a beer and pays for it with a few ones.

The bartender turns his back to ring it in. The cash register pops open. As soon as it does, the guy beside me pulls a knife from his pocket and starts to reach for the bartender – who, I think, sees him making his move in the mirror in front of him.

Again on pure instinct, just as Mr. Trouble starts to reach over the bar, and has himself in an unbalanced position, I reach over, grab the back of his head and help unbalance him even more – face-first into the bar.

Same broken-face, out-like-a-light effect as with the bus punk. Down he goes in front of the bar.

The bartender is now fully turned towards me, watching the doormen rush through the crowd (a crowd that doesn't seem to even notice what's just happened). I stand with my hands in the "I give up" position and maybe it's because they recognize me from earlier, or maybe the bartender's pointing down to Mr. Trouble on the floor, but they never lay a hand on me.

They quickly removed Mr. Trouble from the bar (to where I don't know) and came back to get the quick story on what happened. By now, the bartender handed me another beer, saying it was on the house, along with anything else I might want that night.

Again, I hope I'm never again in such a situation, or worse. But if I am, I'm pretty sure that my wiring will once again choose fight over flight.

The Pearls

Over the years, I've forgotten my wedding anniversary a few times. I've been away on business for some. But I think I've managed to do okay with the big ones.

For our 25th, Gen and I and our two daughters, celebrated in Spain. So five years later, with the 30th fast approaching, I figured I'd have to do something at least comparable.

With four days to go, I still had nothing. It was a Friday and the anniversary was the following Tuesday. But I had a kernel of an idea. I looked up the anniversary "gift" for 30 years and discovered it was pearl. In all the times I'd brought home gifts, I don't think pearls were one of them. So she probably did not have any.

So I called up Russ, a golf buddy and jeweler. Could he help? I knew nothing about pearls, so Russ gave me the clams-eye view. As well as quality, size affects the value. Russ had a selection of pearls in stock and proposed a black pearl pendant and matching earrings, all in custom-made gold settings, with a few diamonds thrown in on the pendant. I gave him my rough budget. He said for that amount he'd go with a 12 mm or so pearl for the pendant and 9 mm for the earrings.

"Great! Let's do it," I said. To which he asked when I needed it by. "Next Tuesday, around noon." Silence. "I was thinking more like which month from now," he finally said. Hmmm. He told me that in order to make it by next Tuesday he'd need to disappoint a couple of brides. My turn to go silent for a spell. "So what's your point, Russ?" I eventually said. He said he'd see what he could do. I knew he'd come through.

So I set about making the other plans.

I booked a table at our favourite little restaurant. I told John, the owner, what was up and that I'd be making arrangements for flowers for the table to be sent over before dinner. I called a florist, told him the occasion, gave him my credit card info and date and time of delivery, and told him to go nuts, so long as there was enough room left on the table for food.

Pearls? Check (or partial check). Resto? Check. Flowers? Check. That just left ... music. Hmmm...

The first dance at our wedding had been to Denver and Domingo's "Perhaps Love." So I made a few calls. Could I hire a country singer / guitar player, and an opera singer, who could rehearse the song in time for a Tuesday performance? Turns out not, at least not according to everyone I called, late on a Friday afternoon. Darn! (I now know someone who could have pulled it off.) So I bought the CD (I only had a vinyl version in my collection) and put a copy onto my iPod Touch. I called John to see if I could plug it into their sound system. He said no problem; they use an iPhone all the time.

So it was (mostly) set.

On the way home from work, I stopped off at a jewelry store. As I said, I had no idea about pearls, and while I knew that Russ would give me a great deal, I was a bit concerned because he was only working off a rough budget, and that meant there was potentially lots of upwards slack. The jewelry store only had one black pearl in stock at that time. They'd cleared out their stock with a sale. The last piece left was a pendant, set in gold, without diamonds, and with a 9.5 mm pearl. Even on sale, they wanted two-thirds of what I'd given Russ as my rough budget. And he was planning on a 12 mm pearl just for the pendant. Call me now a bit concerned.

On Sunday night, Russ called to say that over the weekend he'd made the molds, mixed, melted and poured the gold, and the settings were now ready. He ended up having to use more gold than he originally planned. If I dropped by his place on Tuesday morning they'd be ready. I said I would, cheque book in hand. My concern over price rose a bit more.

On Tuesday morning, I'm at Russ' place and he starts off by telling me that he'd decided to use much larger pearls than originally planned. He said he'd had his in a safe for a few years now and that he felt like using them. I was touched, but still worried about price. He then told me the pendant's pearl measured 19.9 mm and each of the earrings clocked in at 14.0 mm. To be honest, at that point the hand with the cheque book in it was starting to shake. He then produced the set, in a wonderful case, and said he'd thrown in a gold chain for the pendant as well. He explained how to handle and care for pearls but by then I was in agony.

"How much do I owe you?" I blurted out. When he told me the amount, I thought I must have momentarily blackedout and missed a digit. He repeated the number. No, I'd heard right the first time. He wanted an amount less than my rough estimate. In deep puzzlement, I wrote out the cheque. I asked if he could also provide me with an appraisal for insurance purposes. It came as absolutely no surprise to me how much higher it was when I got it a few weeks later, such was the incredible deal that he'd given me.

Any thoughts of guilt at having accepted such amazing generosity from a friend were forgotten at dinner the next day. We arrived on time to be seated at our chosen table, with a huge and gorgeous flower arrangement on it. John served us personally and the food was incredible as always. Just after appetizers, I presented the pearls to Gen, which she wore for the rest of the meal. She loved them! (I had made sure that the dress she chose to wear that night would match – such is the power we husbands hold when asked "how does this look?") After dessert, I nodded to John and he played "Perhaps Love" from my iPod that I'd slipped him earlier. As the song started, volume raised on the sound system, Gen started to say "Isn't that...?" and I rose and asked her to dance. We did. And part-way through, I called for everyone's attention and told them it was our 30th anniversary and this had been our first dance at our wedding. Everyone clapped and Gen shed a tear or two. (I might have stepped on her toes.)

I've told this story to a number of women since then and they've all said how terrific that must have been. I've also told it to a number of husbands. They've pretty much all wanted to kill me, especially when the women I've told were their wives.

Recollections of the Hofbrauhaus

I'm pretty sure that just about every visitor to Munich, Germany stops by the Hofbrauhaus at least once, and for good reason. It's got beer, food, music and tons of atmosphere. I've never missed a chance to drop in.

The most memorable of visits was with Bruce, my regular travel colleague. It was mid-week and the place was not packed. We were able to take a seat at the table nearest the house band. That one is reserved for "regulars" (i.e. locals) most nights, but this time it was open. We joined quite an eclectic mix.

There were a couple of newlyweds from Japan. Their English was as good as my Japanese, so we communicated mostly by hand signs, gestures and lots of smiling and nodding of heads. As the steins of beer flowed, we seemed to communicate even better. They were good fun.

There was also a Canadian couple from Halifax. They had won an "all-inclusive" trip to Munich through a local radio station contest. They brought a great down-east charm to the table. Both were good beer drinkers, but by the end of the night Bruce and I were (sorta) helping her to load him into a taxi.

But the real treat was the pair of retired American gentlemen from the mid-west. They had known each other professionally for years. One owned a chain of hardware stores and the other a nail company. One sold nails to the other, and over the years a friendship developed. They started traveling and vacationing together with their wives. But every so often, like a previous month-long visit to Scotland, the wives would beg out and the boys would hit the road together. This trip was devoted to a month in Germany.

We had a hoot listening to all their travel adventures.

Bruce and I ordered and dug into some plates of German fare, washed down by big steins of beer. The Americans bought everyone a round of beers and we reciprocated. By the way, if you're with a big group, make sure you all order at least one round of beers at the same time, and then marvel at your server's ability to carry them all to your table at once. The band was pumping out all the polka classics, and encouraging everyone to drink drink drink. We'd arrived a little late in the evening but by the time the place was closing I was down three litres. More impressively, Bruce was down five.

That's why I said we sorta helped our fellow-Canadian with her husband. It was more like me helping her husband into the first taxi, and then me making sure that Bruce made it safely into ours.

Touristy as all get out (I've been there when a half dozen tour buses had offloaded), Munich's Hofbrauhaus is still very much a must-visit destination.

Singapore Satisfaction – Part 2

At the conclusion of the first part of this tale, we had arrived at our hotel in Singapore, sans luggage, but deeply satisfied with how helpful Singapore Airlines had been (in contrast to Air Canada). It was nearly midnight and we were soon asleep.

The next day, the Sunday, I was due to give a speech at 11:00 that morning. But Air Canada had messed up our luggage and I had no business clothes to wear. I remembered there was a Marks and Spencer just up the road from the hotel, so Gen and I got over there by 10:00. The store was closed. It would not open until 10:30 that day. That would be too late.

Off in the distance, a clerk was working at a cash register. I called to him through the security fencing. He hurried over and I described my predicament. No problem, sir. He opened the door to let Gen and I in, closed it behind us and called for one of his colleagues to help as well. The two of them had me completely outfitted in no time flat. I'm talking every stitch of clothes: underwear and socks, shoes, pants and belt, shirt and tie, and jacket. It all looked great, and except for the shoes which were a little tight but the best they could do, everything fit well.

A manager happened by while the store was still closed and her only reaction was that she hoped her staff had treated us very well. The clerk cashed me out (Gen stayed to shop for herself) and asked where I needed to be. I had 25 minutes to be in front of a podium at a hotel several long blocks away. I'd be a bag of sweat if I ran. He pulled out a cell phone and said to follow him. He made a call while we found our way through a delivery hallway to a rear exit. A taxi pulled up. It was his cousin and he would get me to my meeting on time, which he did by somehow avoiding the morning traffic.

Later that evening, workday done and Gen and I sipping slings, I composed a message on my laptop to the M&S store manager praising his staff and the amazing service they'd provided that morning.

My bag showed up late that night and was delivered to the hotel. Gen's came in the next day. In both instances, there were again apology messages attached to them from Singapore Airlines. We never ever heard anything from Air Canada.

Pain Relief

When I travel, I pack a pretty good med kit: pills, antiseptics, bandages, that sort of thing. I almost never use it. But on our first trip to Mexico it proved to be very valuable.

We were checking in to the resort late in the afternoon and Gen and I could not help but notice that the young female desk employee was in obvious agony. She was trying her best to tough it out, but the creases in her forehead, red eyes, and gritting of teeth told us something was really wrong.

Her English was only really good enough to handle the check-in procedure and when we asked her if she was ok, she was either too proud, embarrassed, or scared to respond. Scared because I'm sure that time off from work would mean no pay, or maybe even loss of job. Her co-worker came over and in hushed tones translated for us. As near as we could tell, she had had a terrible sinus headache for a couple of days and it was getting worse.

We asked if she'd taken anything for it. She had nothing to take. I asked Gen (who's a nurse) what she thought and as near as she could tell it was indeed a serious sinus congestion – and possibly an infection. There was nothing we could do for an infection (I carry antibiotics but those are a personal prescription). However, back then I also carried the old, but extremely effective, version of Tylenol Sinus.

So I went into my med kit and pulled out six pills. Through her co-worker she was told to take two now, two more at bedtime, and two more when she woke up the next day. We told her we'd drop by the desk at this time the next day to see how she was doing.

The next day I'd only gotten a few steps into the lobby area when she came sprinting over to me and gave me one of the biggest hugs ever. She was smiling from ear to ear and could hardly stop thanking me. Apparently the pills had worked! As effective as the pills had been in making her better, their much stronger effect was in instilling a deep sense of satisfaction in me; it's a feeling that's really hard to beat.

Paintings – The Avenue

I've managed to see many of the world's great paintings, at least those most recognized. The *Mona Lisa*. *The Scream*. *The Night Watch*. *American Gothic*. *Girl with a Pearl Earring*. And *The Voice of Fire*. (That's an Ottawa joke.) But my favourite of all, perhaps familiar to some, is Meindert Hobbema's *The Avenue at Middelharnis*.

Done in 1689, it is considered Hobbema's finest work and depicts a long tree-lined country avenue in the Dutch town of Middelharnis, with its church in the background.

For a number of years, a faded print graced our dining room wall.

It came from Gen's side of the family, and I took little notice of it. Well, I noticed it when it somehow fell from the wall and was slightly damaged. I ended up drawing in a few more seagulls in the upper left corner to cover the small marks. Ironically, apparently that area of the original painting was damaged while undergoing cleaning in the 19th century.

On my first visit to London's National Gallery, I nearly missed it hanging on a wall at the end of one rectangular gallery, so pre-occupied was I at finding paintings by another Dutch artist you may have heard of: Rembrandt. But as I hurried past it, a synapse or two fired in recognition and I came to a dead stop before it. My jaw dropped as I soaked it in.

I remembered Kurt E. Schon's lesson of several years previous (see *Paintings – The Lessons*), and walked to the end of the gallery, turned and faced the painting, and then slowly, step by step, got closer and closer. Of all the paintings I've ever tried this technique on, *The Avenue* has been the best by far. With each step closer comes more and more detail. While the avenue and trees dominate at a distance, as you get closer you notice the hunter and his dog walking towards you. Then it's the farmer tying up small trees to the right. There's a couple standing on the side road that runs off to the right, in front of the farmhouse / barn. As you get closer, you see details of the church and the town's buildings, and people on the avenue in the distance. In the clouds to the left, you see a number of birds. And there's that typical richness of colour and inky blackness of paintings from that period.

Ever since that first encounter, I have always found time to visit the National Gallery and *The Avenue*. I never grow tired of seeing it. In fact just the opposite. And I really can't say that for any other painting.

Chevy Chevette Chills

When I first joined Atomic Energy of Canada, Chalk River Nuclear Laboratories, it was as a shift worker assigned to the NRU Research Reactor (see *D'Oh!*).

During my first year, the company ran a shift bus I could take from home to "The Plant" as it was known. You would do eight-hour shifts: seven night shifts, with two days off, followed by seven evening shifts, with two days off, followed by six day shifts, with four days off – making a 28-day rotation. Start over. The reactor operated every day of the year, so you worked quite a number of company holidays every year. That bus, while not making shift work palatable, at least made it more tolerable. From my end of town to work I could get 50 minutes of sleep each way!

Then the company decided, in its lack of wisdom, to do away with the shift buses. Oh the day-workers would still have bus transportation for many years to come, but not us. Because of the high cost of driving your own car that distance, we scrambled to form car pools with our fellow shift workers. I got in with four other guys and we split up the driving duties.

One of the fellows had a big Ford LTD and we rolled in relative comfort in that. Another had a Chevy Malibu that was a little tight, but still ok. One guy's Volkswagen Vanagon was good-sized, but he hadn't bothered to outfit it with seats other than the two in the front. A picnic table bench was all there was in back. (Seatbelts? Not a chance.) I had a Honda Accord hatchback and I have to admit that I still don't know how the five of us ever fit in that thing. But the worst of all was Gordy's Chevy Chevette hatchback.

It wasn't all that bad in the summer – so long as it wasn't raining so that we could drive with the windows down because the A/C did not work. But in the winter? Well, the reverse was also true: there was no heating either. After one trip up and back when it was -40 degrees out and we almost froze to death, we insisted that Gordy get it repaired. It was so bad that, while we were still breathing, our breath was frosting up the front window as fast as I could scrape it off, while Gordy drove. The three in the back luckily passed out from low-grade hypothermia so did not get to witness the number of times Gordy nearly veered off the road, or into oncoming traffic, during that drive up for a midnight shift.

I think that experience was at least partly responsible for my deciding it was time for a career change. I needed to get off shift work before it quite literally killed me.

Turkey Thief

As I type up this brief tale, another Canadian Thanksgiving long weekend has arrived. Plans to cook a turkey have been made and this triggered a memory of one Thanksgiving past, where some family probably went without turkey, while we had two.

Gen's made a habit of confusing her groceries with the next person's at check-out time. It does not matter if that little plastic separator is on the belt or not, if it's anywhere in the check-out process, from belt to bag, it's fair game.

Take the time when she started feeling up some vegetables and declared them to be "not very fresh." I'm sure she thought they were her veggies, but the poor fellow in line behind her, whose wife had no doubt sent him on the errand, did not know that; after all, he was the one who had picked them out and they were on his side of the plastic separator. Luckily, Gen realized her error and did not tackle him when he yanked his stuff off the belt and headed back to the produce section to replace them.

But her *pièce de resistance* was the year when she got home from buying groceries, including the Thanksgiving turkey, and realized she had two of them. (How you would not notice an extra 25-pound bird still puzzles me.) Her receipt showed that she had only paid for one. Near as we could tell, she had somehow snatched the extra bird from the customer behind her, after it had been scanned and bagged, and somehow placed somewhere within her reach just before she moved away with her own cart of paid-for groceries.

We debated what to do and, in hindsight, probably chose wrong: we kept it and did nothing else. Well, we did stick it in the freezer and a month-and-a-half later, mid-way between Thanksgiving and Christmas turkeys, likely very close to American Thanksgiving, we invited guests over for turkey dinner with all the trimmings.

I told the guests how the bird had come to be on our table. Purloined or not, they all agreed it still tasted great.

The Tradition

Some traditions go back to ancient times. Others? Not so far. Some are deeply rooted in historic events. Others are whimsies created on the spur of the moment to accomplish a specific purpose at a single instant of time. Not buying it? Let me give you a great example.

Bill, a co-worker, and I arrived in Paris a number of years ago on business. Stewart, another member of our group, was to join us later that afternoon. To best pass the time waiting for him, Bill and I retired to my favourite café, from which both Notre Dame and the Eiffel Tower can be seen if you seat yourself at the right sidewalk table.

While I would usually start with a "*pichet de vin*," on this occasion beer seemed much more fitting. Walter, the waiter who had been there for years and who remembered me even after a two-year absence, welcomed me back. I introduced him to Bill and explained that we two Canadians were very thirsty and wanted a couple of beers. Not just regular-size beers but "*grandes bières*." In fact, we told him to bring us the biggest beers they had. Canadian-size, as it were.

And out came two huge steins, which took us a pretty long time to get through. All the better for engaging in that wonderful Paris tradition of people-watching. At one point, Bill and I were actually so distracted by our beers that, I kid you not, when a very pretty Parisienne walked past us and we failed to notice her, she stopped, and cast a scornful gaze at us. When I noticed her and realized what she was doing, I understood the problem immediately. You see the tradition goes both ways: one watches, and one expects to be noticed. So I smiled and with a nod mimed appreciative applause, as did Bill, catching on quickly. Her visage then flashed to a lovely smile, she winked, and carried on her way. The tradition properly restored.

Soon after that, we figured we should head back to the hotel to see if Stewart had arrived. I asked for the cheque and paid. Afterwards I showed Bill the receipt. Beer's not cheap in Paris; it's less cheap at prime locations like where we were; and is even more expensive when you order it by the huge stein. Bill was in shock over what I had paid: 100 Francs a beer (about 25-30 Canadian dollars).

Stewart had not yet arrived so I told Bill that in keeping with a brand-new grand tradition, commencing immediately the newbie to the team must buy the first round of beers. Bill being the newbie must therefore buy the next beers for the two of us. I took him in to a much cheaper cafe, where we ordered and he paid for a couple of very reasonably-priced traditional pint-size glasses of beer. No serious damage done to his wallet.

Then it was back to the hotel and this time, Stewart was there. He suggested we head out for a drink before dinner and I told him I knew just the place. I then informed him of the now time-honoured tradition of the newbie buying the first round of beers and he happily agreed to do that. But first, he said, he needed to visit an ATM to withdraw sufficient funds to cover the round, and his dinner. As he was keying in the amounts, he asked Bill and I if we thought that would cover it, and with straight faces we assured him it would. He took out 300 Francs. Bill was pissing himself trying not to give it away.

We took him back to the first café and Walter greets us again. I introduce him to Stewart and tell him that we would like three very big beers. Stewart would be paying. The large steins arrive. Stewart is impressed. Again after a healthy period of time consuming them, I suggest we head around the corner to another place for dinner. Stewart asks for the cheque. When his eyes light up, Bill and I lose it. Stewart paid with the 300 Francs he had earlier withdrawn, and we headed back to the ATM so that he could top up for dinner.

While perhaps a little miffed at being pranked, he insisted that this tradition be upheld, and every two years afterwards, when he and I were again in Paris together, he would gleefully invite at least one newbie to come out with us for a drink, and oh, by the way, he'd say, "there's a long-standing tradition that you should be aware of..."

Muddy Footprints

When I was growing up, the expectation was that when you borrow the family car, you return it in the same condition it was in when you took it, and with the same amount of gas in the tank. At least, that's what my Dad expected. I'd been tuned up at least once for not filling the tank, but I'm a bit of a neat freak, so I'd always make sure the car was clean. Except for that one time...

It was noonish on a bright sunny Saturday in mid-summer when I was rudely awakened. I was living at home after my first year away at university. I was out late the night before at a dance with my then-girlfriend, who lived a couple of towns away. After the dance we drove to her place. By the time I got back home it was pretty late and I was fast asleep in no time.

Now it's morning and all of a sudden I'm being yanked out of bed by my ear, led through the house out to the carport, my head shoved into the backseat and twisted towards the ceiling.

Dad's telling me how my Mom is so upset at seeing what I was now looking at: women's size-seven muddy footprints all over previously clean roof fabric.

A lot of thoughts are now flying through my mind. Yes, my girlfriend and I had stopped and "parked" at the beach before going back to her place. And yes, we had, at one point, walked along the shore. No, I don't think Mom was upset simply because the car was dirty. And if I didn't find a way out of this fast I probably would not get the keys again all summer long.

I don't know how many microseconds all that thinking took, but my immediate reply to Dad was "Darn that Kirk [my previously-mentioned best friend]! I lent him the keys so that he and Annette could have some private time together. Sorry, Dad. I'll clean it up."

The death grip on my ear was released and I was able to un-pretzel myself from the back seat.

"Sorry, son."

"No problem, Dad. I'm going back to bed. And can I borrow the car again tonight...?"

No Officer

I have a lot of respect for police officers and the work they do. I have a lot of problems with them when they exceed their authority or act in an abusive manner. As recounted in other tales, I've had some good encounters with them over the years, but two come to mind that still leave a bad taste.

About ten years ago, Claude, a colleague of mine, and I were in Vancouver on business. As was my usual practice, we stayed at the Lord Stanley Suites, the closest downtown hotel to Stanley Park and one with surprisingly good rates. It also happens to be located on the edge of the principal gay district of Vancouver.

We had just checked out of the hotel, driven down Denman Street and turned onto Beach Avenue on our way to the airport. A couple of hundred yards down Beach, a short overweight Vancouver motorcycle cop jumps in front of my car with his hands up (like in "I surrender" hands up). I hit the brakes and come to a stop barely inches from his legs. He waddles to my side and starts screaming at me that I was trying to run him over and then, after cursing at us like crazy, orders me to pull into the parking lot off to our right. I turn to him and calmly suggest that he speak much more politely to me, which seems to piss him off.

I then see that he's set up a "speed trap" and had been pulling cars over. Unbeknownst to me, as we turned onto Beach, we passed through a reduced-speed playground area. As I saw later, the only sign saying so was blocked by tree branches. However, given the nature of his expletive-laced tirade I suspected that the speed trap was just a pretense. You see the words "queer" and "gays" and "homos" had been part of his vernacular and I figured this officer had been a gay basher of the worst kind: one in a police uniform. Here were two men in a car together driving out of the gay district so to him we were perfect targets for his abuse. I wasn't having any of it.

I pulled into the parking lot and told Claude to sit tight in his seat. As the officer came storming up to our car, ironically dressed in motorcycle cop gear that could have placed him perfectly as an out-of-shape member of *The Village People*, I calmly got out of my car to face him. He was a good six inches shorter than me and had to look up at me while wagging an index finger. He accused me of trying to run him over. I politely told him he shouldn't be so stupid as to leap in front of a moving vehicle. His red face got even redder. He demanded my driver's licence and registration. I explained that this was a rental car and pulled out my wallet and handed him my licence, at the same time suggesting that he should really be more polite.

As soon as he saw my licence, his demeanor changed completely. I was clearly from out of town, in fact from Ottawa, and his assumption that we were a couple of local gays to bash had now been proven wrong. He calmed down and said to wait while he wrote up a ticket, which he did back at his motorcycle. When he came back to us he was almost apologetic. He said he could have written it up for much more but had given us a break and greatly reduced the offence. I have no doubt that the opposite would have been true had we been a couple of local gay men.

I did not thank him for this "break" but rather took the time to remind him, in many more words this time, that he really needed to be more polite and to treat people with much more respect. His face reddened a bit but he bit his tongue. When I got back in the car, Claude was blown away by the whole incident.

Years later, I was leaving a golf club after a morning round with a group of friends. It was out in the country and it was a beautiful, hot, sunny day. After the round, I was more than a bit dehydrated. Around that time I had developed a bit of a taste for "Beck's 0", a completely alcohol-free beer that I had discovered post-heart surgery when I was on anticoagulants and had to swear off alcohol for a while. I had eight of them in pretty short order while we all watched a golf match on the bar's TV.

Afterwards, I decided to drive through the back country roads, rather than heading straight back to the highway. I pulled out of the parking lot and was less than a half mile down the road, windows down and sunroof open, when a cop, parked along the side of the road ahead, waved me over. I parked ahead of his car on the shoulder. I was a bit puzzled because I had actually been doing less than the speed limit.

He came up to my window and asked where I was coming from. I told him the golf course back down the road. I asked what the problem was and he responded by asking if I'd been drinking. At that point I realized that he was just randomly pulling people over who had come from the golf course, as part of his own unofficial little ride program. This kinda pissed me off and it was at that point that I decided to play this one a bit.

I told him I had been drinking beer. "How much?" I told him I'd had eight bottles of beer to drink back at the bar. He asked me to step out of my car and to have a seat in the back of his. He then pulled a breathalyser out of his trunk and had me blow. I handed it back to him. He looked at the reading and a look of deep puzzlement came over his face. He looked at me and again asked how many beers I'd had? "Eight bottles of beer," was my reply.

He went back to his trunk and pulled out another unit. I blew again for the same result. A perfect zero. He was completely befuddled. I asked him what was wrong. He said that after eight beers I should have been well over the limit, but both units read nothing. I told him yes, but only if they had not been alcohol-free beers. He ordered me out of his back seat and into my car and on my way. As I did, I told him I did not appreciate being pulled over at random, for no reason or cause.

I'm not sure I accomplished anything in either case. I'm sure most readers will think I'm certifiably nuts for having done what I did. But as I said, while I have a lot of respect for police officers, I find it really hard to accept the behaviour of some. At no time was I anything but calm, cool and collected during these encounters, and never raised my voice or resorted to abusive language. I'd probably do the same again.

Lock-in at The Royal Exchange

London, England is soaked in history and tradition. Parks and palaces, museums, theatres, and seemingly a pub on every corner. Close to Paddington Station you will find The Royal Exchange. It's a small "local" with a fine selection of beers, very good traditional pub grub, and friendly service. It is hands-down my favourite.

I first walked through its doors nearly two decades ago. I was staying just up the street, was out for a walk, and wandered in. It's not a big place, basically a narrow bar area up front, and a handful of tables, chairs, and bench seating at the back. I ordered a pint and ham on the bone and both hit the spot. I've been going back on every trip to London ever since.

The Royal Exchange plays an important role in my "no jetlag" strategy when visiting London. I take an early morning flight from Ottawa to Toronto and then connect to an Air Canada flight that gets into London mid-evening that same day. By the time you collect your bags, clear Customs, take the fast train to Paddington Station, and check in to either the Hilton Paddington or the Hilton London Edgeware Road, you have time to make the five-minute walk to The Royal Exchange and drink two pints before the 11pm closing time. Then it's back to the hotel for eight hours of sleep and wake up the next day jetlag-free for the rest of the stay. Trust me, it works like a charm.

The Royal Exchange is also where I experienced my first, and so far only, genuine "lock-in." This a wonderful tradition where the pub owner locks the doors, with some patrons still inside, announces "right then, we're locked-in" and under licensing laws becomes a private party rather than a pub. You can keep drinking so long as the owner says so.

Apparently, tradition also dictates that before the lock in, patrons would set aside some cash behind the bar, to cover the drinks that will be consumed free (i.e. not sold) after the lock-in starts. That's not how it worked, at least not for me, at The Royal Exchange.

The owner is (or was when I last visited) an Irishman who was simply called PJ. Apparently as well as The Royal Exchange, he owns a couple of places in Dublin. I've only seen him at The Royal Exchange twice, although on a few occasions Peter, the regular barman, has told me I just missed him by a day or two.

On the eve of the lock-in, I had started off sitting at the bar and had struck up a conversation with PJ. Business was slow, with a half-dozen patrons in front, and three women in back. I moved to a table in back to eat a sandwich with my pint, and talked to the women, who were social workers and colleagues. Last call came and went and the patrons in front left. PJ came back to join us. It turned out that one of the women's aunts tended bar at one of PJ's Dublin pubs and said she'd love to have a go at pulling a pint. PJ walked to the front door, bolted it, and made the announcement that we were now locked-in.

"What does that mean?" I asked. PJ explained that the bar is now open, to help ourselves, and that no payment was expected, nor would it be accepted. I'd died and gone to heaven!

So the niece pulled her first pint, the first of many, for me. And there we sat and drank and laughed and drank some more. Not excessively, but continuously. The ladies opened a bottle of champagne. PJ stuck to beer. I eventually sampled much of his pretty good selection of single malts.

At one point, one of the ladies asked if there was any coffee. Oddly enough (at least to me), the pub did not have any. So, ever the gentleman, I offered to get some. PJ let me out and bolted the door behind me and I trotted up the street and around the corner to the Hilton. The lobby bar there never closes (at least not to guests) and I ordered a pot of coffee, cream and sugar, which came in a nice service on a tray. I charged it to my room and then whisked the whole thing out the front revolving doors of the hotel, across and down the street, and back to the pub, where PJ let me back in, laughing all the while he was doing so.

When that door was next opened, it was to a sun just rising. We'd spent the whole night inside. I bade farewell to the ladies and PJ, and returned the service to the hotel where I ordered breakfast. I then managed to catch a few hours of sleep before heading out to Farn-borough to set up my trade show booth at the Airshow. I felt a little rough throughout the day but I think it was a very fair price to pay for having experienced my first, and only, lock-in, at The Royal Exchange.

Slow Motion Rollover

I was on the way back from a day of meetings in Montreal with my colleague Terry in the passenger seat of Gen's almost-new Honda Accord, which I had borrowed for the trip. The car never made it home.

It was early December, and as happens in our part of Canada, we were getting hit with a surprise winter storm. It started up as we were a half hour out of Montreal. It was one of those blowing snows that doesn't accumulate on the road but builds up quickly in the ditches. It might have been the first storm of that season.

It was dark out, but visibility was still good. The road was bare and cold. Then I spotted potential trouble ahead: it looked like the road was covered in a layer of hard-packed snow. I disengaged the cruise control, matched everyone else's speed and moved over to the left lane of the four-lane divided highway where there was nobody directly ahead of me.

As we slowly, ever so slowly, passed a car on our right, the steering all of a sudden felt strange. I was getting no road feedback at all. Because Gen's car was brand new, I was running on the factory-original Michelin "all season" tires. Big mistake. Those tires were useless on cold hard-packed snow and the non-feel of the wheel told me so.

Even though we were still in our lane, and pointed straight ahead, I knew we were in trouble. I told Terry so. I think he understood because he checked his seatbelt. Just as we had passed the minivan beside us, Terry able to reach out and touch it if he wanted to, our car started to slowly turn sideways and we soon found ourselves sliding completely sideways directly in front of the minivan. The look on that driver's face? Priceless!

After what seemed like an eternity, we started to drift off the road and towards the right side ditch. We'd shed none of our speed so far. It was a perfectly smooth slide. I said the obvious to Terry: "We're headed for the ditch. Brace yourself." We entered the ditch moving sideways, my door in the lead. We slid like that for a long time, flying snow blocking out the view completely. I said "I think we're going to roll," just as the car's wheels struck something and put the car into a spin along its lengthwise axis.

My left hand had been broken playing basketball a few weeks before and it was still in a heavy cast. All motion stopped. We were lying on the driver's side door, when my hand lost grip on the steering wheel and the cast smashed the window.

Fully at rest, with just the dash lights to see by, I did a quick body check. Okay. I asked Terry if he was alright. He said yes, from his position suspended above me. He then said he could get out of his seatbelt and before I could react. He crashed down on top of me. "Sorry!"

He was able to stand up and we crawled out his window, gathered our briefcases, and climbed out of the ditch to the highway.

A passing driver had noticed our lights in the ditch, stopped, and offered us a ride in to Ottawa. He dropped us off at a gas station and Terry's wife came to pick us up.

I was home when Gen came in. "How was your day?" she asked, not realizing I had not returned her car to our garage. I broke the news to her. She took it reasonably well. The car was a complete write-off. Luckily, our insurance helped me to buy her an even nicer replacement Honda Accord.

For that car, and every one afterwards, we've always had winter tires. And I have never driven the highway between Ottawa and Montreal in winter since then, if there's even a hint of snow to come.

Just Swish It Around

As covered in a few other tales, I've had the good fortune to visit the city/country of Singapore on a number of occasions.

I've often wondered if I could ever live there – at least for a significant period of time each year. It's safe, has predictable and pretty constant weather (hot and humid, clear skies in the morning, clouding over in the afternoon followed by torrential rains, clearing in the evening, repeat) and the people are great. I am most impressed by their dedication to education.

Walk into any North American bookstore. Measure the number of shelf-feet dedicated to books on religion, bibles, "Christian" fiction, spirituality, astrology, the occult, etc. Now do the same for books dedicated to math, science, engineering etc. The ratio of the former to the latter is almost always at least three to one and the farther south you go the higher it gets. The highest I ever measured was in Tampa, Florida, where I came up with 40 to 1 in one bookstore. I call that calculation the scientific illiteracy index.

In Singapore, the exact opposite is always the case. They have huge collections of scientific, engineering, medical, and architectural books, a large number of which are textbooks, and comparatively none on religion etc. When I visited one bookstore in Singapore on a Sunday, I was amazed to see entire families sitting around together, with the father and mother reading to their children. In a few cases they were reading children's books, but in many cases they were reading math and science books to them. I was impressed!

But I think I'd quickly become bored if I lived in Singapore. Eating, shopping, "pubbing" (and working) is just not enough for me.

Worse yet, I'd probably end up in jail for violating their laws regarding criticising their government. You see, their court system has ruled that, because they pay their politicians a lot of money, they cannot possibly be corrupt. So any time a member of the (very small) opposition makes an allegation of corruption (even if armed with irrefutable evidence), it's the accuser that gets charged with libel or slander. This keeps the governing party in power. It would drive me nuts.

I'm also not a fan of censorship. And Singapore has got it in spades. I once went to see a Bruce Willis film in a movie theatre over there. It was so butchered that I had to see it again as soon as I returned to understand what the heck happened in it.

But the one thing that convinced me more than anything I did not belong was the toilet customs. I'll explain.

All my trips have been for business, specifically to attend what is now known as the Singapore Airshow. On my first trip, they were using exhibit halls co-located at the airport. The first day of the show, I headed to the men's room to do my duty. After seeing that the available "toilets" consisted of two footprints in front of a hole in the floor, I decided to wait until the end of the day when I was back at my hotel. However, they had your typical bank of urinals along one wall, so I figured partial relief was better than none at all.

As I was doing my thing, a local, attired as I was in a nice business suit, took the position to my left. Now we guys try to avoid noticing what goes on next to us in these situations but curiosity got the better of me. You see my fellow reliever had decided to combine his relief with a wash. He was hanging over the bowl, flushing constantly with his left hand, and reaching into the urinal stream with his right to cup water and then wash his junk.

Most guys, having noticed this, would have quickly finished their business, tucked and zipped, and hurried away. But me? Nope. I kept myself hanging over the bowl, turned my shoulders toward him, and said "You know what I do instead of sticking my hand in there to wash my balls? I grab a handful of toilet paper and plug the drain at the bottom of the bowl. Then when it fills up I just swish it around [now with hands on hips making Elvis gyrations] in the pool until it's clean."

I don't know if it was my words or my motions that scared the poor fellow, but I've never seen anyone tuck, zip, and scamper out of a washroom so fast!

Flying Drunk

I've taken too many flights in my life to count. Most have been short haulers, but a good number have been longer cross-continent, or cross-ocean, ones. On the shorter hops, I almost never drink alcohol; water or orange juice are it. On the longer ones, especially when there's a dinner served, a glass or two of wine are fine. I've learned the hard way that anything more just doesn't work.

I have trouble sleeping on long flights (although I'll be asleep even before take-off on a short haul!). My buddy Bruce and I were awaiting an evening flight on Air Canada from Toronto to Frankfurt, where we would then connect the next morning to Hamburg. I mentioned my sleeping woes. He had the same issue. We decided to try something a little different on this trip.

I'd managed to get Air Canada to upgrade us both to business class. That was back before they introduced those personal recliner / compartment seats that fold down flat into beds. As soon as we got on the plane, we'd start drinking. When we got pretty darn tipsy we'd stop, fall asleep for several hours, and wake up refreshed and well-rested. Well, that was the plan.

We started with champagne (and orange juice) before take-off. As soon as the plane leveled out they were setting us up for dinner. We ordered cocktails and downed them. We went through most of the wine list during dinner, at a fast-enough pace that we had to "bing" the flight attendant a few times for refills. He finally left us a couple of bottles. Port accompanied dessert, and a cognac or three helped with digestion. Then it was recline the seats and pass-out time. That part worked like a charm.

I was jostled awake by a rather hard landing. Looking over at Bruce, I saw he looked a little rough. Or was I looking in a mirror? We'd slept (if you could call it that) through breakfast an hour or so beforehand. My seat was in the upright position; my guess is that the flight attendant had done that for me. As we taxied to the gate, I struggled to find my shoes and put them on. I vaguely remembered a male flight attendant offering to remove them during the flight. I think he also offered to rub my feet, but I hoped I had only imagined that part – as I checked to make sure my belt was still fastened. When the cabin door was opened, we left the plane and headed to passport control and our connecting flight.

My head hurt. My tongue kept sticking to the roof of my mouth. Could someone please turn down the lights in this airport?

After what seemed like a much longer-than-normal grilling by the passport control officer (who probably noticed that my shoes were on the wrong feet) we got to the departure gate for our next flight. Bruce and I compared notes. It was unanimous. We wouldn't be flying drunk ever again.

Well, I guess never sometimes does not mean forever. I did stick to my commitment to not have more than the usual glass or two of wine at dinner on the flight. But what about arriving at the airport already half, or in my case, fully cut?

I'd been in Munich (what is it with Germany, me, and booze?) for a week on business, and this time Steve was my travel buddy. We'd been out really late the night before and topped it off with single malt scotch at the hotel lobby bar. Not a glass or two; the bottle. I managed to stumble back to my room, set a wake-up call, and get maybe two hours of sleep. I somehow caught a quick breakfast in the hotel's restaurant, got packed, and met Steve at the appointed time in the lobby. He looked okay. His expression when he looked at me told me I was not.

By the time we got off the commuter train from the city of Munich to the airport, I was sicker than a dog. Waiting in line at check-in was torture. I never get sick to my stomach (a blessing sometimes, sometimes not) but this time, the nausea was so severe I was sure I would. As soon as I could, I headed to one of the duty-free stores to ask for a plastic shopping bag – just in case I couldn't make it to a toilet in time. I guess my non-existent German and the saleslady's non-existent English were not a great match because she handed me one of those wee little plastic baggies that one uses to house one's carry on liquids and gels. My breakfast into _it_ would surely not _fit_!

I tried sign language and theatrics instead of English. I must have done a great job of acting out projectile vomit, or maybe I looked the part rather well, because she got it that time and handed me one of those multi-gallon handled bags you could fit a small car into. Just having it in hand made me feel less like having to use it.

As I boarded the flight, I begged two bottles of water from the attendant and headed to my seat. She must have shown some concern for how I looked, because later Steve told me that he had to explain to her that although I was not feeling well, I'd likely live. I buckled myself into my window seat in the last row, downed the water, and only came to when we were pulling up to the gate in Frankfurt.

I was feeling somewhat better by the time I strapped in on the next flight. More bottles of water were consumed and I managed to eat the offered food on the flight to Toronto. We cleared Canadian Customs and were waiting for our connecting flight to Ottawa when I mentioned to Steve that I felt pretty good. He was amazed at my recovery. More so when, as the drink cart was passing by on that Ottawa-bound flight, I ordered a beer.

I've since managed never again to fly drunk, and I only need to think back on either of those trips to remind myself why it's such a bad idea. No more flying drunk!

Four Floors of Whores

In other tales, I've touched on my overall thoughts about the city-state of Singapore: its cleanliness, inhabitants' emphasis on education, its politicians, its bathroom habits. However, one of the most striking things about Singapore is the dichotomy between what is allowed and not allowed within its borders, and how one building can be such an outlier to the norm.

Singaporeans are subject to all sorts of censorship, most of it involving not only sex, but sexuality. The internet is monitored and if you happen to stray too close to a site that offends, up pops a very visible warning of your transgression. If you go to a bookstore in search of the *Sports Illustrated* swimsuit edition you are out of luck. Don't even bother looking for *Playboy*. If you go to a movie at a Cineplex, one of the first things to appear on screen is a censor's message and stamp of approval, and almost any scene containing nudity or sexuality will have been expunged, although violence and mayhem are just fine. And if you are bringing videos to show in your trade show booth, you need to submit them well in advance so that they may be properly vetted by the authorities.

[I should note at this point that these are all personal observations from my travels to Singapore. I do not know the most current state of censorship, so things may have changed. But they didn't over the many years that I visited.]

Given these examples, (and there are likely many more) how does one explain Orchard Towers, better known as the Four Floors of Whores? If ever there was a most-glaring example of the difference between what one would expect, and what one actually finds, this is it.

Outwardly, it's an office / residential tower just like any other. It's located on Orchard Road, right across from the Hilton Singapore, and in the heart of the shopping district. Its bottom floors consist of a mix of commercial businesses: jewelry and electronics shops, clothing and apparel stores, tailors and cleaners, and bars. As you come in the front doors, there is a set of escalators to take you between its floors.

During the day, the "regular" shops are open and shopper traffic is brisk. You might assume, however, that overall business is not great because many storefronts (basically all of the bars) are shuttered with steel rollups. You might also get a feeling that all is not what it seems when you are invited into one of the massage parlors as you walk by, a promise of "happy endings" pitched more quietly than the initial invitation.

Now come back in the evening and things have changed. As the shutters go down on all those shops you've visited (but not the massage parlours!) the shutters go up on the others. All of a sudden, the foot traffic changes. With the sun fully down, the place is hopping. There's music coming from bars on all levels, more so as you get to the higher floors, and hundreds of patrons swarm in. So too are hundreds and hundreds of young women dressed in the skimpiest and sexiest of outfits.

Yes. Those floors are now chock-a-block full of whores.

Word of warning: unless you are shopping for one, do not enter any bar alone, because you will be hit on continuously and mercilessly no matter how many times you say "no, thank you." I was with a largish group of people on my one and only visit (inside) and we were able to circle the wagons, so to speak, and have a beer in relative peace. (But at the prices they charge, don't go for the beer!)

Those escalators out front become the conduit of unattached patrons and girls going up to the bars, and matched pairs heading

back out to the long but fast-moving taxi queue out front. And by the way, "girl" might be in appearance only; apparently some have outdoor plumbing for those who are into that sort of thing.

To get back to my original point, with all of this happening in very plain sight, what's the explanation of how puritan Singapore, so active in censoring down to the minutiae level, allows such activity? Does it generate too much sex-tourism money (à la mini-Thailand?) Do a bunch of people in power get a cut? Or does Singapore, such an effective censor in pretty much every other area of life, unofficially admit that nobody can control the world's oldest profession? Does it, with that resignation, allow it to flourish in this one building (although it apparently gets raided by police, for show, every so often), in this "four floors of whores", as it is known by locals and visitors alike? I don't know.

And by the by, if you're actually looking to drink beer, I suggest that you visit Muddy Murphy's Irish Pub located on the ground floor of the office tower across the street. They have an excellent selection of beers, very good food, and nobody will harass you while you enjoy it.

Swiss Alps

I'm not much of a downhill skier. I've never taken lessons, and it shows. I've relied on natural athleticism to pick up many sports, and skiing was no exception. I've skied much less as I've gotten older. I think knowing how easily I could hit a tree or catch an edge and break my neck has played a part in keeping me off the slopes, as has a lowering tolerance for the cold.

But when a chance arose to ski the Swiss Alps about ten years ago, I couldn't pass it up. Even though it was ultimately the reason I've never skied again, I still consider it well worth it.

I happened to be heading to Europe on business. My employer was buying a big piece of equipment from a Swiss company and needed someone to "inspect" the work to date. Since I was already going to be in the neighbourhood, I volunteered to spend a day visiting the factory.

The factory visit was scheduled for near the end of the week, so the Swiss company invited me to stay over for the weekend and get in some skiing. They assigned three of their employees to be my guides. To keep things above board, I paid for my own lift tickets, ski rentals, meals, etc. I packed all manner of warm and dry clothing. I was both looking forward to it, and more than a bit anxious.

The first day, I decided to play it safe and wore multiple layers of clothing. After all, if the temperature was just below freezing at the bottom of the hill, surely it would be much colder up on the glacier at 10,000 feet, would it not? Wrong assumption. It was a sunny, cloudless day, just below freezing at every altitude. By halfway through the day, I was in distress. Real trouble. We stopped at the highest chalet, where it took bottles and bottles of water, and a couple of bowls of goulash, to overcome my dehydration. A touch of altitude sickness did nothing to help either.

It was at the chalet that I committed a major etiquette faux-pas that left my hosts horrified. You see, the chalet had a lot of picnic tables set out in an area on the glacier. All around the tables were people lounging in various state of undress on chaises, soaking up the sun. Having perspired myself into a state of dehydration, while still at the picnic table, I stripped down, removed my last two sweat-soaked layers of shirts, and put the others back on. It was during that moment of shirtlessness that my hosts' jaws dropped: apparently, while the chaises were the equivalent of being on a beach at a resort, the picnic tables, right beside them, were considered the equivalent of fine dining at a five star restaurant in Zurich – and one would never "strip" in such an establishment, now would one? Suitably chastened, I finished out the day.

The next day, I dressed more appropriately (and stayed so), and saw no repeat of the problems of the day before. It was an amazing day of skiing that left me with three enduring memories.

The first was starting off our ascent to the top in a cable car, transferring to a chair lift for the next part of the ascent, and then finishing the last stage on a good old-fashioned T-bar. Problem was, while the locals are used to riding those up a near-vertical climb, where falling off would bring great harm, rather than just embarrassment, I was not. My legs and arms were burning by the time we got to the top.

Once there, we did a traverse across the mountain's peak, to the other side, before starting our descent. I did not think much of it at the time, but we were going at a pretty good clip on that traverse, with inside leg much higher than outside due to the almost 45-degree slope. At the end of the traverse, we faced a very steep long run down to the beginning of the tree line. My hosts attacked the hill, tips pointing straight down the hill, like the lifelong expert skiers they were. I carved hard, tips running parallel to the descent and then reversing (after a brief stop), ever-mindful that a fall would likely see me rolling down the hill for several hundred metres. I finally reached my hosts, patiently waiting for me. It was then that I looked back up to see what I had descended and noticed that the traverse was actually a pretty narrow path whose downhill side ended abruptly in a 1,000-metre sheer cliff. No safety railing or fence. Had I caught an edge and tumbled only 20 metres or so to the edge, that would have been it. I guess there aren't many personal injury lawyers in Switzerland.

At the end of the day, I was ready to jump into a cable car and ride to the bottom. I was beat. One of the hosts said she'd guide me across the mountain where we could take a nice long leisurely trail to the bottom. I should have consulted a map. She took a wrong turn. We got to a point where there was no going back or alternate routes: just a steep, narrow, rock-infested, mogul-populated "trail" that ran for 1,000 metres vertically, straight through the trees. Terror! I don't know how long it took me, but I carved (and stopped) and carved (and stopped) as hard as I could down the whole thing. Never fell. Never hit a tree. Close but no concussion!

And while I felt a huge sense of relief when we finally emerged from the trees at the bottom of the hill, that impression of fear was so powerful, that was the last time I ever put on a pair of downhill skis. I guess if you're going to quit, quitting after an amazing two days on the Swiss Alps is the time to do it.

The Richard-Out Award

Sometimes in life one witnesses an achievement so special you feel it needs to be recognized in a special way. Such was the case during the 2004 inaugural year of a company golf tournament I had a hand in organizing.

Years and years ago, the aerospace part of Canada's National Research Council was an especially great place to work because of the esprit de corps that went along with being there. While the work was engaging and challenging (and rewarding) there were a number of events organized by staff that made working there all the more special.

There was a Christmas Gala (which we called the "Seasonal Gala" for political correctness) that brought together over 300 people at its peak. There was a summer picnic for staff and their families, which included a water shower for the kids courtesy of one of the airport's fire trucks, and a flyover by some of our aircraft. There was an annual hockey game between our two largest campuses, the winner getting to claim the "Braggin' Rights" trophy. And there was a golf tournament that, at first, was mostly for aerospace staff only, but grew to include clients and other NRC personnel over the years.

On that inaugural round of golf, one member of the foursome was Sid. Like most of us, Sid's not a bad golfer; he makes some good shots and misses a few others. But he was having a particularly rough time that day, especially off the tees.

Now there's a tradition of sorts amongst male golfers. If off the tee you fail to drive the ball past the ladies' tees, it's called a dick-out. You are to unzip and whip it out, and walk the rest of the hole, with putter exposed. Of course, it's almost never done in practice, mostly because nobody else in the foursome really wants to see that happen, and also because, while it's one thing to treat the trees on a golf course like a man's urinal park, it would be quite another to flash other foursomes, marshals, neighbours, and bar-cart girls for a reason other than personal relief.

During that round, Sid had numerous dick-outs, too numerous to recall. He even had two on the same hole, his second shot failing to make it past the ladies' tee as well.

In the intervening year between the first and second annual offerings of the tournament, I decided to commemorate Sid's achievement by ordering the largest trophy to be awarded for the tournament. While I was very tempted to name it after him, I instead had a plaque engraved with his name in recognition of his first year's accomplishment. The trophy itself was called "The Richard-Out Award" and Sid would have the distinction of winning it again in 2011.

He's been quite a good sport about it over the years, accepting the good-natured ribbing that goes along with it. At the tournament dinner every year, I would always let everyone know the genesis for the award, and it was no surprise how honest people were in reporting their own dick-out tally, given that Sid led the way.

The tournament last took place in 2012, a victim, like all the other events mentioned above, of a change in leadership and attitude within NRC. But through this tale I figured I'd honour Sid one last time: that first year really was something to watch!

The Vasectomy

I love all three of my children to bits. I can't imagine a life without them. But before they were born, in fact right after they were conceived, I must confess I did not feel quite the same way. I think each time Gen told me she was pregnant my reaction was "You're having a what!" and "Is it mine?" The latter was not accusatory; more like some very deep denial.

By the time she was pregnant with our third child, in fact throughout the entire pregnancy, I was very much convinced I would father no more. (Of course the moment she entered the world and into my arms, Allie became "my most favourite youngest daughter.") The solution was that either Gen or I would get "fixed."

Like the athletes we were, we decided to hold the "Neutering Olympics." This consisted of a series of events, some sports like badminton, swimming, and basketball 21, as well as non-sports games like Trivial Pursuit, and Scrabble. The winner got the operation.

Now because it was safer for me to get snipped than Gen, I of course tried hard, and won. Mind you, I wanted it to be a close competition, so for some sports where I had a decided advantage I took steps to even things up a bit. For example for basketball 21, I shot with my left hand while holding a kid with a poop-filled diaper in my right. I think I still won 21-0. After my victory, I went to my family doc, who said he'd refer me to a surgeon. The surgeon's office sent me two consent forms to fill out: one for each of the hospitals where he might perform the deed.

At that time in Pembroke, there were two hospitals: the General Hospital (which was Catholic and was where both my parents and Gen worked) and the Civic (which was essentially Protestant). The one-page consent forms for both hospitals were identical, except that the one for the General had a disclaimer on the reverse side which read (and I paraphrase only slightly): "By having this operation you are committing a mortal sin in the eyes of The Almighty God and for this you shall rot in Hell for all eternity." I added a handwritten line to it saying something like: "The foregoing is not applicable to atheists or other free-thinking individuals." As luck would have it, they scheduled the surgery for the General, despite my obvious insolence.

The day of the operation, I had my Mom drive me over, since Gen was working and was using the one car we owned at the time. Mom came in with me. She must have headed to the cafeteria for coffee after that, and let everyone know where I was and what I was having done. You see there's something special about not only living in a small city, but also being in a hospital where both your parents and your wife work. Everybody knows you, and everybody seems interested in you.

This was evidenced by the two nurses who "prepped" me: one I knew from high school and the other was a friend of Mom's. It's tough making small talk when someone's got a razor poised over your privates. It's even tougher when you know them quite well. Then the parade, I mean surgery, began. On several occasions throughout the operation, the operating room door would open a bit and a head would peek in and wish me good luck, or ask me how I was doing. (There was no need to ask what I was doing since, thanks no doubt to Mom, word had spread quite fast.) The head of radiology dropped by. Several nurses. And two cooks from the cafeteria, one of whom I went to school with for years. I masked my slight discomfort with jokes like

"It feels like the Doctor's tiring a bit. Want to take over for him?" and "A stitch in time saves four" (which was an oblique reference to my not wanting a fourth child).

About the operation itself... it's pretty much a non-event. Just a tugging sensation after the first freezing. With one exception. When he finished the first side, the doc said he was now going to freeze the other and that some patients feel a little more pain when the freezing goes in. Little! Talk about the understatement of the century. Right up there with the most painful thing I've ever felt, which is passing kidney stones.

Afterwards, Dad drove me home and cracked funny about the sack of ice I had on my crotch. I was annoyed because I missed playing my regular basketball game that night. But by a week later, all was back to normal.

Now you might be wondering why I'd want to tell everyone about this experience. Well, to be honest, the readers of this book are by far not the first to hear this tale. You see, for years I would use it as a test of sorts: to see if my daughters' new boyfriends were worth keeping or not. The first time they were at the family dinner table with us, I'd launch into the tale of my vasectomy. I could tell a lot about them by how they reacted, or not. One boyfriend of Nat's, who went on to become a medical doctor, passed with flying colours, blending inquisitiveness and humour as he got engaged in the story with me. I knew I needed a better "test" with him.

That opportunity came not too much later. I am very liberal in my attitudes and it was not uncommon, on a Sunday morning, to be downstairs making my traditional Sunday morning pancake feast for anyone who happens to have slept over. On some occasions, I did not know who would emerge from what bedroom, and with whom. So I always made extra just in case. On this one morning, that same boyfriend was the first down, having spent the night in my daughter's room. Coffee was on and I offered him a cup. It was just him and me in the kitchen, so I asked him how he slept last night. He said fine.

"I'm only asking," I said, "because I was worried. With all of the moaning and groaning coming from my daughter's room in the middle of the night, you might not have been able to sleep very well."

He didn't bat an eye. "Nat warned me about you," he said with a laugh. He was a good one.

Cuban Cigar Hangovers

I love a good Cuban cigar. The problem is they don't love me. It seems that every time I've smoked one, I wake up with a massive hangover. No amount of teeth (or nostril) brushing could take away the leftover taste making me ill. At least I think it was the cigars.

Take, for example, the time my buddy Tony and I were in Paris together. The morning after the first night in the city together, we rendezvoused in the hotel lobby at the appointed time to head to Le Bourget to get our booth set up for the Paris Airshow. I was feeling terrible.

As we were riding the train, Tony and I mused about why I was feeling so crummy. I suggested we retrace our steps from the previous evening.

We'd started off at my favourite café (see *The Tradition*) for a couple of large steins of beer. Then we'd moved from its sidewalk to the restaurant proper. We'd had a couple of bottles of wine between the two of us with the always-excellent meal, and when it came time to order a glass of port with dessert, our server simply brought us a full bottle.

After its consumption, we did the short walk across the *Pont au Change*, *Île de la Cité* and then *Pont Saint-Michel* and into the Latin Quarter. We soon found a table at a sidewalk café and had a couple of beers to take care of the thirst we'd worked up on our walk. No more than a few steps past that, we sat down at my favourite Greek souvlaki place in Paris and had a few ouzos. I think I had some baklava as well. Then it was farther down the street and a stop at a café for more port.

We closed that café, and eventually walked back to our hotel, through streets mostly empty, with all establishments now closed, and had to ring the bell for the night desk clerk to let us in. I'd come to know him over a number of visits to Paris and his hotel, and Tony and I sat down with him for a chat in the lobby. As we were feeling a little thirsty, he poured us a couple of glasses of port from the lobby bar's selection. I then went up to my room and retrieved a full bottle I had purchased the day before and was intending to take back home with me. Tony and I drank that over the next hour or two. Then we retired for the night and met back in the lobby a few hours later for a trip to the show site.

"I'm still not sure why you feel so crummy," Tony mused, as the train slid past Le Stade de France. It was then I had the eureka moment. I knew what had happened. At that last café, Tony had pulled out two huge Cuban cigars from his pocket humidor. We clipped, lit, and smoked them until the café was past closed. That was it! Clearly, I was sick from the cigars.

I then swore off them until just two years ago. Never had a problem. Until...

It was on Canada Day that I swung by Kirk and Annette's place. Months before, they'd had a new big front window installed, with an integrated granite bench/sill in front of it. Kirk had done the caulking to finish off the job. However, even from across the room, it looked like it had been done by a drunken baboon. I'm actually really good at caulking (hey, if you have to be good at something...) so I offered to fix it for them. On that Canada Day, I brought over my tools and set to work.

As it was a holiday, I had a few beers while doing the job. This might have slowed me down a bit, but in the end it was some of my best caulking. Annette was impressed, and Kirk had to admit it looked pretty good. I was invited to stay for dinner as compensation, and since Gen was out of town, I said yes.

Annette's a great cook and whatever she whipped up hit the spot, washed down with lots of wine. After dinner, we started sampling Kirk's single malts. By the end of the night, he and I were in his hot tub, staring at the stars, drinking a bottle of his finest. The problem was that he also pulled out a couple of Churchill cigars. Against my better judgement, (at least what was left of it by that time) I smoked one. I ended up crashing in one of their guest bedrooms afterwards.

When I awoke the next day, my head was killing me. Clearly, a Cuban cigar had done its nastiness on me once again.

Which is why I have since been cigar-free and intend to stay that way, at least for the foreseeable future. I'm sure that will take care of my next-day headaches. Reasonably sure, at least.

The Pool That Wasn't

Gen and I tried to have a backyard pool. Honest! But despite our best efforts it just wasn't meant to be.

We moved to our Ottawa home in 1989 with our three kids. The property has a pretty good-sized backyard, at least as far as most homes in the burbs go. Gen and I are both ex-lifeguards and swimming instructors, and we raised our kids, as much as possible, as water babies. We'd take them to community pools year-round, and one year we figured we'd make the investment in a backyard pool that the whole family could enjoy throughout the summer months. So I called the biggest, and what I thought was the best, pool company in the city and asked them to send a salesperson over.

We met with him a few days later. I explained that we were looking for a complete turnkey project. We would agree on exactly what we wanted. He would look after everything. I would pay them. We'd hop into the completely finished pool.

Our vision included the biggest pool that could be fit into our backyard, custom sized to be deeper than usual. Because of all of the below-ground services running along the back and sides of our property (including cable, phone, and electrical), cable location would be required. He started to recite who I'd have to call to have this done. I interrupted and reminded him this was to be a turnkey project. He would look after it. I would pay him for having done so. Okay. We moved on.

An upgraded electrical service would need to be installed to handle the pump. He told us we'd need to get an electrician. I again reminded him what turnkey meant. Same with building permits from the city. And a bunch of other similar things. He kept trying to tell me what I'd need to do. I kept telling him that all I was going to do was to sign the contract and then the cheque.

We talked about landscaping. I told him we might as well have the whole backyard done at the same time, including a new back fence, since the old one had to come down to allow access for construction. He said he could provide landscapers' numbers. I again said I expected him to do that subcontracting; I would pay him all of the cost and a tidy mark-up on top of it. Such was the nature of a turnkey project.

After a couple of hours, and lots of note-taking on his part, we shook on the deal. He was to drop off the contract, itemized as discussed, and fully-costed, the next week, and I'd sign it right away. It was still spring, and he said that even though they had quite a number of jobs ahead of ours, they should be able to tackle it in time for us to enjoy at least half the summer with the new pool.

A week came and went. I called and left a message for him. No reply.

Another week went by. Same thing.

After the third week, I did not call again.

After the fourth week, the neighbours, who all had kids as well, began opening their pools. Our kids started to get invited to play in them with their friends. The neighbourhood was alive with the sounds of diving and splashing and "Marco!"

In the end, we gave up on our plan to have a pool built. We gradually landscaped and planted gardens and trees to the point where, within a couple of years, it would have been a shame to dig it all up. So we never did.

But I still wonder what it was we'd done to scare that salesman away. Was a client with a cheque book open and ready to pay whatever price really that terrifying? I guess maybe business was simply way too good that year.

But I also sometimes wonder what it would have been like having the pool that wasn't in the backyard.

Paintings – Vermeer

I've just watched a superb documentary film called *Tim's Vermeer*. It's a Penn and Teller film that deals with inventor Tim Jenison's multi-year quest to discover how Vermeer managed to produce such photo-realistic paintings, in his day and age, and then to use those same techniques today to paint a Vermeer as Vermeer himself did.

I have long been fascinated by Vermeer's work, and many of the paintings shown in the documentary were familiar to me, as I have had the very good fortune to see them, up close and personal.

It was many moons ago (1995-96) when I was in Washington D.C. on business with Jamie, a media relations hired gun I had under contract, who eventually became a good friend. We were downtown in the McGraw Hill building for a meeting with *Aviation Week* staff. We were finishing up in Ed's office (the newsletter publisher). (see also *The Scotch Night* for another tale involving Ed.) He asked when we were flying out. Not until the evening, I said, so were looking to kill some time, possibly over at the Air & Space Museum.

Jamie mentioned that he would have liked to see the Vermeer exhibit running across the street in another Smithsonian building, but he had been told it was sold out. No problem, said Ed. He picked up the phone, got someone on the line by first name, and asked him to bike-courier a couple of VIP tickets over to him. It turns out he'd called the Washington-based rep for a huge aerospace firm that was one of the prime sponsors of the exhibit. Fifteen minutes later, we were shaking hands goodbye with Ed and on our way by taxi to the exhibit.

Now these tickets were as good as gold. Make that platinum.

There was a special entrance door we got to use. "Regular" ticket holders were queued in a line that stretched way down the block. Our door had no line. Rather, we were welcomed with a glass of champagne and an assortment of cheeses and crackers, while a curator gave us an overview of what we were about to see. She then spent the next hour or more walking us through amazing galleries, with beautiful lighting and hardwood floors, close to each of the 23 Vermeer paintings on display. This was an amazing assemblage, given that there are a total of only 36 works attributed to Vermeer.

The collection came from galleries around the world, and included the Queen's own Vermeers, which normally hang in Buckingham Palace. (These included "The Music Lesson", which is the same one that Tim decides to reproduce in the documentary.) To call the collection breathtaking would be a gross understatement.

Our "guide" was fabulous, but at the end of the tour I could not help but mess with her, just a bit. When she asked how we liked it, I said it was fantastic, but I was a bit disappointed. A look of genuine concern crossed her face and she asked why. I told her I was originally from a small lumber town in Canada with a big plywood-producing factory. I had really been looking forward to seeing "the veneers," but that all I'd seen were hardwood floors. Jamie managed to keep a straight face until her jaw dropped. Then he broke up and she, catching on immediately, joined him and me in a guffaw.

VIP tickets to THE Vermeer exhibit: truly priceless.

Arab Conflict

Disclaimer: I have next to no personal experience with Arab persons "of power." That's why it is somewhat disappointing that two of the experiences I have had did not go off so well. In defense of the Arabs portrayed in this story, I have trouble with respecting people in positions of power, simply because of their position, and I don't suffer fools gladly.

In *Hilton Hookers*, I did not mention that one guilty pleasure, and pretty fun pastime, is to sit in the lobby of the Hilton London Metropole and watch the large Arab entourages come and go. The men (I assume some with "princely" status) would sweep in, dressed from head to toe in their white robes, led by their dark-suited and beefy bodyguards, and followed by a handful of women in black burqas, or similar attire, with the occasional small child.

After checking in, they'd all head to the elevators and their rooms.

After that, more often than not, the bodyguards would return to the lobby. A hooker or two would approach, and moments later the prince would re-appear and exit with the whole bunch for a night of fun on the town. (I saw a few of them at the casino down Edgeware Road on a number of occasions, drinks and chips in hand, and hookers on their arm.) Other than making for good theatre, my overall feeling was "hey, they're just like anybody else," which is why I probably had that thought in mind when I was ordered off an elevator by a pair of bodyguards.

I had gotten into one and had hit the button for my floor when I saw two no-neck bulldogs in suits leading a prince to my elevator. So I courteously pressed the open button and waited for them to enter. The guards stopped at the door's entrance, a foot or two from where I was standing off to one side, and said "You. Out!"

It took a microsecond or two for my synapses to connect the dots and realize that they were saying they wanted the elevator all to themselves and the prince. That dirty dog infidel (me) had better listen to them and leave. Those same synapses, as they sometimes do (see *Fight or Flight*), also set my digital temper from "0" to "1."

I stepped to the middle of the elevator, flashed the universal "c'mon, let's go" hand signals, telling them they were welcome to try to remove me. They started towards me and I braced for impact. Then the prince barked out some instructions and they stopped, looked at me in disgust, and backed out of the elevator. As the doors were closing, I smiled at the beef-buddies and told them it was a good thing their daddy saved them from a good old-fashioned ass-kicking.

When I got back to my room, it took a few bottles from the mini-bar to stop the shakes.

It was many years later, when I found myself at the Dubai Airshow, that I had my second unpleasant encounter, which could have resulted in a nice international "incident."

On the second day of the show, the shuttle bus from my hotel dropped me off at the main entrance to the halls. There was quite a long set of lineups at all of the security screening points. They are much the same as those found at airport security checks.

I was in the right-most line that was open. There was one further to my right, but that was signed for VIPs and military personnel only. None of us "regular" visitors used that line, and neither did anyone else. Or so it seemed. A security guard who was standing by that open check-in called to a bunch of us to come over and get checked through. It was an act of intelligence and kindness, given how slowly our own line was moving. It was also really badly timed, because moments after a dozen or so of us moved over, a military bus pulled up outside behind us and started unloading its occupants.

The security guard saw this and motioned for us to move quickly through the screening. He didn't care what alarms were triggered. He just wanted us through and out of the way pronto. I reached the front of the line and was about to step through when an Arab officer of some self-importance came up from behind. Leading his bus-mates and wanting to show his obvious superiority, he grabbed me by the shoulder and, actually yelling in my face, demanded to know what I was doing in "his" line.

A fair question. I glanced at the security guard, who turned twenty shades of white. I figured if I ratted him out, he'd face either lashes or a beheading. So I turned slowly to face the officer, who was a little shorter than me and not as heavy, and told him calmly to please, be more polite.

This fired up another round of yelling. Then a poke of the one index finger to my chest. You know what's coming.

I went to a "1" again. I told him, calmly and coolly, that if he touched me again I would break his arm and likely other body parts. The guy next in line behind me reacted well to hearing this. In a classic Australian Mick Dundee accent, he said: "Go ahead, mate. Have a go at him. I've got your back." I had no doubt that he did.

The officer then considered his options. His troops were all studying the floor and ceiling, while several dozen fellow visitors turned towards us, focused on what would happen next. I think they had my back as well.

The officer blinked first. He stepped back, muttering to himself. I stepped through the portal and his chattering picked up again. I took off my jacket and handed it to the security guard. Then I stepped back towards the portal. Good idea or not, I was pissed. The officer blinked again. He ordered all of his team back out the main door and onto the bus, which attracted several snide comments, in multiple languages, from the crowd of visitors.

Yeah, they had my back.

Strangely enough, I did not get the post-adrenalin shakes that time. Perhaps my previous Arab conflict had inoculated me. To tell the truth, I'd prefer not to ever have to test my immunity again.

The Dive Knife

As I've mentioned in another tale, my son Nick is a commercial diver. Soon after he graduated and was diving professionally, I was at a conference in Virginia Beach. I had a few hours of free time and headed over to a dive shop not far from the hotel. I was looking to get Nick a present and after looking around and talking to the manager of the store for a while, I decided on a dive knife.

I bought the best they had. Titanium. Sharp as all get out. Strong enough to pry stuff with. It came with a locking sheath.

For my return trip, I packed it in a large suitcase. As is my usual practice, I had my laptop bag and another small bag as carry-ons. Upon check-in, things did not go well. I was told that my big suitcase was over its weight limit of 50 pounds and I must pay some ridiculous penalty as a result. I argued that my frequent flyer "status" gave me a limit of 75 pounds. I was told that the weight increase only applied to my Air Canada flights, not to partner airlines – of which this was one. Pay up.

Undeterred, I pressed on. Ok, what about the number of checked bags allowed? Even though the limit was 50 pounds per bag, how many bags could I check? The answer was three. So I took my almost-empty small carry-on and added a bunch of heavier items from the big checked bag to it. The dive knife, in a box, and in a plastic bag, went into the side zippered pocket. I then checked that small bag, both checked bags now being under 50 pounds each. I proceeded to security, boarding pass in hand.

The departure gate was jam-packed. Looked like another case of overbooking, so I was happy to use my "status" to be one of the first to board, take my seat right near the rear of the plane, and find a spot for my computer bag in the overhead bin of the jet I was flying on. It was destined for some other American airport, where I would then connect to Ottawa.

I had noticed something strange while boarding: the ground crew were bringing some small suitcases and bags up from the baggage cart down on the tarmac and putting them on the jetway, near the front door of the airplane. When all of the passengers had boarded and had taken their seats, or were in the process of stowing their carry-ons, a harried flight attendant came over the intercom and asked that the passengers who had left their luggage on the jetway to please identify themselves. She repeated this a minute later. Nobody raised their hand. Eventually she came trundling down the aisle holding a bag in front of her and yelling for the owner of the bag to identify them-selves. A little old lady sitting across the aisle from me put her hand up with trepidation and the flight attendant set upon her, grilling her about who she thought she was leaving her bag there. The old lady, terrified and quivering, managed to stammer words to the effect that she had not left it there – she had checked that bag on check-in.

I pointed to the baggage tag. The flight attendant gave me a dirty look and took off for the jetway in a huff. A minute later, she announced that because the hold was full to the brim, the ground crew had brought up a bunch of small checked bags and suitcases. She was now going to have to find places in overhead bins for them. Thus began ten minutes of huffing and puffing and grousing by said attendant. Bags were not matched to customers; no time for that since there was a schedule to adhere to.

Now, I'd normally ignore all that sort of commotion, open a book and zone out. However, I saw her coming down the aisle with my bag in hand. She got about a third of the way before putting it in an overhead bin. I made note of where she put it. Then I stared at that bin for the duration of the flight.

You see, I knew that inside that bag was the dive knife. It was a finely honed weapon. With it in hand, I could have killed and dismembered a passenger or crew member. I might have even been able to use it to gain access to the flight deck. And while I would never do such things, in the post 9/11 world of flying I did not doubt that there were some who would. As we were taxiing for take-off, I debated telling the attendant about it but, given her abuse of and no apology to, the little old lady, I figured she'd likely accuse me of hijacking or some such thing. So I vowed not to take my eyes off the bin.

It was a short flight and when we landed, I took my time to make sure that not only was I the last one down the aisle, but every other passenger had already left. Retrieving the bag from the bin, I walked slowly to the front where the two attendants, the pilot and the co-pilot were standing. I asked the same attendant if she could please ensure my bag got back into the checked-bag process, and made it safe and sound onto my next flight.

This set her off on a mini-tirade about her not being my servant etc. etc. I ignored her and asked the Captain for a moment of his time. He said no problem. What could he do for me? I placed the bag on the seat next to him. Took a few steps back. Then I asked him to open the zippered pocket, reach in and take out the plastic bag. He did. I then asked him to take the box out of the bag and open it. He did. I then asked him to take out its contents. In his hand was a very dangerous-looking dive knife, in its sheath. I asked him to take the knife out of the sheath.

I asked him how he felt knowing this had flown in an overhead bin on his flight. He was turning a bit white by now. He asked how I got it on board. I pointed to the tag on the bag. Apparently, the attendant never told him about the checked bags coming up from below. Then, in an admittedly politically incorrect manner, I asked him what he thought would have happened if I was not who I am, but rather my name was Mohammed and for months I had been contemplating jihad on Americans, when, in what was surely a sign from Allah, my checked bag miraculously appears in the cabin and nobody but me knows its contents. I ask him to imagine the damage that might have been done. He was even whiter now.

I asked him to please re-pack my bag and see it got checked through to Ottawa. He promised he would. As I left the plane, I gave that attendant the deepest scowling look I could muster. She uttered no apology, and not even the customary "have a nice day."

A week later, I was still stewing over those events. I couldn't let it go. I was in the aerospace industry and could see how such things should never happen. But if, for this airline, it happened on my flight, who was to say it could not happen again. I did not think that flight crew would have reported it. So I decided to contact the airline myself.

I used the fact I was an employee of the Government of Canada to great advantage, getting through to the office of the airline's senior VP in charge of security. But his assistant said that he was busy, and probably too busy for the rest of the week to call me. Standard blocking technique. So I upped the ante, saying that if he did not come on the line immediately, it would cost the airline big-time in fines. Would she like to be responsible for this happening? He came on a minute later, none too happy about it.

I then recounted, non-stop, my whole experience, including my discussion with the Captain. I named no names. Named no flights or destinations. I simply said I believed this to be a potential airline-wide issue. If it happened to my flight, it could happen again elsewhere unless someone took steps to prevent it. There was initial silence, then he thanked me very much for bringing this to his attention. He asked if I had spoken to "the authorities." I said no, but I would unless he proved to me that he had taken steps to prevent this from happening again. He asked how he could do that. I said, by sharing with me the internal communication that he would now need to send to the appropriate people in his operation. I gave him a couple of weeks. Later that day, he emailed me a copy of a notice he had drafted and sent to his head of ground operations and others, telling them how checked luggage should never end up in a plane's cabin.

I kept my end of the bargain, knowing I'd done my bit to make air travel just a little bit safer.

My Standard Fee

As also mentioned in *The 21-Year-Old Springbank*, I like my single malts, and I like to share them. While I stocked my collection through countless duty-free travel purchases over the years, a pretty good number were compensation of sorts. They were my standard fee for services rendered above and beyond the call of duty. I'll explain.

If you were a friend and business associate and through my efforts I was able to, say, put you in touch with a potential client, and that client and you then did a deal, I'd drop the hint that thank-you was great, but single malt said it greater. The catch was that it would be shared between us, at a mutually convenient time.

I'd only drop the hint once, and the future relationship was never affected by whether the bottle was paid or not.

I once recommended an excellent contractor to a colleague in another government department who really needed his services. The contract was issued. That contractor knew of my standard fee and sure enough, on an occasion when we found ourselves at the same conference in some foreign city, he presented me with a 700ml bottle. We sat in the lobby of our hotel and finished it over the course of the evening.

On many an occasion, the bottle would only be partly consumed, sometimes only a very little. In that case, it would be added to my office credenza collection, to be shared after 4pm on Fridays with whoever dropped by. In the "old" days that was everyone right up to and including Vice-Presidents. In the latter years, when puritans ruled, it was working-class only.

I once helped a colleague collect a bonus he was fully entitled to, but which he knew nothing about. NRC had completely overlooked him and it was only by chance, as I was reading through a bunch of files, that I put two and two together and saw that he'd been inadvertently screwed. It took me a few months of working behind the scenes, but eventually the wrong was righted and he received a cheque for a few thousand dollars. When I dropped the hint of my standard fee, and the condition that he join me in partaking, he laughed it off. I thought nothing else of it. Later that year, we were sharing a dinner table at a banquet. I noticed he was not drinking – because he had never done so. So that was it. But a few months after that, while we were all assembled in a museum for an annual staff awards ceremony, he slipped me a brown paper bag containing my standard fee.

The standard fee bottles were put to other uses as well. One year, we had a big charity fundraising event at work. Somehow I ended up "volunteering" to be the subject of the dunk tank. I'd checked out the water earlier in the day and it was freezing. So I took over a bottle –

just in case a nip was necessary to warm the cockles. The tank was set up at home plate on a baseball diamond and people threw from the pitcher's mound. There were a few hits leading to some dunkings, but I could get out fast enough that I never needed the antifreeze. Later, though, the throwers started to dwindle and I figured we needed to raise more cash. So I pulled out the bottle of single malt and made an offer: the bottle to the first person who could hit the bulls-eye from second base, at double the price per throw. Someone eventually won it after a lot more money was raised.

After I was laid off from NRC, I was packing up my things. I'd brought in an empty wine bottle box for the single malts. Each bottle brought back memories of favours done, and glasses raised. And thoughts of tradition and the importance thereof.

Zap Three Times

Every several years, it seems that I do something major to my body, or it to me, which requires some serious medical intervention. In January of 2009, it was the ticker.

I went in to work one morning feeling out of sorts. I had not slept well the night before, and woke up very tired, with a feeling of dread hanging over me. I made it to work in time for a monthly three-hour management team meeting and was not my usual self. (A colleague would later say he knew something was wrong with me because I had failed to stir things up during the meeting.) I noticed that my pulse seemed to be higher than usual, and erratic. I felt a bit faint.

So after the meeting I did what nobody should do in that situation: I drove myself to an urgent care clinic (rather than dialing 9-1-1). I'd been there many times before, but usually for sports-related injuries. This time, when asked about the reason for my visit I said it was my heart. I'd said the magic word. No waiting room stay this time! Faster than you can spit I was hooked up to an EKG. Almost as fast, the doctor told me an ambulance was on the way. No need to panic, but they felt it best to get me to an ER. I was in A-fib. As I learned later, my heart was being short-circuited by some rogue electrical signals generated by tiny muscles at the base of some blood vessels attached to my heart. These signals caused an irregular and more rapid heartbeat, which resulted in decreased blood flow. It was not supposed to be really dangerous, except if left untreated, as the risk of stroke increases dramatically if you are in untreated A-fib for more than 24 hours. So it was off to the ER.

Along the way, things were pretty calm. No lights or siren. The tech riding in back with me had me hooked up to an EKG machine. He was listening to my heart and taking my blood pressure. I was passing the time watching the irregular heart pattern on the display when I saw the line go flat. Two thoughts crossed my mind: someone must have pulled the plug on the machine; and (as I was feeling myself passing out) shite, my heart just stopped! Which it did. I died.

Well, not like brain dead (although Gen would disagree.) Just no-heartbeat dead, and will-stay-that-way dead unless said heart gets fired back up. No angels. No tunnel. No heaven (or hell.) Just nothing. Like the deepest no-dream sleep you've ever had.

When I came to, it was to the sight of a long flat line moving off to the right of the monitor being chased by a bunch of squiggles. Squiggles good; flat line not so much. The tech welcomed me back. I noticed that the siren was now on.

At the hospital, it didn't take long to end up in a bed with a bunch of docs, nurses, and other techs hovering over me. I was told that my heart needed to be rebooted (cardioverted) as I was still in A-fib. They tried doing it chemically, which had no effect. Then they decided to do it by zapping me with a defibrillator. But first they would be prepping me with propofol, a drug sometimes referred to as "milk of amnesia." It puts you out and makes you forget the pain you are about to receive. As I found out, it also acts as a truth serum.

You see, I was surrounded by nothing but women. After getting the drug, I apparently told them that I wanted to ...date...all of them (that's how I remember it!). Gen was less than impressed, but they'd heard it all before, I'm sure.

The zapping worked. The propofol? Not entirely, because I have a vivid, and real, memory of sitting up immediately after being zapped and saying (à la Tony the Tiger) that I felt grrrrrrreat! My next memory was 30 minutes or so later, when they told me I would soon be ready to leave the hospital.

Throughout the rest of 2009, I would go into A-fib eight more times and need to be cardioverted twice more. (Those times without Gen at my side!) The other six times, I used a variety of techniques to self-cardiovert. This was more than an inconvenience, so my cardiologist referred me to a surgeon.

The protocol that the cardiologist and the surgeon had to follow was that they first had to try to convince me to not have surgery, but to instead live the rest of my life on drugs, to help prevent A-fib occurrences and to reduce the risk of blood clots. Not the type of lifestyle I wanted to live. So after they'd gone through the required spiel, surgery was then discussed. It turned out I was an ideal candidate for ablation surgery.

In a nutshell, ablation surgery involves getting to your heart, using catheters inserted through your wrist and groin blood vessels, and then burning away those small muscles at the base of those blood vessels attached to the heart that I mentioned earlier. Typically ablation surgery takes two to four hours and has a 75-85% success rate – success meaning you'll never go into A-fib again. If you do, they do the surgery again, with the same probability of success. Statistically, they get it all by the third time in, if need be. I was on the operating room table for nine-and-a-half hours.

You see, I didn't like the idea of going through the hassles of the prep, surgery, and recovery more than once, so I asked the surgeon why he didn't just hang around in there until he was sure he'd identified and zapped all possible problem sites. He said it was usually because it was hard on the patient. I countered with the supposition that the "typical" patient was not in as great shape as I was. I could endure a lot more time on the table. He agreed. He found three sites to ablate. One complication was that I apparently have a one-in-20 kind of heart. When they try to punch through a wall to get from one side to the other, it's so soft and flexible that they can't. So they spent a couple of hours finding an alternate route (hopefully not by using iPhone Maps).

The actual zapping was quite the experience. They want you a little more alert during the procedure, so they back off on the sedation a bit. The sensation is like feeling a stick of dynamite going off in your chest in super slow motion: there's a gradual explosion of heat that rises to a very high intensity before slowly dissipating. After feeling it three times that day, I'd prefer never to have it happen again.

I went through the usual post-surgery routine of blood thinners and regular blood tests. This meant no basketball or other contact activities for a while. After six months, there were no more A-fib episodes and the surgery was deemed a complete success.

I have often said that being cardioverted was one of life's really neat experiences. However, if any of you ever need to have it done, it's really best if your loved ones are not at your side after you've been given propofol.

§

Acknowledgements and Credits

Catherine Betz, who was once an all-too-brief co-worker, and who remains a very dear friend of mine, did a tremendous job of editing this book, and of providing amazingly insightful comments and myriad suggestions that led to a greatly-improved final version. She even knows Bugs Bunny cartoons better than me!

My daughter Natasja Mackwood who's recollections fleshed-out *Rumble in Toronto*.

A special thanks to the members of the online audio/video forum called "The Audio Annex," who, in the early days of writing this book, each undertook to read and provide feedback on a draft story of my choosing:

Zing

Babs

Batman

Mrs. Batman

mudder17

heeman

Botch

MattB

PaulyT

And to everyone whose real-life exploits formed the basis for *Most of These Stories Are Somewhat True.*

Photo credits are as follows:

Danny Zingone contributed the *Maxi-Me* photo. The photo was taken by Russell Sanders, using Danny's camera.

The photo of me that accompanies *Swimming – The Hot and the Cold of it* was taken with my camera by a Scandinavian Amazon whose name I unfortunately never got.

Rebecca Eadie took *The Kilts* photo.

Credit for the photo that accompanies *How Much for that Guy in the Window* goes to M. Trujillo.

The watercolour of Notre Dame Cathedral in the story *A Crasher's Tale – Part 2* is an original work by Olga Milliken.

The back cover author photo is by DaZi Photography.

All other photos were taken either by me, or a family member.

About Me, the Author

It will come as a big surprise to anyone who knows me, when I say that I am, at heart, a shy and introverted person. At least that's how I feel. But in order to cure myself of those traits, I have adopted an outward appearance that's the complete opposite. There - I've outed myself!

Being the class clown, or the one to stand up in front of a crowd to tell a tale, has been my way of dealing with it. I can agonize for days over an impending speaking engagement, but have found ways to turn that around and feed off the resulting nervous energy.

I possess neither a singing voice, nor the ability to play music (despite a couple of years of piano lessons as a child). So stories became my instruments. Stories can be played over and over again; in different keys if need be. They can be tuned, even on the fly, to deal with audience feedback. They can be original compositions, or variations on old ones. I can be both the conductor and lead soloist at the same time.

After years and years of performing them, I felt it was time to collect and preserve these tales.

Despite the disclaimer at the front of the book, this collection will give the reader an accurate, albeit partial, representation of who I am, and what I believe in.

Above all else, I value friendships deeply. I trust that nothing in this book, nor excluded from it, will in any way diminish any of those friendships.

Writing this book has been therapeutic. It has brought memories forth that had long ago been forgotten. It has also gotten me thinking about two previous attempts at writing, attempts that were squashed by other priorities. I just might get around to revisiting them: an action/adventure original movie screenplay, and a sci-fi novella.

Speaking of movies, I'd like to end this book with the final monologue from the film *Big Fish* (2003):

Have you ever heard a joke so many times you've forgotten why it's funny? And then you hear it again and suddenly it's new. You remember why you loved it in the first place. That was my father's final joke, I guess. A man tells his stories so many times that he becomes the stories. They live on after him. And in that way he becomes immortal.

CPSIA information can be obtained
at www.ICGtesting.com
Printed in the USA
LVOW01s1849290216

477002LV00005BB/10/P

9 780994 931009